CRITICAL INSIGHTS

Southwestern
Literature

CRITICAL INSIGHTS

Southwestern Literature

Editor
William Brannon
Collin College, Texas

SALEM PRESS
A Division of EBSCO Information Services, Inc.
Ipswich, Massachusetts

GREY HOUSE PUBLISHING

Publisher's Cataloging-In-Publication Data
(Prepared by The Donohue Group, Inc.)

Southwestern literature / editor, William Brannon, Collin College, Texas.
  -- [First edition].

    pages ; cm. -- (Critical insights)

    Edition statement supplied by publisher.
    Includes bibliographical references and index.
    ISBN: 978-1-61925-842-6 (hardcover)

    1. Southwest, New--In literature. 2. Southwest, Old--In literature. 3. American literature--Southwest, New--History and criticism. 4. American literature--Southwest, Old--History and criticism. 5. American literature--Mexican American authors. 6. Indians in literature. I. Brannon, William, 1972- II. Series: Critical insights.

PS277 .S68 2016
810/.9/979

First Printing

PRINTED IN THE UNITED STATES OF AMERICA

Contents

Resources

About This Volume

William Brannon

This volume collects fourteen original essays with a goal of providing an overview of scholarship regarding Southwestern literature. Following an introductory essay on Southwestern literature, four "context" essays are intended to provide a general introduction to the volume's theme and facilitate the immersion of readers into the more focused ten "critical readings" chapters that follow. A historical background essay addresses how Southwestern literature has been influenced by different time periods, and examines what makes the literature of the Southwest relevant to a modern audience. A critical reception essay reviews the history of the critical response to Southwestern literature, surveying the major concerns that critics of the region's literature have addressed over the years. A critical lens essay uses a feminist approach to offer a close reading of the work of Sandra Cisneros. A comparative analysis essay examines how different writers have considered Glen Canyon.

The next ten essays provide an in-depth study of representative Southwestern authors and related themes, examining the role the Southwest region plays in not only inspiring writers, but also providing a tableau aptly suited to depicting the challenges encountered by individuals who negotiate the sometimes blurred boundaries between the different cultures that comprise the region, as well as the multiple contradictions characteristic of the Southwest.

In "The Polychotomous Southwest," Mark Busby traces the development of Southwestern literature as it evolved from Cabeza de Vaca's account in the 1500s to explorers and travelers such as Frederick Law Olmstead in the nineteenth century, the increased prominence of Southwestern authors in the twentieth century, and finally the varied voices appearing during the first two decades of the twenty-first century. Busby also defines some of the major themes of Southwestern literature. The subsequent essay, "Understanding Southwestern Literature: Critical Approaches and Major Works," provides a general overview of the different areas of critical approaches to Southwestern literature. Useful areas of critical inquiry within the field of Southwestern literature include not only focusing on how history has impacted Southwestern literature, but also how writers have responded to the natural world and the challenges depicted in Native American literature and Mexican American literature. T. Jackie Cuevas argues in "Chicana 'Feminist Architecture' in the Works of Sandra Cisneros" that considering the selected works of Chicana writer Sandra Cisneros provides evidence of what Chicana cultural theorist Gloria Anzaldúa called building a "feminist architecture." Focusing her critical reading on the collection *Woman Hollering Creek and Other Stories* and on the novel *Caramelo*, Cuevas argues that Cisneros explores and expands what constitutes Mexican identity "in and beyond the Southwest." For Laura Smith, the place of a literary *ecological* imaginary in environmental politics and political discourse provides a critical context to the study of Southwestern literature, and so, Smith's "Writing (and Righting) the Desert Southwest: Literary Legacies and the Restoration of Glen Canyon" focuses on tensions between the particularities of a literary Glen Canyon and the revalorization of the political landscape of Glen Canyon. Smith investigates the growing calls for 'Glen Canyon restoration' and discusses the cautionary tales of Katie Lee, Edward Abbey, Ellen Meloy, Terry Tempest Williams, and others, while considering the 'ecology of influence' and lasting legacy of these writers in the Glen Canyon controversy. Smith concludes that "an environmental politics at Glen Canyon is not only influenced by the literature, but in some sense is also produced by the literature."

Literature of the Southwest includes many different genres. In her essay "The Indian Captivity Narrative: A Genre of the Southwest," Randi Lynn Tanglen suggests that while the Puritan Indian captivity narrative of New England has often been recognized as the first unique form of American literature, the first published account of Indian captivity in the Americas actually took place in the Southwest. Tanglen also argues that the captivity narrative is still present and influential in shaping the contemporary literature of the

Southwest. Tanglen cites examples of how the captivity narrative set in the Southwestern region has provided the basis for movies and television shows, among them the western film *The Searchers* and the popular television series *Hell on Wheels*. Tanglen devotes special attention to Leslie Marmon Silko's short story "Yellow Woman" (1981) and its modern reinterpretation of the captivity narrative about a Pueblo woman kidnapped by a *ka'tsina* mountain spirit.

Leslie Marmon Silko is also the subject of critical attention for Wilma Shires in "Balances and Harmonies Always Shifting: An Ecopostcolonial Borderlands Reading of Silko's *Ceremony*." In her reading of *Ceremony*, Shires recognizes that one of its central themes involves healing and progressing, while maintaining a changing traditional culture and this is evident in the plight of the novel's protagonist, Tayo. Consequently, Shires suggests that the elements of transition, change, becoming, balance, and harmony in *Ceremony* are used by Silko to convey a restoration of health to both the earth as well as to the novel's protagonist, Tayo.

Mexican American literature is an important part of the Southwest's literary culture and the next three essays focus on different texts within this field of study. Paul Guajardo provides a survey of Mexican American memoirs in "Mapping the Territory: Mexican American Memoir" and argues that these narratives grapple with important questions of identity for Mexican Americans. Guajardo declares "minority memoirs are not just immigrant stories, they are universal narrative about life and about the human condition," and as a result, Guajardo presents a compelling case that these merit increased critical attention. In "Resisting Dominant National Narratives: Recovering María Amparo Ruiz de Burton's *Squatter and the Don* and (Re)writing Mexican American History" Annette Portillo challenges what she describes as "the notion of America's 'eastern-centered' historical origins and the myth of a cohesive, self-contained 'American' national narrative" by focusing on Ruiz de Burton's *Squatter and the Don*, a "recovered" novel, originally published in 1885. According to Portillo, Burton's novel reveals "the hypocrisy of a 'democratic' America but also portrays instances of assimilation and integration." Portillo argues that "in order to complicate the very tenets of American literary history we must re-read and critique such authors as Ruiz de Burton who complicate our understanding of not only Chican@ history and literature, but dominant narratives of Southwestern American literature and culture." Mike Lemon claims in "Ecological Martyrs: Ecocritical Considerations in Ana Castillo's *So Far from God*" that "for most readers and theorists...*So Far from God* has a discernible shift within the text, from magical realism to ecocritical and political considerations." As a result, Lemon argues that "a transition in terminology, from magical realism to spiritual imagery, should occur." Lemon also considers Castillo's portrayal of what he identifies as the spiritual movements within the novel and explores how the spirituality attributed to each character affects their environmental discourse.

The next two essays focus on Willa Cather. In "Willa Cather and Southwestern Aesthetics" John Samson proposes that "by examining Cather's views of the Southwest evident particularly in *The Song of the Lark*, but also in *The Professor's House* and *Death Comes for the Archbishop*, in light of statements contemporaneous to them" readers can gain insight into Cather's fiction by being able to "understand more fully and precisely how the Southwest is for Cather a place of aesthetic development." According to Samson, the fusion of these elements also allows insight into better understanding how Cather and the Southwest were involved with the emerging literary and aesthetic movement of modernism. The creative role of the Southwestern landscape for Willa Cather is also the focus of Max Despain's "Creative Genius: Willa Cather's Characters and the Influence of the American Desert Southwest." Despain observes that following Cather's initial visit to Arizona in 1912, "the American Southwest would subsequently be an important site of creative and artistic growth for characters in three of Cather's novels." Despain suggests that Cather found the Southwest to be a source of inspiration since "the expansive, complex landscape rich with ancient heritage and untamable land formations were a perfect proving ground for her philosophical ideas about how creative genius grows." Despain concludes that Cather uses the landscape of the Southwest to inspire her characters to their versions of creative genius, be it as an artist, an engineer, or a priest.

The next two essays provide critical readings of Cormac McCarthy's western novels. Maria O'Connell's "Of Judges and Fairybook Beasts: The Male Mentor and Violence in Cormac McCarthy's *Blood Meridian*" interprets the unrelenting violence in *Blood Meridian* as not resulting from any conventional conception of conflict, but instead, O'Connell proposes that Glanton's gang acts as a corporate unit consisting of men from different ethnicities and backgrounds unified in attempting to impose their own ideas of masculinity and nationality along the Mexican border. These attempts to exert control over the surrounding natural world as well as to demonstrate 'appropriate' male behavior lead to the carnage depicted in the novel. In "The Haunted Frontier: Cormac McCarthy's Border Trilogy," Cordelia E. Barrera, on the other hand, chooses Cormac McCarthy's decidedly less grim Border Trilogy, comprised of *All the Pretty Horses*, *The Crossing*, and *Cities of the Plain*. Barrera observes that the two characters whose exploits form the basis of the trilogy, John Grady Cole and Billy Parham, "assume mythic roles common to historical western narratives situated between two key frontier paradigms: the myth of progress and the primitive-pastoral myth." Barrera proposes that in the trilogy, "the boys' willful dreams are continually overshadowed by powerful Mexican and indigenous realties," and this leads to the boys being "haunted by unsettled, unresolved histories of collective violence and cultural and social issues signified by their crossings into Mexico."

The concluding essay in the volume turns the reader's attention to the literary output of another important Southwestern author, Larry McMurtry. In "Coming to Terms with Death in the West: Anticipation of Death and the Effects of Loss in the Novels of Larry McMurtry" Roger Walton Jones notes that McMurtry "like Mark Twain or William Faulkner, is very much identified with the particular region of the country where he grew up even as he transcends it," and consequently, Jones argues this results in "while McMurtry may be said to transcend his environment and the simplistic macho stereotypes often associated with it via Western pulp fiction and film, he nevertheless finds ample means to exploit his rich Western heritage and his intimate familiarity with its desolate landscape." Jones suggests McMurtry accomplishes this by using fiction as a means to depict "the enduring strength of Southwestern men and women as they face the undeniable reality of death in their lives," and this is evident in all of McMurtry's work.

The Southwest is a region with a rich history, often the product of interplay between multiple cultures. Southwestern literature, then, is made up of assorted voices in an array of genres conducive to a variety of critical approaches. This collection provides a sampling of the seminal works of the Southwestern literary canon and the scholarship that continues to shed light on these works and their authors.

On Southwestern Literature

William Brannon

The Southwest region offers contrasts. The adobe ruins of settlements abandoned centuries ago exist within a short driving distance of modern cities laced with concrete highways filled with automobiles taking workers to jobs in sleek office buildings. Cattle graze on prairies oblivious to the steady churn of oil pumps. Massive wind farms visible from the interstate greet travelers journeying cross-country.

Southwestern literature may evoke images of desolate, windswept mesas or majestic snow-capped mountains. It may also suggest narratives of Apache warriors ruthlessly pursuing hapless outlaws following a bank robbery gone awry or a determined rancher seeking to recover a lost cow. Taken as a whole, it simply consists of literary works focused on the southwestern region of the United States. Understanding the complexity of southwestern literature, however, necessitates considering the term regionalism in depth, as well as defining what constitutes the geographic region itself. In *Region and Regionalism in the United States*, Michael Steiner and Clarence Mondale recognize the potential for controversy among scholars when discussing regions and regionalism, noting, "Mere mention of the word 'region' among a group of historians is likely to provoke a flurry of emotionally weighted words as 'sectionalism,' 'balkanization,' 'antimodernism,' 'provincialism,' 'antiquarianism,' 'federalism,' 'decentralization,' and 'environmental determinism.'" (234). In spite of these potential objections, Steiner and Mondale conclude, "The spatial diversity of our culture—the dramatic differences, for example, between New England, the South, and the Far West—is an essential feature of the American experience, and regional analysis provides a further framework for understanding the development of such a multifarious society" (243). In "Literary Cultures of the American Southwest," Daniel Worden notes, "The American Southwest complicates many of the common notions about 'the region' in American literary history," adding that while "regional writing in America is often considered to be hostile to modernity, nostalgic for small-town life, and detached from the literary experimentations central to modernism and postmodernism," it also stands in stark relief since "the American Southwest, in contrast, connotes both ancient and radically contemporary cultures" (81).

Defining any particular region presents immediate challenges. Will every definition be based on strict geographical boundaries, or will culture provide the basis for defining traits? Perhaps a definition of the Southwest will include some combination of geography and culture, along with other attributes? If geography is the guiding characteristic used when defining the Southwest, then which states should be included? How should we consider a large state like Texas whose far eastern edge shares more in terms of landscape and cultural attributes with those associated with the American South than it does with the American West? What about California? Does only the southern half of California merit inclusion in the Southwest? David King Dunaway and Sara Spurgeon note in *Writing the Southwest* that "the Southwest's range could be expanded in all directions: North to Utah, South to Mexico, West to California, and East to Texas and Oklahoma" (xxii). With these factors in mind, a broad definition of the region known as the Southwest can (and should) encompass Oklahoma, Texas, New Mexico, Arizona, Utah, Colorado, Nevada, and California.

The challenges inherent in defining the parameters of the Southwest also occur when considering what constitutes the region known as the American West—not surprising since the Southwest may be considered a sub-region within the American West. However, while the Southwest does share much of the same geology, inhabitants, and history as the larger Western region, and hence overlap does occur, some important differences do exist, and these are reflected in southwestern literature. For example, while the history of the western half of the continental United States beginning in the middle of the nineteenth century features Anglo-American westward migration resulting in the displacement and relocation of many native peoples, this same process not only occurred in the

Southwest, but it included an added dimension to the potential conflict in the form of Anglo-American confrontations with other European settlers intent on possessing the same lands, the Spanish, whose own earlier arrival precipitated ongoing conflict with native inhabitants.

In addition, aridity, or lack of rainfall, is a characteristic frequently attributed to the western region of the United States, yet the eastern portions of Oklahoma, Texas, Kansas, Nebraska, and the Dakotas, all of which can be labeled as part of the western United States, receive ample rainfall, as do the western areas of the states of Washington and Oregon. Still, due to an average of between four and sixteen inches of annual rainfall in many parts of the region, the allocation of water resources in the Southwest continues to be an ongoing concern, and the adaptations of the Southwest's inhabitants to this challenge infuse much of the region's literature.

Major Authors & Seminal Works

Two significant authors associated with the Southwest include Willa Cather and Cormac McCarthy. Cather, who is originally from Virginia and subsequently relocated to Nebraska as a child, found inspiration in the Southwest's landscape and multiple cultures after visiting her brother in Arizona. She channeled these experiences into her novels *The Song of the Lark*, *The Professor's House*, and *Death Comes for the Archbishop*. Cormac McCarthy was born in New England and subsequently grew up in Tennessee, which was the primary setting for his first four novels. McCarthy's relocation to the Southwest was paralleled in his fiction, resulting in his critically acclaimed Border Trilogy. While Cather and McCarthy are examples of authors not originally from the Southwest who wrote books inspired by and set in the Southwest, other important southwestern writers have drawn inspiration from their having been born in the Southwest. Ralph Ellison, a native Oklahoman, utilized his formative experiences in the Sooner State to compose *Invisible Man*, although the novel's setting is Harlem. An enrolled member of the Kiowa tribe who was born in Oklahoma, N. Scott Momaday draws upon his childhood years in the Southwest for material for his novels and poetry. A native of New Mexico, Rudolfo Anaya has produced novels and poetry that reflect his growing up there, while Texan Larry McMurtry uses the Lone Star State as a setting in his fiction, with the action taking place in small towns, large metropolitan areas, as well as the open prairie.

The impact of multiplicity of cultural influences present in the Southwest is evident in the region's contributions to popular culture. The Southwest can certainly claim ownership of 'the cowboy,' recognizable worldwide in literature, television, music, and film, for better or worse, as a symbol associated with the United States. The long trail drives that introduced the cowboy into the popular consciousness in the nineteenth century originated in the Southwest, while the language and customs associated with the American cowboy can be traced to the Spanish *vaqueros* whose arrival in the sixteenth century introduced the cattle industry and its use of horses to North America. Southwestern folklore has introduced creatures such as the chupacabra, the mythical creature alleged to kill animals, especially goats. The isolated landscape of eastern New Mexico made possible the Roswell Incident, thus providing popular culture with one of its most enduring narratives of extraterrestrial sightings. Furthermore, the popularity of the television series *Breaking Bad*, set and filmed in Albuquerque, provided an antidote in popular culture to the stereotype of the Southwest as merely a sparsely populated desert whose few inhabitants concentrate on ranching or farming.

Since the history of the Southwest is rooted in successive settlements by different cultures (and their inevitable conflict), the Southwest is thus an area where different cultures not only exist but blend together and where inhabitants must deal with internal and external contradictions. These contradictions are often the subject of well-known novels by southwestern authors. In *Blood Meridian, or That Evening Redness in the West*, for example, Cormac McCarthy chronicles the adventures of a nameless fourteen-year-old boy known as the kid, who, after running away from his home in Tennessee, arrives in Texas. The novel traces the kid's journeys from Texas to Mexico to California and then back to Texas in the middle of the nineteenth century. The kid joins a brutal gang of scalphunters led by Captain John Joel Glanton. The gang is paid to collect the scalps of the Apaches who raid Mexican settlements. McCarthy's portrayal of the unrelenting violence resulting from the gang's barbaric acts and their journeys throughout the Southwest collecting scalps allows McCarthy to challenge the ideologies supporting the Anglo territorial expansion into the American Southwest.

The conflicts precipitated by Glanton's gang during the course of *Blood Meridian* arise from the exploitation of other peoples. The scalphunters indiscriminately murder to provide the scalps sought by the Mexican government. Upon returning to Chihuahua, the scalphunters initially receive a welcome fit for heroes "as they bore on poles the desiccated heads of the enemy through that fantasy of music and flowers" (McCarthy 165), but the grateful reception soon turns ugly. Repeated episodes of public debauchery after the gang's banquet with the governor result in "these scenes and scenes like them were repeated night after night. The citizenry made address to the governor but he was much like the sorcerer's apprentice who could indeed provoke the imp to do his will but could in no way make him cease again" (171), and the embrace extended by the grateful citizens soon turns to fear and rejection. The gang's initial mission to aid in the protection of the Mexican frontier by collecting Apache scalps soon clashes with the more basic need of the gang to satisfy their greed, thus leading to the gang's subsequent murder of innocents to provide the necessary scalps.

The citizens whom they, ostensibly, are helping protect become unwitting victims of the Glanton gang's brutal wrath. The gang, in turn, incurs the wrath of not only the Apaches but also the Mexican authorities in its attempts to cheat the Mexican officials and substitute Mexican scalps for those of Apaches. The depiction of the murderous exploits of Glanton and company allows McCarthy to appropriate narrative structures associated with the western genre and subsequently challenge the ideologies supporting the Anglo territorial expansion into the American Southwest. The unceasing conflicts that provide the basis for the plot of *Blood Meridian* can be interpreted as representative of a microcosm of this period in southwestern history, with representatives of multiple cultures seeking the fulfillment of opposing goals motivated by very different belief systems. The anonymous kid, who is ostensibly the novel's protagonist, can only attempt to make sense of the carnage surrounding him even as he bears some responsibility for what happens.

In another celebrated novel associated with the Southwest, *Ceremony*, Leslie Marmon Silko depicts the struggle of Tayo, as he tries to resolve feelings of alienation and depression after he returns to the Laguna Pueblo reservation following the conclusion of World War II. Tayo's difficulties are complicated by the depression and estrangement he experiences as a result of his combat experiences in the Pacific Theater during World War II. Tayo feels guilt from not only watching as Rocky, his childhood companion, dies in combat, but also guilt as a result of his being involved in the war effort and not assisting his uncle, Josiah. Josiah's death results in Tayo's hallucination, which places Josiah on the battlefield among a group of Japanese prisoners whom Tayo has been ordered to shoot. Paralyzed by the apparent physical manifestation of the guilt he feels for abandoning his uncle, Tayo can only watch as the other American soldiers fire upon the prisoners. Confronted with the prospect of coping with the losses of Rocky and Josiah, each of which he indirectly attributes to his participation in the war, Tayo finds himself in direct opposition to many of his fellow Native American veterans, like Harley, Leroy, and Emo, who spend time trying to relive their wartime experiences at the Dixie Tavern, their "good times courtesy of the U.S. Government and the second World War" (Silko 40).

As someone of mixed ethnic heritage, Tayo seems to realize that part of the other veterans' intense desire to drink away their present existence results from an awareness of the realities of life on the reservation mixed with racial prejudice outside the boundaries of the reservation. This prejudice permeates even the Army recruiter's speech to Rocky and Tayo when he informs them that "anyone can fight for America" and adds further insult in the lines, "even you boys. In a time of need, anyone can fight for her" (Silko 64). The observations of the blond woman picked up by the veterans in Gallup reinforce this rejection that the Laguna veterans feel for "they had been treated first class once, with their uniforms. As long as there had been a war and the white people were afraid of the Japs and Hitler. But these Indians got fooled when they thought it would last. She was tired of pretending with them, tired of making believe it had lasted" (165–66). For the Laguna men, including Tayo, the return from the war means renewed subjugation at the hands of the white men with whom they fought side by side in the recently concluded war.

In "I Don't Know, But I Ain't Lost," Mark Busby suggests, "one of the major features of southwestern writing is ambivalence—the act of being at once torn in several directions and crossing varying borders" (49). The ambivalence Busby observes occurs in different thematic concerns addressed by southwestern writers and also informs the often hybrid forms of writing adopted by southwestern authors, especially American Indian and Mexican American writers. The multiple cultures present in the Southwest result in different languages filling the pages of southwestern literature. So within a southwestern text, it may not be uncommon for more than one language to be used by a protagonist and often without translation. For example, in its depiction of the ritual ceremonies Tayo undergoes in his attempts to seek inner peace, Silko's *Ceremony* includes multiple languages. In Cormac McCarthy's Border Trilogy, characters switch from speaking English to Spanish to English. This linguistic switching, sometimes within the same paragraph or sentence, while potentially posing difficulties for the reader, can successfully convey the multicultural layers of the Southwest region. As another example, to ensure Tomás Rivera's *...y no se lo tragó la tierra / And the Earth Did Not Part* was accessible to his intended predominantly Spanish-speaking audience, the novel was available at first only in Spanish.

Frequently associated with scenes depicting cultural conflict played out often on horseback against the backdrop of a harsh landscape, southwestern literature often defies the common associations given to the region and increasingly utilizes urban settings. For example, in contrast to his acclaimed *Bless Me,*

Ultima and its primary setting of a rural village in New Mexico, Rudolfo Anaya's *Heart of Aztlán: A Novel* depicts life in a barrio in Albuquerque, while Terry McMillian's *Waiting To Exhale* examines the friendships of four African American women in twentieth-century Phoenix.

Classifying Southwestern Literature

Categorizing the different types of literature within the Southwest proves as difficult as debunking long-held associations of the Southwest. An obvious system of classifying southwestern literature involves doing so based on genre (e.g., poetry, short stories, novels, drama, nonfiction, etc.). This approach would accommodate such writers as dramatist Preston Jones, whose three plays, *The Last Meeting of the Knights of the White Magnolia*, *The Oldest Living Graduate*, and *Lu Ann Hampton Laverty Oberlander* comprise *A Texas Trilogy*. But since many prominent southwestern authors have experimented with multiple genres, this approach can be problematic. Sandra Cisneros, for example, has published short story collections, like *Woman Hollering Creek and Other Stories*; collections of poetry, like *My Wicked, Wicked Ways*; and novels, like *The House on Mango Street* and *Caramelo*. N. Scott Momaday is known for his novels *House Made of Dawn* and *The Way to Rainy Mountain*, but he has also published several collections of poetry.

In an effort to find a better solution to how best to categorize southwestern literature, some critics have identified three broad categories based on the three cultures that have exerted the most influence over the Southwest: Native American, Mexican American, and Anglo American. Prominent Native American authors include not only Leslie Marmon Silko and N. Scott Momaday, but also poets Simon Ortiz, Joy Harjo, and Luci Tapahonso. Mexican American authors besides the aforementioned Sandra Cisneros and Rudolfo Anaya, include Américo Paredes, Tomás Rivera, Denise Chávez, Arturo Islas, Ana Castillo, and Dagoberto Gilb. A category devoted to Anglo American authors might be filled with not just Willa Cather and Cormac McCarthy, but might also include prominent authors ranging from Mary Austin to Edward Abbey to

Larry McMurtry. This way of categorizing southwestern literature poses its challenges indeed since writers are grouped solely on perceived cultural affiliation without much regard for the content. For example, significant differences exist between the thematic concerns of Edward Abbey and Larry McMurtry. Such an approach also minimizes the contributions to southwestern literature of writers not easily identified as being aligned with one of these three cultural groups. This includes African American authors, ranging from earlier writers like Sutton Griggs and J. Mason Brewer to contemporary authors like Jewell Parker Rhodes and Anita R. Bunkley. It also includes Asian American authors, like Kim Ronyoung, Kren Tei Yamashita, and Hisaye Yamamoto.

Another possible way of categorizing southwestern literature would be based on thematic concerns. Since the natural environment of the Southwest has served as inspiration for many writers, it is indeed convenient to create a thematic category of southwestern literature devoted primarily to nature writing. Doing so would include many authors associated with the Southwest, such as, for example, Charles Lummi, John C. Van Dyke, as well as Mary Austin, Roy Bedichek, Joseph Wood Krutch, Edward Abbey, and Terry Tempest Williams. This type of categorization would have merit due to its allowing for comparison of Van Dyke, whose novel *The Desert* (1901) details a fictional visit he made to the Southwest, with Mary Austin, who not only traveled the Southwest, but resided in the region. Another benefit would be to show the contrasts between those authors like Austin—whose work praises the southwestern landscape and, in doing so, encourages visitation by outsiders—and the writing of Edward Abbey, who, while not discouraging others from appreciating the natural beauty of the Southwest landscape, complains about the systematic containment of the natural world in the form of natural parks intended to be used by tourists.

Here again, classifying southwestern writers thematically poses challenges. Barbara Kingsolver's novels all deal with urban themes, but settings in Larry McMurtry's novels, for instance, range from declining small towns to large urban centers. Then there are those southwestern writers from Texas, like Katherine Anne Porter,

William Goyen, William Humphrey, William Owens, Leon Hale, and Mary Karr, whose literary output depicts the ties of Texas to southern culture instead of the concerns often associated with the Southwest. Such divergent thematic content can lead some to exclude these writers from the southwestern canon.

A possible resolution to the myriad of issues in differentiating the various branches of southwestern literature would be to perceive the Southwest not as a monolith but instead as a tapestry. And such a tapestry should comprise not just novels, short stories, and poetry produced in the Southwest, but also the accessible writings that continue to be published in regional newspapers and magazines to this day.

Southwestern Literature as an Academic Study

The advancement of southwestern literature as an area of academic study can be traced to institutions of higher learning within the Southwest. J. Frank Dobie is often cited as being among the first members of academia to attempt to include representative texts from the Southwest in the academic curriculum as part of a class, entitled "Life and Literature of the Southwest," which he taught at the University of Texas at Austin in the early twentieth century. Dobie provided the following rationale for his establishing the course in his *Guide to Life and Literature of the Southwest*:

> It is designed primarily to help people of the Southwest see significances in the features of the land to which they belong, to make their own environments more interesting to them, their past more alive, to bring them to a realization of the values of their own cultural inheritance, and to stimulate them to observe. (9)

A tireless advocate for promoting appreciation of the Southwest's literature and culture, Dobie was later instrumental in the establishment of the *Southwest Review*, one of the first academic journals whose focus was literature of the Southwest.

Other academic publications were established following the lead of the *Southwest Review*, including, in 1971, *Southwestern American Literature*, which provided an additional venue for scholarly work in the form of essays, fiction, poetry, and book reviews focusing on the literature of the Southwest. In addition, The Center for the Study of the Southwest (CSS) at Texas State University—which seeks to foster scholarly appreciation of the Southwest region, including its literature, through sponsored conferences and symposia—publishes another regional journal, *Texas Books in Review*, which surveys books about Texas, while Texas State University houses The Wittliff Collections, repositories of literature, film, music, and photography of the Southwest and Mexico. Included in The Wittliff Collections is the Southwestern Writers Collection, which houses the artifacts of notable southwestern writers, including John Graves, Cormac McCarthy, Rick Riordan, and Sam Shepard.

Texas State University is a member of The Consortium of Southwest Centers, a group consisting of a wide variety of institutions in different states sharing a common southwestern regional focus. Other member institutions include Ft. Lewis College, Austin College, Colorado College, Southern Methodist University, Texas Tech University, the University of Arizona, the University of New Mexico, and the University of Texas at Arlington. Each member institution maintains a center devoted to some aspect of the study of the Southwest. Examples of these centers include the Center of Southwest Studies at Ft. Lewis College, the Center for southwestern and Mexican studies at Austin College, the Hubert Center for Southwestern Studies at Colorado College, the Clements Center at Southern Methodist University, the aforementioned Center for the Study of the Southwest at Texas State University, the Center for the Southwest at Texas Tech University, the Southwest Center at the University of Arizona, the Center for Southwest Research at the University of New Mexico, and the Center for Greater Southwestern Studies and the History of Cartography at the University of Texas at Arlington.

Academic journals with a focus on the Southwest include *American Indian Quarterly: Journal of the Southwest, Borderlands Texas Poetry Review, ISLA: Interdisciplinary Studies in Literature and Environment*, and *Western American Literature*. Important archival collections include the Strong Collections for Texas and the SW, part of the Center for American History at the University of Texas and the Southwestern Children's Literature Collection at the University of Texas, El Paso.

Significant contributions to southwestern literature have also been made by a number of university presses, including University of Texas Press, University of New Mexico Press, University of Arizona Press, and Texas Tech University Press. These academic presses have published important southwestern writers who otherwise may have been overlooked by traditional, larger publishers.

Also noteworthy is the contribution made by Arte Público Press, based at the University of Houston. Founded in 1979 with a goal of providing a publishing venue for Hispanic literature, Arte Público Press and its imprint, Piñata Books, which focuses on children's literature, have provided a forum showcasing Hispanic literary works, among them Sandra Cisneros's iconic *The House on Mango Street*. The contribution of Arte Público is not limited to the discovery of emerging new Hispanic authors, however. In 1992 the press initiated the Recovering the U.S. Hispanic Literary Heritage project with the goal to recover and archive previously lost or undiscovered Hispanic writings from the colonial period of the United States to 1960.

Conclusion

In 1973 in *My Blood's Country: Studies in Southwestern Literature*, William T. Pilkington analyzed the impact of the Southwest on writers, noting, "historically, the Southwest is a paradox. In a commercial sense most of it is new and undeveloped country, but on the other hand, its rich and storied past transports one back through the centuries" (2) and as a result Pilkington claims, "it is not surprising…that Southwestern writers, again and again, draw their raw materials from the region's undeniably colorful history" (2–3). Pilkington goes on to write, "quite simply many Western and Southwestern writers, by yielding to the temptation to be romantic about the past or lyrical about the landscape, fall victim to the very qualities that attracted them in the first place" (3). Unfortunately, it has been this tendency Pilkington identifies that, in the past, resulted in the relegation of southwestern literature to a lower status within the American literary canon.

Southwestern literature is best appreciated as texts reflecting the Southwest, a region heir to not just the rich past Pilkington and others acknowledge, but also one containing multiple cultures whose shifting boundaries create a type of vibrant multilayered writing that rewards readers. These characteristics of the Southwest that make categorizing its literary output difficult are conducive to the creation of literature emblematic of the region's cultures. Momaday's *House of Dawn* utilizes a nonlinear narrative structure not as a nod to the tenets of modernism, but in fidelity to Native American narrative traditions. The ambivalence Busby identifies as present in much of southwestern literature manifests in Cormac McCarthy's *All the Pretty Horses* and John Grady Cole's fateful decision to cross the border and seek an idealized lifestyle in Mexico only to return empty-handed at the novel's conclusion, having learned that not only does the idealized pastoral world he sought not exist in Mexico, but the land across the border represents a culture very different from the one he has known in Texas.

In his examination of postmodernism's potential effect on regionalism in "American Regionalism in a Postmodern World," Charles Reagan Wilson observes that "postmodern regionalists still see value in regional life, even in the postmodern world that knows of the constructed nature of social identities" and Wilson contends this occurs because "people within American regions continue to invest their regional cultures with significance" (158). He concludes, "Postmodern regionalism rests in the sense that even in a global village geographical places still differ and the people who live in them find meaning in the social groups they claim and the local experiences that continue to abide" (158). Wilson's observations are especially appropriate when engaging with southwestern literature. Considered in the past to be merely part of western American literature, southwestern literature demands recognition by virtue of not only place, but also its people, who, as Wilson suggests, can attribute meaning to the cultures with whom they identify even as the demarcation lines between those cultures blur. This meaning can exist in literary form in its broadest sense in popular periodicals focused on a specific locale, like the *Texas Highway* and *Arizona Highway* magazines produced by their respective state highway departments, or it can be found in the mystery novels of Tony Hillerman and the mash-up of traditional Navajo culture with the mystery genre.

Whether it's the traditional western tale of lawmen on horseback pursuing outlaws into a canyon, an essay describing a visit to an isolated canyon, or a narrative portraying a detective's pursuit of a killer on a Native American reservation, southwestern literature reflects the experiences of people who live in the region, while welcoming those who value the dizzying cultural diversity of the Southwest as simultaneously a geographic location as well as a literary place.

Works Cited

Busby, Mark. "'I Don't Know, But I Ain't Lost': Defining the Southwest." *Regionalism and the Humanities*. Eds. Timothy R. Mahoney & Wendy J. Katz. Lincoln: U of Nebraska P, 2009. 44–55.

Dobie, J. Frank. *Guide to Life and Literature of the Southwest*. Dallas: Southern Methodist UP, 1952.

McCarthy, Cormac. *Blood Meridian, or That Evening Redness in the West*. New York: Vintage, 1986.

Pilkington, William T. *My Blood's Country: Studies in Southwestern Literature*. Ft. Worth: Texas Christian UP, 1973.

Silko, Leslie Marmon. *Ceremony*. 1977. New York: Penguin. 1986.

Steiner, Michael & Clarence Mondale, eds. *Region and Regionalism in the United States*. New York & London: Garland Publishing, 1988.

Wilson, Charles Reagan. "American Regionalism in a Postmodern World." *Amerikastudien / American Studies* 42.2 (1997): 145–158. *JSTOR*. Web. 16 Aug. 2015.

CRITICAL CONTEXTS

The Polychotomous Southwest

Mark Busby

Ricochets from the Southwest's frontier past pierced the twenty-first century as Americans who focused on their second amendment rights favored open-carry bills. In 2015, in support of such a bill, proponents openly wandered near the State Capitol in Austin, Texas, with Glocks on their hips and AR-15s slung over their backs; one group even threatened a South Texas legislator for lack of support. The ghost of the old Southwest rose up in a postmodern showdown. Southwestern writers dramatize the irony of western settlers advancing civilization but losing the wilderness that beckoned them. Into the twenty-first century, powerful southwestern mythology looks back to the old, simultaneously summoning postmodern attempts to reexamine, explode, or supplant that old dichotomy, with many voices of a polychotomous Southwest.[1]

Regional American literature began receiving extensive critical attention in the late-twentieth century when critics led by Michel Foucault recognized the "turn to spatiality." Foucault observed that "[t]he great obsession of the nineteenth century was…history: with its themes of development and of suspension, of crisis, and cycle, themes of the ever-accumulating past…. The present epoch will perhaps be above all the epoch of space" (22). Literature about region necessarily focuses on the "spatial turn," which moves from literary time to literary space and place. Hsuan L. Hsu noted in *American Literary History*: "The relation between literature and regional production involves not only the production of literature about regions but also the ways in which literary works produce, reimagine, and actively restructure regional identities in the minds and hearts of their readers…" (62).

This essay identifies major elements in the imagining and reimagining of Southwestern literature and surveys it from Cabeza de Vaca in the 1500s, to the popularity of cowboy narratives in the nineteenth century, the flowering of southwestern literature in the twentieth century, and the varied voices of the first two decades of the twenty-first. Traditionally, western and southwestern American literature have been defined in relation to the East, the counter region, creating a cornucopia of opposing themes growing from freedom/restriction to individuality/community, etc. Recently, a more complex view of the West as transitional space (liminal space)[2] between opposites (binaries) has evolved. As Steve Tatum noted in *Modern Fiction Studies*, "instead of Turner's concept of the westward-moving frontier as a line of demarcation conceptually grounded by East/West and savage/civilized binaries, contemporary critics are more likely to view the frontier as an intercultural contact zone...." (462). These approaches draw from older images to reinvent the Southwest as a space characterized by a cacophonous variety of polychotomous voices.

Defining the Southwest is as varied as the landscape. W. Eugene Hollon in *The Southwest: Old and New* says, "the term 'Southwest' as hereinafter used refers only to the four large states of Texas, Oklahoma, New Mexico, and Arizona" (6). William T. Pilkington in *My Blood's Country* is more specific: "Texas, New Mexico, and Arizona, plus parts of Oklahoma, Colorado, Utah, Nevada, and Southern California (excluding Los Angeles)" (8). J. Frank Dobie's definition in his *Guide to Life and Literature of the Southwest* is the most elastic: "The principal areas of the Southwest are...Arizona, New Mexico, most of Texas, some of Oklahoma, and anything else north, south, east, or west that anybody wants to bring in" (14).

Understanding the Southwest requires knowing how the diverse, polychotomous southwestern voices—Native American, Mexican American, African American, and Euro-American—have transformed traditional attitudes about the region and the natural environment and requires recognizing the relationship between the region and the broader national identity. The harsh southwestern landscape historically led southwesterners to venerate a frontier individualism that led settlers to view nature as their resource. Some southwestern writers questioned individuality over community and created accounts of communal, supportive societies suggesting the fragile connections between human and natural worlds in hybrid, contradictory narratives.

SOUTHWESTERN HISTORY

Prehistory to Contact: Alvar Núñez Cabeza de Vaca

The region's history reflects the interaction of diverse peoples. The Southwest fell into history at first European contact with Álvar Núñez Cabeza de Vaca. His *Relación* told how, after an ill-fated expedition with Spanish explorer Pánfilo de Narváez, Cabeza de Vaca was shipwrecked and captured by native people along the Texas coast near Galveston in 1528. After wandering through Texas, New Mexico, and Mexico early in 1535, Cabeza de Vaca and the three other survivors reached a Spanish settlement on the Sinaloa River in Mexico in 1536 and then returned to Spain. His account of the expedition with tales of Zuñi villages and the Seven Cities of Cíbola encouraged other explorers, Hernando de Soto and Francisco Vázquez de Coronado, who searched for the cities of gold in 1540. *Relación*, the first book recounting confrontation and reconciliation between European explorers and native peoples, has all the literary elements—structure (escape and return, journey), mythic parallels, frontier myth, regeneration through violence, and the fundamental theme of a man's survival after having been stripped of resources except for his mind and imagination.

For literary scholars, *Relación* is the prototype for much American literature. As Pilkington notes, the book's theme of the "physical, emotional struggle for an accommodation between races" is "a conflict that has never been very far removed from the American consciousness and one that has always been a factor in the works of our best and most vital writers…" (145–46). Literary scholars embrace Cabeza de Vaca's recognition that American Indians were real people, not the *Other*. Frederick W. Turner in *Beyond Geography: The Western Spirit against the Wilderness* concludes that *Relación* is the first captivity narrative.

The Frontier Southwest, the Cowboy, and the Modern Southwest, 1821–1960

The southwestern story reflects the larger western one—the powerful narrative of being drawn to a dream of paradise. The cowboy, dominant icon of the frontier myth, is primarily a Texas and southwestern figure. After the Civil War, when enterprising Texas veterans discovered their homes destroyed and herds of cattle roaming wild, they rounded up the cattle, beginning the trail drives of cowboy legend that lasted from about 1870 to 1895, when barbed wire, railroads, and economic declines ended trail driving. Still, the cowboy is internationally identifiable as an American symbol—an image of frontier freedom and independence.

In *Virgin Land,* Henry Nash Smith traced cowboy narrative's popularity in late nineteenth-century dime novels, reinforced in Pinkerton agent Charlie Siringo's memoir *A Texas Cowboy* (1886) and in Alfred Henry Lewis' *Wolfville* (1897) about his experiences on ranches in Texas and Arizona. The early twentieth century saw increased interest in cowboy frontier values, particularly after Frederick Jackson Turner's famous 1893 address questioned if the end of the frontier signaled the end of America's defining traits. Dime novels pointed the way to serious literature, such as Owen Wister's *The Virginian* (1902); Andy Adams' trail-drive novel, *The Log of a Cowboy* (1903); much of the work of New Mexico's Eugene Manlove Rhodes, especially *Good Men and True* (1910) and his novella, *Pasó por Aqui* (1927); and Emerson Hough's *North of 36* (1923). Texas travels led to Stephen Crane's southwestern short stories, such as "The Bride Comes to Yellow Sky" (1898), where train and bride enter the frontier world and change everything. William Sydney Porter (O. Henry) drew from his sheep-ranching experiences in South Texas, especially in surprise-ending stories like "The Last of the Troubadours." Mollie E. Moore Davis also wrote about cowboys in *The Wire-Cutters* (1899), predating Wister and Adams' novels, which are usually identified as the first modern westerns. These works established elements of the major American genre, the western—set in the nineteenth century, with cattle, cowboys, horses, Indians, and outlaws.

As raconteur and compiler, J. Frank Dobie extended cowboy story popularity. Most Texas literature collections begin with Dobie's books, which are neither fiction nor scientific folklore. Dobie's correspondence with a cowboy named John Young led to *A Vaquero of the Brush Country* (1929). Other Dobie cowboy story collections are *The Longhorns* (1942) and *The Mustangs* (1952). He also collected Spanish Southwest stories of searches for ancient treasure. *Coronado's Children* (1931), his first book about lost mines, was the first book by a non-Eastern writer selected by the Literary Guild.

While Mollie Davis wrote about the cowboy, Annette Kolodny in *The Land Before Her* demonstrated how pioneer women fundamentally transformed the male frontier archetype. Early twentieth-century southwestern women writers affected literary history. Mary Austin wrote of two areas, the eastern Sierra Nevada desert region of California and the high plateau country of northwestern New Mexico. *The Land of Little Rain* (1903) describes the Sierra Nevada, and *The Land of Journey's Ending* (1924) is about New Mexico, where Austin thought Indian, Spanish, and Anglo hybridity would produce a new civilization.

Austin depicted her own experiences within the region, while Willa Cather drew from visits rather than from living in the region. Cather visited her brother Douglass, a Santa Fe Railroad employee in Winslow, Arizona, in 1912, producing Cather's major southwestern works: *The Song of the Lark* (1925), *The Professor's House* (1925), and *Death Comes for the Archbishop* (1927). A visit to Santa Fe in 1925 led to Cather's interest in Jean Lamy, first Bishop of Santa Fe, after she found a biography of Joseph Projectus Machebeuf, first Bishop of Denver and Lamy's friend. Cather dramatized how well-educated, civilized men were radically transformed by primitive frontier life.

Not all early twentieth-century southwestern writers sang praises of the Southwest as Austin, Cather, and Dobie did. Katherine Anne Porter obscured her past, shaving four years off her age and claiming to have been brought up among a southern, "white pillared" crowd. Porter's southwestern past was unhappy, and she got out of Texas "like a bat out of hell" as soon as she could. But her strong, ambivalent women, like Miss Sophia Jane Rhea of *The Old Order* (1955) come from that past, and "The Grave" and "Noon Wine" portray the region's strengths (ingenuity, democracy, strong-mindedness) and weaknesses (sexism, racism, anti-intellectualism).

Notable southwestern African American and Hispanic writers during this period include Texas-born Sutton E. Griggs whose *Imperium in Imperio* (1899) and *Unfettered* (1902) foreshadowed later works calling for full rights for black citizens. Dobie also encouraged Mexican American writers, especially Jovita González who served as president of the Texas Folklore Society from 1931 to 1932. Arguably the most important southwestern writer of color during this period was Ralph Ellison. His early stories and posthumous novel, *Three Days Before the Shooting...* (2010), are often set in Oklahoma, while his major work, *Invisible Man* (1952), is set mainly in Harlem, but concerns the themes of freedom and restriction raised by Ellison's southwestern past.

The Renaissance in Southwestern Literature, 1960 to the Twenty-First Century

After important publications at the end of the 1950s, in the 1960s the full southwestern literary renaissance began. Fiction, much of it about the cowboy frontier past, continued, but drama, poetry, and, particularly, environmental literature demonstrated a dynamic presence. In 1961, Larry McMurtry, the dominant Texas writer for the past fifty years, published his first novel. He grew up in the small town of Archer City, south of Wichita Falls, and became a prolific writer of novels, nonfiction, screen- and teleplays, and hundreds of book reviews. Several novels have been made into movies and television miniseries. Some of the most important works are *Horseman, Pass By* (1961), *The Last Picture Show* (1966), *In a Narrow Grave* (1968), *Terms of Endearment* (1975), Pulitzer Prize-winner *Lonesome Dove* (1985), *Duane's Depressed* (1999), and three late memoirs—*Books* (2008), *Literary Life* (2009), and *Hollywood* (2011). With his writing partner Diana Ossana, McMurtry won an

Academy Award for the film *Brokeback Mountain* (2006) adapted from an Annie Proulx story.

More recently, the southwestern writer focusing on the cowboy is Cormac McCarthy, whose powerful novels recast the traditional western story. McCarthy's enigmatic southwestern novels, including *Blood Meridian* (1985), the Border Trilogy—*All the Pretty Horses* (1992), *The Crossing* (1994), and *Cities of the Plain* (1998)—and *No Country for Old Men* (2005) use repeated border crossings as a metaphor for a complex, oxymoronic amalgamation of good/evil, optimism/nihilism, and similar binaries that ultimately suggest a nihilistic optimism. Thus, the border metaphor reimagines binaries through a polychotomous melding of the forces of life and death, rationality and irrationality, old and new.

Environmental Literature

In 1960, Texan John Graves published *Goodbye to a River*. His subtle, distinctive style—a fusion of fiction, folklore, philosophy, history, nature, personal experience, and allusion presented with sentence fragments, ellipses, and dashes—makes his work memorable. Graves balances high and low, using a quotation by Shakespeare or Thorstein Veblen then regional dialect. In *River*, *Hard Scrabble* (1974), and *From a Limestone Ledge* (1980), he laments the passing Southwest with regional specificity balanced by cosmopolitanism and a subtle environmentalism. Graves' concern with nature is mirrored by other southwestern nonfiction writers, including Rick Bass, Charles Bowden, Stephen Harrigan, Terry Tempest Williams, and especially Edward Abbey.

Although Abbey achieved success with novels, *The Brave Cowboy* (1956), filmed with Kirk Douglas as *Lonely Are the Brave* (1961), and with *The Monkey Wrench Gang* (1975), his nonfiction, particularly *Desert Solitaire* (1968), is the bedrock of his work. An examination of wilderness and freedom, *Desert Solitaire* is "Cactus Ed's" masterpiece, combining philosophy, autobiography, fiction, observation of nature, and attitude. Abbey, like Thoreau, condensed three seasons as a park ranger at Arches National Monument in Utah into a single year.

The Urban Southwest

An important southwestern writer of urban Texas was Billy Lee Brammer, whose one novel, *The Gay Place* (1961), is the classic Texas political novel. (The title reflects its time and refers ironically to the state legislature as a happy place.) Brammer, once an assistant to Lyndon Johnson, imagined Texas with a Johnson-like character as governor. Edwin "Bud" Shrake's novels set in Texas cities are *But Not for Love* (1964) and *Strange Peaches* (1972). Shrake was a sportswriter in Dallas and an acquaintance of Jack Ruby before John Kennedy's assassination, and his work reflects that fatal day. More recent works about the urban Southwest include Ben Fountain's *Billy Lynn's Long Halftime Walk* (2012), winner of the National Book Critics Circle Award, a satirical examination of sexuality, professional sports, advertising, and the Iraq War that focuses on an American Army squad brought to Texas Stadium to receive an award at halftime of the Dallas Cowboys football game on Thanksgiving 2004. These urban works counter southwestern literature that has often romanticized the wilderness and the frontier.

Mexican American Literature

Since the mid-twentieth century, Mexican American writers have gained prominence, initially by Américo Paredes, a folklorist at UT-Austin. Paredes collected *corridos* (folk ballads, many about encounters between Mexican Americans and the Texas Rangers) to illustrate Mexicanos' resolution to resist the oppressive Rangers. Paredes collected ballads about Gregorio Cortez, a turn-of-the-century South Texas *vaquero* whose exploits form the basis for Paredes' book *With His Pistol in His Hand* (1958), later filmed as *The Ballad of Gregorio Cortez* (1982).

Another important South Texas Mexican American author is Tomás Rivera, whose book *...y no se lo tragó la tierra/And the Earth Did Not Devour Him* (1971), was filmed by Severo Pérez as *And the Earth Did Not Swallow Him* in 1994. The loosely connected vignettes follow a migrant family from Texas to Minnesota in 1952. Both the book and Rivera were highly influential, as he became chancellor of the University of California at Riverside in 1979, the first Chicano chancellor in American higher education.

Rivera's life and work were significant for Rolando Hinojosa, writer of a series about the South Texas Valley: *Estampas del valle y otras obras/Sketches of the Valley and Other Works* (1973), *Klail City y sus alrededores/Klail City and its Environs* (1976), *Mi querida Rafa/My Dear Rafe* (1981), *Rites and Witnesses* (1982), *The Valley* (1983), and *The Useless Servants* (1993).

New Mexico's Rudolfo Anaya is the author of *Bless Me, Ultima* (1972), the bestselling Mexican American novel, filmed in 2013. It concerns Tony Marez, who grows up in New Mexico and witnesses various deaths before he chooses to become a shaman of the hybrid religion of the Christlike Golden Carp. He escapes becoming a Catholic priest by following the example of Ultima, a *curandera* (healer) who uses her magic to cure Tony's uncles of the *brujas'* (witches') curse and shows Tony the natural world's power.

Other Mexican American writers have also published significant works. A journeyman carpenter in El Paso with an MA in art history, Dagoberto Gilb published acclaimed collections of stories, *The Magic of Blood* (1993) and *Woodcuts of Women* (2001), concerned with the Mexican American experience. More recently, he published *The Flowers* (2008) and a short-story collection, *Before the End, After the Beginning* (2011), about the effects of a stroke.

Other important Mexican American authors include Denise Chávez, author of a story collection, *The Last of the Menu Girls* (1986), and novels *Face of an Angel* (1995), *Loving Pedro Infante* (2001), and *The King and Queen of Comezón* (2014); and McArthur "Genius" award-winner, Sandra Cisneros, who gained fame for *The House on Mango Street* (1983), about growing up in Chicago. Cisneros moved to and wrote about San Antonio in *Woman Hollering Creek and Other Stories* (1991). She also published *Caramelo* (2002) and *Have You Seen Marie?* (2012), an illustrated fable about women searching for a cat.

American Indian Literature

Southwestern American Indian literature received national attention with N. Scott Momaday's Pulitzer Prize-winner, *House Made of Dawn* (1968). Momaday, a Kiowa who grew up on Navajo, Apache, and Pueblo reservations, received a PhD from Stanford. His works reflect Euro-American literature and the Native American oral tradition. Momaday's success inspired works by others, especially the now classic *Ceremony* (1977) by Leslie Marmon Silko, a Laguna Pueblo. Silko also published *Laguna Woman* (1974), *Almanac of the Dead* (1991), *Yellow Woman and a Beauty of the Spirit* (1996), *Gardens in the Dunes* (1999), and *The Turquoise Ledge: A Memoir* (2010). Ethnic and women writers tell their stories from the inside, and they counter historical racist and sexist themes in southwestern literature.

Southwestern Drama

American drama since 1960 demonstrates two developments—the emergence of powerful regional theaters and Off-Broadway and Off-Off-Broadway playhouses. Southwestern playwrights like Preston Jones, Sam Shepard, Horton Foote, and recently Tracy Letts established themselves as significant American dramatists. Minority and women southwestern playwrights, including J. California Cooper and Hanay Geiogamah, also influenced the look of post-1960 southwestern drama.

Preston Jones' plays, including those comprising *A Texas Trilogy—The Last Meeting of the Knights of the White Magnolia* (1973), *Lu Ann Hampton Laverty Oberlander* (1973), and *The Oldest Living Graduate* (1974)—demonstrate a deep ambivalence toward the impermanent values of the mythic and portray comically small-town southwestern life with stock characters speaking dialect.

Sam Shepard's earliest plays, *Cowboys* and *The Rock Garden*, presented in 1964 at New York's Theater Genesis show the importance of Southwest images, especially the cowboy. Since then, Shepard has written numerous plays, won many Obie awards and a Pulitzer Prize for *Buried Child* (1979). Other important Shepard plays are *Operation Sidewinder* (1970), *The Tooth of Crime* (1972),

Geography of a Horse Dreamer (1972), and *True West* (1980). Shepard has also published five memoir and fiction collections including *Cruising Paradise* (1996) and *Day Out of Days* (2010), which, like his plays, reimagine southwestern themes.

Horton Foote became one of the most acclaimed writers about small-town America, especially Wharton, Texas, his hometown and subject of numerous plays, several filmed: *Trip to Bountiful* (1985), *1918* (1985), *On Valentine's Day* (1986), and *Convicts* (1991). He won the Best Screenplay Oscar for *To Kill a Mockingbird* and a second for his original screenplay, *Tender Mercies* (1982). *The Young Man from Atlanta* won the 1995 Pulitzer Prize.

Probably the most successful recent southwestern playwright is Tracy Letts, who received the 2008 Pulitzer Prize, the Drama Desk Award, and the Tony Award for *August: Osage County*. Other Letts' plays with southwestern settings are *Killer Joe* (1993), filmed with Matthew McConaughey, and *Bug* (1996) filmed in 2006 with Ashley Judd.

Perhaps the most significant southwestern American Indian playwright is Hanay Geiogamah, a Kiowa-Delaware, who established the American Indian Theater Ensemble in the 1970s. Later called the Native American Theater Ensemble, the company toured presenting Geiogamah's plays, most of which focus on contemporary Indian life with glimpses into the past. *Body Indian* (1972) examines the way the Indian body politic undermines itself as Bobby Lee, an alcoholic who lost his legs to the American "Machine in the Garden" (the train), gets drunk, and is robbed by friends. *Foghorn* (1973), referring to the foghorns used to harass Indians occupying Alcatraz in 1969, presents Indian stereotypes—from Pocahontas to activists at Wounded Knee—in order to exorcise them, and in *49* (1975), police break up an Indian celebration.

Houston playwright Celeste Bedford-Walker's most successful play is *Camp Logan* (1991), a historical drama based on the all-black 24th Infantry, assigned to construct Camp Logan in Houston in 1917. The soldiers anticipated going to France in World War I; instead, Houston police assigned them as laborers and subjected them to racial attacks, harassment, and beatings. The production concerns the soldiers' court-martials. Bedford-Walker's *Distant Voices* (1998) includes voices of sixty people buried in College Memorial Park Cemetery near Freedman's Town, Houston's Fourth Ward.

Poetry

Looking back at southwestern poetry from midcentury, J. Frank Dobie declared it "mediocre," but afterwards, poetry has flourished across the diverse groups that constitute the Southwest. Vassar Miller's poems, collected in *If I Had Wheels of Love* (1991), are often philosophical and religious and reflect Miller's lifelong affliction with cerebral palsy. Naomi Shihab Nye of San Antonio gained prominence through a Bill Moyers television profile. Her works include *Different Ways to Pray* (1980), *Hugging the Juke Box* (1982), *Red Suitcase* (2013), novels and stories, and works for children. Walter McDonald of Lubbock, an Air Force pilot who taught at the Air Force Academy and Texas Tech, has been a prolific Texas poet since the 1970s whose work juxtaposes the harsh landscapes of Vietnam and West Texas. His works include *Caliban in Blue and Other Poems* (1976), *Rafting the Brazos* (1988), *Counting Survivors* (1995), *Blessings the Body Gave* (1998), and *Climbing the Divide* (2003).

Among other notable Texas poets are Dave Oliphant, also a jazz historian, critic, translator, and publisher, author of *Footprints* (1978), *Austin* (1985), *Backtracking* (2004), and *The Pilgrimage* (2012); and Jerry Bradley, *Simple Versions of Disaster* (1981), *The Importance of Elsewhere* (2010), and *Crownfeathers and Effigies* (2014). R.S. Gwynn combines humor with poetic form in *The Narcissiad*, a satirical poem (1982); *No Word of Farewell* (2001); and *Dogwatch* (2014).

Southwestern poetry by ethnic poets has exploded recently, especially Mexican American and American Indian poets. Discussed above, Sandra Cisneros, Denise Chavez, N. Scott Momaday, and Leslie Silko also publish poetry. Tino Villanueva's *Scene from the Movie GIANT* (1993) concerns the effect of watching the film in the 1950s in San Marcos, Texas, Villanueva's hometown. Other notable Chicana poets are Sarah Cortez, Carmen Tafolla, and Pat Mora.

New Mexico's Jimmy Santiago Baca is the author of *Black Mesa Poems* (1995), *In the Way of the Sun* (1997), *Winter Poems Along the Rio Grande* (2004), and *Spring Poems Along the Rio Grande* (2007). His memoir, *A Place to Stand* (2001), examines his prison years, where he learned to become a poet.

Alberto Ríos grew up in Nogales, Arizona, the subject of *Capirotada: A Nogales Memoir* (2008). His poetry includes *Whispering to Fool the Wind* (1982), winner of the Academy of American Poets Walt Whitman Award; *Five Indiscretions* (1985); *The Lime Orchard Woman* (1988); *The Theater of Night* (2005), which received the PEN/Beyond Margins Award; and *The Dangerous Shirt* (2009).

Southwestern American Indian poets focus on cultural experiences, drawing from Native American myth and legend. Among the important poets are Joy Harjo, a Mvskoke, author of *She Had Some Horses* (1983), *The Woman Who Fell from the Sky* (1996), and *How We Became Human* (2004). Simon J. Ortiz, an Acoma Pueblo, uses Southwestern images in such works as *Woven Stone* (1992), *From Sand Creek* (2000), and *Out There Somewhere* (2001). Like other Indian writers, Ortiz looks to a tribal past and ancient oral traditions.

Luci Tapahonso, a Navajo, born in Shiprock, New Mexico, grew up on the largest U.S. Indian reservation and learned English as a second language after her native tongue, Diné, often included in her poems and stories. She attended the University of New Mexico, studying with Leslie Marmon Silko. Her works include *One More Shiprock Night* (1981), *Seasonal Woman* (1981), *Blue Horses Rush In* (1997), and *A Radiant Curve* (2008).

Ofelia Zepeda, a member of the Tohono O'odham Nation, was born and raised in Stanfield, Arizona, near the Tohono O'odham (formerly Papago) and Akimel O'odham (formerly Pima) reservations, and is the foremost authority in Tohono O'odham language and literature. Her works include *When It Rains* (1982), translations of Tohono O'odham and Akimel O'odham poetry; *Home Places* (1995); *Where Clouds Are Formed* (2008); and *Jewed 'i-Hoi/Riding the Earth* (2009).

Southwestern Themes

Over years studying southwestern literary history, I have identified repeated themes: journeying, frontier binaries, ambivalence, primitivism/pastoralism, *ubi sunt,* sexism, racism, violence, and spirit. Travelers from Cabeza de Vaca to nature writers, like John Graves and Ed Abbey, roamed the Southwest pondering the natural and cultural phenomena. Traveling is a natural act in a region with vast spaces. Texas is 801 miles from the Panhandle in the north to Brownsville in the south and 773 miles from the easternmost bend in the Sabine River to the westernmost point of the Rio Grande near El Paso. The journey's archetypal power increases where vastness summons and impedes.

Southwest narratives also reflect American frontier mythology's constellation of images, values, and archetypes resulting from the confrontation between the uncivilized and civilized worlds, what Frederick Jackson Turner called the "meeting point between savagery and civilization" (4). The binary, dichotomous mythology actually includes a gathering of polychotomous terms, such as wilderness/civilization, rural/urban, individual/community, past/ present, and others. Binary tension, like thesis and antithesis, results in an oxymoronic synthesis, the liminal space, such as restricted freedom and communal individuality.

Still, southwestern geography generates profound ambivalence. The term "Southwest" simultaneously points both south and west. On one hand, southwestern vastness makes distinguishing borders difficult. On the other, being positioned on the edge of southern and western culture and along the border with Mexico fortifies an awareness of borders. Both borders and the frontier evoke a boundary where conflicting cultures, attitudes, and factions meet. Early settlers both conquered nature and felt immediately at one with it, exhibiting the ambivalence Larry McMurtry admitted cut him "as deep as the bone" (166) in his radiant essay, "Take My Saddle from the Wall: A Valediction." The ambivalence of being stretched at the same time between such other polychotomous forces as good/evil, optimism/nihilism, among others, is central to the southwestern legend. Often southwestern writers examine the divisions derived from the frontier myth that live inside and the diminished outside natural world.

Historian Larry Goodwyn examined elements of the southwestern frontier myth and concluded that the "frontier legend is pastoral" (161), emphasizing the primitivistic belief that being outdoors promotes living moral lives. Primitivism idealizes older societies and is related to pastoralism, involving raising livestock in the countryside. Literature has extolled the positive values that living close to the land breeds and is related to the nostalgia of *ubi sunt*—literature lamenting transience. Grieving the loss of the older, primitivistic open range of cowboying has become a cliché in southwestern literature, but writers like John Graves in *Goodbye to a River* dramatize contemplative and complex narratives evoking the old while recognizing the progressive nostalgia of the new, polychotomous Southwest.

Goodwyn also concluded that the legend is sexist and inherently masculine and is "primitively racialist." These early statements of Otherness have elicited important counterarguments from southwestern women and ethnic writers and from others sensitive to this ugly heritage. Such women as Mary Austin, Katherine Anne Porter, Carolyn Osborn, Sarah Bird, Sandra Cisneros, Naomi Shihab Nye, Leslie Marmon Silko, and other Indian, Mexican American, and African American writers, such as N. Scott Momaday, Rudolfo Anaya, Rolando Hinojosa, Dagoberto Gilb, Ralph Ellison, and Reginald McKnight have addressed these issues from their particular perspectives.

Violence is another legacy of the frontier; the gun on the hip sadly continues. In spring 2015, a fight among rival motorcycle gangs in Waco, Texas, left nine dead with over one thousand weapons confiscated. In a 1975 *Atlantic* essay, McMurtry upbraided Texas, noting that frontier violence was a vestige of the old world. Richard Slotkin also examined the myth of violence in three books—*Regeneration Through Violence* (1973), *The Fatal Environment* (1985), and *Gunfighter Nation* (1992).

Finally, in "The Spirit of Place" chapter in his idiosyncratic, but influential, *Studies in Classic American Literature* (1923), D.H.

Lawrence wrote that "[e]very continent has its own great spirit of place…. [T]he spirit of place is a great reality" (10). Lawrence was drawn to the American Southwest as a place where the human spirit, crushed by the Industrial Revolution, could be reborn like the phoenix, his personal symbol. No doubt the Southwest's association with American Indian cultures fueled the belief that spirit speaks louder and more powerfully in the Southwest. Southwestern literature, from early myth to Anaya's *Bless Me, Ultima* to McCarthy's *The Crossing*, hint of the region's spirit.

Conclusion

Marginalized until the latter half of the twentieth century, southwestern American literature moved out of the shadows as literary historians and critics, following Foucault's "turn to the spatial," found southwestern writers' diverse voices and borderland liminality a distinct part of the American literary scene. With the rising emphasis on Mexican American, American Indian, and environmental writing and a postmodern interest in the spatial turn, southwestern literature received particular focus in American literature anthologies and critical discussions of national literature. To illustrate: in 2015, Southern Californian, "Half Mexican" poet Juan Felipe Herrera, son of migrant workers, was named American poet laureate for his poems of hybridity.

Notes

1. I have adapted the term "polychotomous" from the biological system of classification, which expands upon the single binary—a dichotomy—to suggest a constellation of binaries in creative tension. See Weiss, David J. "Polychotomous or Polytomous?" *Applied Psychological Measurement* 19.1 (Mar. 1995): 4.

2. "Liminal," "hybrid," and "mestizo" are references to mixture—of space, of materials, of ancestry—all related to concepts derived from an ambiguous border.

Works Cited

Dobie, J. Frank. *Guide to Life and Literature of the Southwest*. Dallas: SMU P, 1952.

Foucault, Michel. "Of Other Spaces." Trans. Jay Miskowiec. *Diacritics* 16 (Spring 1986): 22–27.

Goodwyn, Larry. "The Frontier Myth and Southwestern Literature." *American Libraries* (Feb 1971): 161–67; Rpt. in *Regional Perspectives: An Examination of America's Literary Heritage.* Ed. John Gordon Burke. Chicago: ALA, 1973. 175–206.

Hollon, W. Eugene. *The Southwest: Old and New.* New York: Knopf, 1961.

Hsu, Hsuan L. *American Literary History* 17.1 (Spring 2005): 36–69.

Kolodny, Annette. *The Land Before Her: Fantasy and Experience of the American Frontiers 1630–1860.* Chapel Hill & London: U of North Carolina P, 1984.

Kurtz, Kenneth. *Literature of the American Southwest, A Selective Bibliography.* Los Angeles: Occidental College, Ward Ritchie P, 1956.

Lawrence. D. H. *Studies in Classic American Literature.* New York: Viking, 1923.

McMurtry, Larry. *In a Narrow Grave.* Austin, TX: Encino, 1968.

_____. "The Texas Moon and Elsewhere." *Atlantic* 235.3 (March 1975): 29–36.

_____. *Lonesome Dove.* New York: Simon & Schuster, 1985.

Pilkington, William T. *My Blood's Country: Studies in Southwestern Literature.* Fort Worth: TCU P, 1973.

_____. "Epilogue." *Cabeza de Vaca's Adventures in the Unknown Interior of America.* Trans. Cyclone Covey. Albuquerque: U of New Mexico P, 1961. 145–52.

Tatum, Steven. "Postfrontier Horizons." *Modern Fiction Studies* 50.2 (Summer 2004): 460–468.

Turner, Frederick Jackson. "The Significance of the Frontier in American History." *The Frontier in American History,* 1920. *Project Gutenberg.* Web. 19 Jun 2015. <http://www.gutenberg.org/files/22994/22994-h/22994-h.htm>.

Turner, Frederick W. *Beyond Geography: The Western Spirit against the Wilderness.* New York: Viking, 1980.

Understanding Southwestern Literature: Critical Approaches and Major Works_____

William Brannon

In "The Author as Image Maker for the Southwest" in *Old Southwest/ New Southwest*, Arrell Morgan Gibson notes, "the Southwest is a land of changing images; at times it has been held in low esteem, at others in high esteem, from extremes of scorn and rejection to respect, even affectionate embrace" (25). Gibson goes on to suggest, "no other region in the United States has been the subject of such extended and contradictory literary and partisan attention" (25). The Southwest is a region of contradictions. The critical concerns that have garnered the attention of those studying southwestern literature result, in part, from these contradictions.

Southwestern literature encompasses texts diverse in form, as well as subject matter, and these are representative of the southwestern region and its inhabitants. Prominent among the initial major critical concerns that have been the focus of scholars of southwestern literature over the years includes anxiety regarding the consequences of the disappearing frontier that attained mythic status in the United States by the second half of the nineteenth century. This historical approach to studying the critical concerns of southwestern literature includes the western genre and its central figure, the cowboy. The sometimes unforgiving natural environment of the Southwest invokes appreciation of its beauty and has subsequently lent itself to questions about the individual's role in the environment and responsibility to preserve the natural world for subsequent generations. Beginning in the second half of the twentieth century, critical concerns have considered the portrayal of the lives and cultures of those residing in the American Southwest, specifically the portrayal in Native American literature of those struggling to negotiate the challenges inherent in attempting to maintain fidelity to one's cultural heritage while living in the larger culture and Mexican American literature with its similar attendant concerns regarding the challenges confronted by the living in those areas adjacent to the US-Mexican border.

A glance at books focusing on literature of the Southwest reveals the wide variance in how different authors have attempted to define the region. In the introduction to *Southwest Heritage*, Mabel Major and T. M. Pearce observe that while the "the Southwest as an area of American culture has been variously defined" and "at the beginning of the nineteenth century the name was given to the lands occupied by the Five Civilized Tribes of Indians east of the Mississippi, the lower Mississippi Valley, and the lands to the west of it," for many people, the region "includes the region from the Mississippi Valley westward to the valley of the Colorado River, and from the broad watersheds of the Arkansas on the north to the Mexican border on the south" (1). In his introduction to *The Southwest: The Greenwood Encyclopedia of American Regional Cultures*, Mark Busby, although acknowledging "the greater Southwest is a physical region that runs from the piney woods of East Texas to the Gulf Coast" and extends geographically "across the rolling Texas Hill Country to the dry deserts and arroyos of Trans-Pecos West Texas, New Mexico, Arizona, Nevada, Utah, southern Colorado, and southern California" opts to "primarily follow the National Endowment for the Humanities' designation of the Southwestern region as Texas, New Mexico, Arizona, and Nevada" (xix). Given the difficulty of defining the boundaries of the Southwest region, defining literature of the Southwest can prove a bit less problematic if the Southwest's literature is considered as representative of the region's diverse cultures linked by multiple critical concerns.

Expansion into the western half of the United States accelerated in the nineteenth century, culminating in the contiguous lower forty-eight states. The relentless territorial expansion was motivated in part by narrative myths justifying the subjection of native peoples and the subsequent commercial exploitation of the environment for agricultural purposes and mining and, subsequently, for water supplies for fast-growing urban cities. The inevitable conflict resulting from this territorial expansion and the effects of this environmental intrusion are nowhere more pronounced than in the Southwest, and this is reflected in Southwestern literature, particularly in the exploits of the cowboy prominent in narratives in the late nineteenth century and continuing into the early twentieth century.

In his essay "The Frontier in American History," initially read at a meeting of the American Historical Association in Chicago on July 12, 1893, Frederick Turner laments the potential loss of the benefits he and others associate with the American frontier, and he goes on to suggest that the collective experience of westward expansion contributed to the positive development of the American temperament, for, according to Turner, it is to "the frontier the American intellect owes its striking characteristics" (37). Turner buttresses his argument by listing several of these following traits attributable to the frontier:

> That coarseness and strength combined with acuteness and inquisitiveness; that practical, inventive turn of mind, quick to find expedients; that masterful grasp of material, lacking in the artistic but powerful to effect great ends; that restless, nervous energy; that dominant individualism, working for good and for evil; and withal that buoyancy and exuberance which comes with freedom—these are traits of the frontier, or traits called out elsewhere because of the existence of the frontier. (37)

For Turner, the closing of the frontier portends potential dangers for the country, and crucial to appreciating Turner's anxiety over these perceived dangers is understanding the myths associated with the frontier in the American West and, by extension, the Southwest.

In *Regeneration Through Violence: The Mythology of the American Frontier, 1600–1860*, Richard Slotkin defines myth as "a process, credible to its audience, by which knowledge is transformed into power; it provides a scenario or prescription for action, defining and limiting the possibilities for human response to the universe" (7). For Slotkin, "as a vehicle of myth, literature enjoys the advantage of formal permanence," but a downside to this attribute of literature as vehicle of myth is that "literature is subject to the movements of the literary marketplace" (*Regeneration* 20), and in the case of the settling of the frontier, according to Slotkin, writers inevitably over the years embellished narratives to conform to myth and, by doing so, this led to, "introducing characterizations of their material which have little to do with the American colonists' attempts to understand their situations in their own terms" (20). In the case of southwestern literature, the result was that for years Southwestern literature was largely overshadowed and subsumed by the western genre and its stock depictions of conflicts between cavalry and Native Americans, lawmen and outlaws, and similar formulaic plots. Slotkin argues in *Gunfighter Nation* that "myths are formulated as ways of explaining problems that arise in the courses of human experience" (6) and goes on to assert that "in each stage of its development, the Myth of the Frontier relates the achievement of "progress" to a particular form or scenario of violent action" (11). This requirement for literature to convey violent action necessary to justify perceived American progress has posed problems for Southwest literature, especially in light of the history of the region and its representative cultures.

Daniel Worden discusses the impact of the assorted cultures in the Southwest in "Literary Cultures in the American Southwest," observing, "the many Native American cultures in the Southwest—including the Pueblo communities, Navajo, Apache, Ute, Sioux, and many others—have unique oral traditions, accessible to the modern scholar through a history of translation, transcription, and ethnographic projects," and Worden asserts that these narratives are "central to the history of the Southwest, its people, and its literature" (85). Important, too, Worden says, are the "first published accounts of the Southwest" in the form of "the many travelogues and journals published by Spanish explorers and missionaries" (85). Of these documents, Álvar Núñez Cabeza de Vaca's *Adventures in the Unknown Interior* is among the most notable.

Cabeza de Vaca's book offers a conduit to many of the critical concerns that would eventually arise in southwestern literature. In its narrative of de Vaca's ordeal involving his journeys with four companions through the interior of present-day Florida, Texas, New Mexico, Arizona, and northern Mexico after surviving being shipwrecked, the book anticipates subsequent texts concerning later exploration of the region. On a basic level, Cabeza de Vaca's book provides a model for other texts by authors to follow when recording their travels and adventures in the Southwest. De Vaca's description of his travels foreshadows the later narratives of authors ranging from subsequent Spanish explorers to authors such as Mary Austin, in the early twentieth century. In addition, Cabeza de Vaca's period of captivity by Native Americans represents the first captivity narrative in the Southwest. Another important component of this model provided by de Vaca's book involves the initial motivation for the Spanish expedition, one whose mission involved exploring the region with the goals of acquiring wealth from gold and other mineral resources as well as territorial expansion, goals that anticipated the frontier myths underlying later Anglo-American expansion in the same region.

Prior to 1900, much of the literature of the Southwest had as its focus the frontier. This literature took the form of the previously mentioned travelogues, memoirs, and similar kinds of writing, or else manifested itself in the form of examples of the western genre, including the dime-store western novel. Coping with frontier life also formed the basis for folktales detailing the daily challenges of existence in the Southwest and thus evoking again the Myth of the Frontier and the struggles inherent in progress. In *The Great Frontier* (1951), Walter Prescott Webb identifies 1890 as "usually accepted as marking the date when there was no more frontier available, when the new land was no longer new" (4). Webb echoes Frederick Jackson Turner's speech in extolling the benefits of the frontier, claiming "the effects were present everywhere, in democratic government, in boisterous politics, in exploitative agriculture, in mobility of population, in disregard for conventions, in rude manners, and in unbridled optimism" (5). Webb, though, fails to take into account several aspects of the frontier and its attendant myths. The mobility of population he mentions as a benefit resulting from westward expansion of the frontier does not take into consideration the dislocation of the native peoples to allow for the repopulation of areas by settlers. Similarly, the democratic government he mentions excluded segments of the population, most notably women, during this period in history. This exclusion of women, as well as other demographic groups occurred in narratives conveying the myths of the frontier. Ironically, the closing of the frontier would lead to some American writers to consider the value in preserving the natural world and call into question the costs of reckless exploitation of natural resources. The definition J. Frank Dobie offers for "literature of the Southwest" in his *Guide to Life and Literature of the Southwest* includes "writings that interpret the region, whether they have been produced by the Southwest or not. Many of them have not. What we are interested in is life in the Southwest, and any interpreter of that life, foreign or domestic, ancient or modern, is of value" (13). For many writers, what has been most interesting about life in the Southwest is the natural environment.

Sections of the Western region of the United States may be characterized by the relative lack of rainfall compared to those areas east of the Mississippi River, and this aridity of the land often has been a signature trait assigned to the Southwest region. In *Southwest: Three Definitions*, Lawrence Clark Powell recognizes the importance of nature to southwestern writers, insisting one should, "Start with the land. It was here first and it will be here last" (37). Powell goes on to refer to the attributes of the natural environment in the Southwest as "Climate and configuration. Absence of abundant rainfall, Vastness of mountains, deserts, and distance under the clear skies" (37). Despite the harsh, often austere, conditions imposed upon the region's inhabitants by the frequently dry, natural environment, the Southwest offers a diverse landscape recognized by authors for its beauty. Powell identifies "two kinds of Southwesterners: native and adopted" and categorizes as "the former group were here first—Pimas and Papagos, Yumas, Apaches and Navajos, to name the chief tribes," while members of what he labels adopted Southwesteners "can't contain the joy with which the Southwest fills them" (37). Mary Austin may also be placed into this latter category. The author of thirty-two books, Austin was born in Illinois, but later moved with her family to California following her graduation from college. In *The Land of Little Rain* (1903), Austin describes the appeal of the Southwest, specifically its natural environment, noting, "The rainbow hills, the tender bluish mists, the luminous radiance of the spring, have the lotus charm. They trick the sense of time, so that once inhabiting there you always mean to go away without quite realizing you have not done it" (6). Elsewhere in *The Land of Little Rain*, Austin explains the importance of water to all inhabitants of the natural world, including man, by detailing the visitors to a water-hole. Among the visitors are coyotes, rabbits, cattle, rats, chipmunks, owls, quail, sparrows, and other animals (Austin 9–16). Austin prefaces her description of the visitors to the water-hole by observing that if humans adopted a different perspective and attempted to view nature through the lens of its other residents, then the trails leading to the water source would appear "as country roads, with scents for signboards" (9). In doing so, Austin suggests not only the need for an appreciation of the natural world, but the necessity of reconsidering human attitudes toward nature. The natural world that provided creative inspiration for Austin, not only affected in a similar manner later writers like John Graves and Edward Abbey, but led those writers to question the effects of ongoing human intrusion on the natural world and urge corrective action lest the region's fragile ecosystems be irreparably damaged. Hence, in *Goodbye to a River* (1959), Graves muses early in the book how "few people are willing to believe that a piece of country, hunted and fished and roamed over, felt and remembered, can be company enough" (16). Graves later remarks, "there is a pessimism about land which, after it has been with you a long time, becomes merely factual. Men increase; country suffers" (58). Abbey expresses sentiments similar to Graves when he opens *Desert Solitaire* by stating "this is the most beautiful place on earth" (1) and then adds to the description of the Moab desert by detailing a location where "lavender clouds sail like a fleet of ships across the pale dawn, each cloud, planed flat on the wind, has a base of fiery gold" (4). Abbey vents his resentment at those who do not fully appreciate the scenic beauty offered by the natural world, though, arguing those tourists who visit national parks are shortchanging themselves, since "so long as they are unwilling to crawl out of their cars they will not discover the treasures of the national parks," and as a result, Abbey claims these tourists "will never escape the stress and turmoil of those urban-suburban complexes which they had hoped, presumably, to leave behind a while" (51). Abbey's exhortations to not only appreciate nature but to take action to prevent man's destruction of the natural world become more urgent and take the form of encouraging ecological sabotage in his novel *The Monkey Wrench Gang* (1975).

Critical focus regarding the individual's appreciation of the environment and subsequent responsibility to preserve the natural world from exploitation at the hands of humans parallels similar critical responses to the situation of indigenous peoples evident in literature set in the Southwest. Just as the period of time following World War II witnessed an increase in the publication of literature concerned with preserving the natural landscape of the Southwest, the same period saw an increase in Native American writers, such as N. Scott Momaday, Leslie Marmon Silko, Simon J. Ortiz, and Paula Gunn Allen whose novels, short stories, poetry, and essays addressed the challenges faced by Native Americans in the Southwest in the twentieth century as they attempted to adjust to living in an increasingly industrialized, secular society that emphasized very different values. If writers expressed concern that the natural world was under assault by commercial interests bent on reaping the land's resources without any concern for the consequences, then Native American writers not only drew upon traditional cultural beliefs promoting the importance of maintaining harmony with the natural world, but also depicted people who not only had often been marginalized from the larger American society and relegated to tribal areas, but whose culture was subsequently in danger of being lost due to the imposition of the social values conveyed by Anglo-American culture.

In her essay "Language and Literature from a Pueblo Indian Perspective," Leslie Marmon Silko argues that an important difference exists between how the Pueblo and other Native American peoples view narrative compared to Anglo-American culture. Silko asserts that for the Pueblo and other Native American peoples, "language *is* story" and elaborates on this difference by describing how "at Laguna Pueblo, for example, many individual words have their own stories" (50). According to Silko, this idea of language yields situations "so when one is telling a story and one is using words to tell the story, each word that one is speaking has a story of its own, too," and she suggests, "this perspective on narrative—of story within story, the idea that one story is only the beginning of many stories and the sense that stories never truly end—represents an important contribution of Native American cultures to the English language" (50). As a result, Silko proposes this different conceptualization of storytelling results in "something that comes out of an experience and an understanding of that original view of Creation—that we are all part of a whole; we do not differentiate or fragment stories and experiences" (50).

Silko's observations regarding the differences in perceiving the function of language are present and echoed in a novel by another prominent Native American writer, N. Scott Momaday. In *House Made of Dawn*, Momaday chronicles the struggles of a young Tano named Abel, home from a foreign war, as he attempts to reconcile the differences between the world of his grandfather with its emphasis on oral tradition and the world of postwar industrial America. Momaday examines the role of language in the two cultures as a means of underscoring Abel's position caught between the two cultures.

Upon returning to the town where he was raised, Abel's inability to communicate using the language of his people reinforces the sense of dislocation he experiences regarding his surroundings since "he could not say the things he wanted" (Momaday 57). Abel endures frustration at his ability to even exchange common greetings, since "Had he been able to say it, anything of his own language—even the commonplace formula of greeting 'where are you going'—which had no being beyond sound, no visible substance, would once again have shown him whole to himself; but he was dumb" (57). Abel's inability to communicate illustrates his frustrations trying to negotiate the gulf he experiences between the native culture that forms the basis of his identity and the industrialized dominant culture in which he has been immersed due to his military service. The horrors of war he has witnessed have contributed to his being left "inarticulate" or unable to communicate exactly what forms the basis for the disgust he feels that motivates him to drink incessantly. Ironically, Abel's inability to verbalize his anger using his native tongue demonstrates the extent to which he has become distanced from the tribal culture with its emphasis on oral tradition and storytelling.

The importance of words becomes apparent in the novel's conclusion. As Abel runs after the other runners, he begins to sing under his breath. Momaday suggests that this act of singing does not involve strictly a literal sense, since "there was no sound, and he had no voice; he had only the words of a song" (191). Instead, Abel continues "running on the rise of the song," and the singing suggests that Abel has developed an awareness of the importance of remaining faithful to the usage of words encouraged by the tribal culture and knowledge that he must avoid becoming ensnared by the ways words are used in the manner of the dominant culture. In doing so, Abel must continue the journey running after the past represented by the stories and prayers associated with the tribe's history even as he continues to seek a cure for the disgust he feels regarding the dominant industrial culture.

Just as Abel encounters difficulty in navigating between two cultures in Momaday's *House Made of Dawn*, characters in narratives by Mexican American writers confront similar challenges. These challenges can be especially problematic for female characters, and this confronting of multiple cultures necessitates what Gloria Anzuldúa describes in *Borderlands/La Frontera: The New Mestiza* (1987) as a new mestiza consciousness resulting from "racial, ideological, cultural, and biological cross-pollination" (77). Consequently, Anzuldúa notes that *la mestiza* confronts an array of cultural messages. According to Anzaldúa, this clash of cultures necessitates that *la mestiza* must cope "by developing a tolerance for contradictions, a tolerance for ambiguity" (79). Anzaldúa suggests that *la mestiza* "can be jarred out of ambivalence by an intense, and often painful emotional event which inverts or resolves the ambivalence" (79). Only after experiencing a type of jarring emotional event akin to that Anzaldúa describes can the mestiza develop a new mestiza consciousness, whose "energy comes from continual creative motion that keeps breaking down the unitary aspect of each new paradigm" (80).

In her story "Bien Pretty" from *Woman Hollering Creek and Other Stories*, Sandra Cisneros depicts a mestiza, Lupe, who undergoes a jarring emotional experience similar to that mentioned by Anzaldúa, one that provides the foundation for Lupe to begin the development of a new mestiza consciousness.

The jarring event for Lupe Arrendondo in "Bien Pretty" occurs when her Mexican lover, Flavio Munguia, abruptly ends their relationship and returns to Mexico to the children from his two marriages. Although hearing the news makes Lupe feel as if "my Torres Special felt like it wanted to rise from my belly," Flavio responds to Lupe's hasty excuse that she needs to check on her clothes in the dryer by stating simply, "Es cool" (Cisneros 159). Flavio then exits from the story. The narrative of "Bien Pretty" can be read as Lupe's attempt to work through her distress by identifying and sorting those facets comprising her identity as she copes with Flavio's departure. Lupe's behavior reflects the assorted cultures whose presence exists in her life. These cultural influences include music featuring Amazon flutes, Tibetan gongs, and Aztec ocarinas. Lupe's impulse to draw upon Chicano culture as she copes with the jarring experience of Flavio abandoning her includes her visiting Casa Precidio Religious Articles, the Mexican voodoo shop, in search of votive candles. Illustrative of her acceptance of the contradictions between cultures, Lupe chooses "a Yo Puedo Mas Que Tu from the pagan side and a Virgin de Guadalupe from the Christian" (159). Lupe's situation requiring her to negotiate the problems of living in multiple cultures may be seen as representative of a recurring critical concern in Mexican American literature set in the Southwest: the realization that for many residents of the Southwest, the multiplicity of cultures in the region requires developing an ability to adjust to the conflicting demands and expectations of these different cultures.

In *The Cultures of the American New West*, Neil Campbell suggests that the New West, or one defined as a "complex, multifaceted, cultural text" (5) allows for fluidity, since this conceptualization of the West "is always relational, dialogic, engaged in or capable of reinvention—and, therefore, contradictory, irreducible, and hybrid" (164). As an area within the larger western region that possesses a distinctive cultural heritage, the Southwest embodies these attributes Campbell associates with the New West. As a result, southwestern literature rewards critical inquiry that considers the Southwest as a cultural text emerging from the past and informed not only by myths associated with the frontier, but also revealed in literary responses to nature and exploration of the challenges associated with living in a multicultural society.

Works Cited

Abbey, Edward. *Desert Solitaire: A Season in the Wilderness*. New York: Touchstone, 1968.

Anzaldúa, Gloria. *Borderlands/La Frontera: The New Mestiza*. San Francisco: Aunt Lute, 1987.

Austin, Mary. *The Land of Little Rain*. 1903. New York, Penguin, 1988.

Busby, Mark, ed. *The Greenwood Encyclopedia of American Regional Cultures: The Southwest*. Westport, CT: Greenwood, 2004.

Cabeza de Vaca, Álvar Núñez. *Adventures in the Unknown Interior of America*. Albuquerque: U of New Mexico P, 1983.

Campbell, Neil. *The Cultures of the American New West*. Edinburgh, UK: Edinburgh UP, 2000.

Cisneros, Sandra. *Woman Hollering Creek and Other Stories*. New York: Vintage, 1992.

Dobie, J. Frank. *Guide to Life and Literature of the Southwest*. Dallas: Southern Methodist UP, 1952.

Gibson, Arrell Morgan. "The Author as Image Maker for the Southwest." *Old Southwest/New Southwest: Essays on a Region and Its Literature*. Ed. Judy Nolte Lensink. Tucson, AZ: Tucson Public Library, 1987. 25–37.

Graves, John. *Goodbye to a River*. 1959. New York: Vintage, 2002.

Major, Mabel & T. M. Pearce. *Southwest Heritage: A Literary History with Bibliographies*. 3rd Rev. ed. Albuquerque: U of New Mexico P, 1972.

Momaday, N. Scott. *House Made of Dawn*. 1966. New York: Harper Perennial, 1977.

Powell, Lawrence Clark. *Southwest: Three Definitions*. Benson, AZ: Singing Wind Bookshop, 1990.

Silko, Leslie Marmon. *Yellow Woman and a Beauty of the Spirit: Essays on Native American Life Today*. New York: Touchstone, 1997.

Slotkin, Richard. *Gunfighter Nation: The Myth of the Frontier in Twentieth-Century America*. New York: Atheneum, 1992.

_____. *Regeneration Through Violence: The Mythology of the American Frontier, 1600–1860*. Norman: U of Oklahoma P, 2000.

Turner, Frederick Jackson. "The Significance of the Frontier in American History." 1947. *The Frontier in American History*. Tucson: U of Arizona P, 1997. 1–38.

Webb, Walter Prescott. *The Great Frontier*. 1951. Lincoln: U of Nebraska P, 1986.

Worden, Daniel. "The Literary Cultures of the American Southwest." *A Companion to the Literature and Culture of the American West*. Ed. Nicolas S. Witschi. West Sussex, UK: Wiley-Blackwell, 2011. 81–97.

Chicana "Feminist Architecture" in the Works of Sandra Cisneros

T. Jackie Cuevas

Although the mainstream view of southwestern literature has historically been constructed as the domain of Anglo writers, such as Larry McMurtry and Cormac McCarthy, Mexican American and other ethnic minority writers certainly have been a significant part of the cultural milieu of the US Southwest. As David King Dunaway asserts in *Writing the Southwest*, "[T]he core, or canon, of contemporary Southwestern literature (if not the bestseller lists) is solidly multiethnic, a reflection of a Southwestern, and indeed American, social reality which publishers have only belatedly acknowledged" (xxii). Among this multiethnic canon of US southwestern literature are Chicana/o, or Mexican American, writers such as the highly acclaimed author Sandra Cisneros.

Although born in Chicago and raised there as well as in Mexico City, Sandra Cisneros can rightfully be considered a writer of the US Southwest. Cisneros lived in San Antonio and the central Texas area for several years (Saldívar-Hull 105), and the region certainly crept into her work, such as in her short story collection *Woman Hollering Creek,* featuring places such as San Antonio and Seguin, Texas. Cisneros' work is also of the Southwest not only because of her Texas connection, but also because of her transnational connections to Mexico and the border region between Mexico and the US. While writers such as Rodolfo Anaya may have laid groundwork for situating southwestern Chicano experience in the American literary imagination, Cisneros infuses Mexican American women's fictional narratives into the US southwestern canon. Cisneros' works are among the Chicana/o texts that "help reconceive the region as multi-ethnic, multi-lingual, and multi-cultural" (Wrede 98). By producing narratives that situate Mexican Americans as transnational inhabitants of the US Southwest, Cisneros expands the geographic and metaphoric boundaries of what southwestern can mean.

One of the defining features of Sandra Cisneros' work is its emphasis on the interlocking struggles of existing in the US/Mexico borderlands, of being a woman in a male-dominated world, and being of Mexican descent in an Anglo-centric US. Responding to these struggles, Cisneros' young female protagonists enact various forms of Chicana-feminist cultural critique. Deborah L. Madsen remarks that "Chicana feminism has arisen largely from this need to contest the feminine stereotypes that define machismo, while at the same time identifying and working against the shared class and racial oppression that all Chicanos/as—men, women and children—experience" (108). Chicana cultural theorist Gloria Anzaldúa describes her own response to navigating life in the US/Mexico borderlands as strategically taking elements of her various cultures and making something new of them. In *Borderlands/La Frontera*, she asserts her form of Chicana feminism: "I will have to stand and claim my space, making a new culture—*una cultura mestiza*—with my own lumber, my own bricks and mortar and my own "feminist architecture" (Anzaldúa 44). Through resisting dominant ideas about gendered limitations and Chicana biculturalism, Cisneros weaves such a feminist architecture throughout her writing in various genres, such as novels, short stories, children's books, essays, and poetry. These narrative strategies interplay to allow for imagining new possibilities for self-construction for Cisneros' Chicana protagonists, particularly in her books *Woman Hollering Creek* and *Caramelo*.

Chicana Resistance in "Woman Hollering Creek"
The title story of *Woman Hollering Creek* examines the struggles of a young woman from Mexico who falls in love with a Mexican American man from Texas and naively expects him to whisk her away from poverty to a lavish American dream. Not knowing the exact details of her fiancé's line of work or the town where they will live, Cleófilas imagines Seguin, Texas—in reality, a small rural town—through the romantic lens of the *telenovelas* (Mexican soap operas) she watches on television: "*Seguín, Tejas.* A nice sterling ring to it. The tinkle of money. She would get to wear outfits like

---

the women on the *tele*" (Cisneros, *Woman Hollering* 45). After they marry and move to Seguin, Cleófilas' husband unexpectedly starts physically abusing her. By setting up Cleófilas' Mexican family home as a safe place compared to her home north of the US border, Cisneros' representation challenges the popularized misconception that Mexican men are somehow more patriarchal or domineering than American or Mexican American men: "In her own home her parents had never raised a hand to each other or to their children" (47). The story also subverts the dominant narrative of Mexicans going north for a "better life," as Cleófilas decides to return to the safety of her father's home in Mexico.

Cisneros cleverly manages Cleófilas' response to the abusive situation by reworking the folkloric legend of *la Llorona*. *La Llorona*, the Weeping Woman or Wailing Woman, "is an imporant part of Mexican storytelling traditiona on both sides of the US/Mexican border" (D. Perez ix). *La Llorona*, according to folk legend, is a ghostly woman said to haunt bodies of water, such as creeks and lakes. Various versions of the tale abound, but in many versions, *la Llorona*, out of misguided mercy or vengeance, has drowned her children and now roams around wailing for them. Across many variations of the story, a man is somehow involved, such as a husband who has abandoned or abused the woman who becomes *la Llorona*.

When Cleófilas and her husband first drive across Woman Hollering Creek as newlyweds traveling to Seguin, the husband refers to the creek as "La Gritona," (the shouting woman) a synonym for *la Llorona* (D. Perez 18), and Cleófilas wonders if the woman yells because of "pain or rage" (Cisneros, *Woman Hollering* 47). After the husband becomes abusive, Cleófilas struggles with what she should do. At a doctor's visit, a medical professional and her friend agree to help Cleófilas and her child leave her abusive situation by giving her a ride to the bus station so that she can return home to Mexico. The women make a plan to help Cleófilas leave her husband, and when she does, she lets out a loud wail of relief as she crosses back over the creek towards her home in Mexico. Cleófilas herself becomes the wailing woman; however, she escapes the fate of the ghostly *Llorona* of the cultural myth and instead becomes a figure of Chicana women's agency, connecting with other women to push back against patriarchal violence.

As Cisneros reworks the *Llorona* tale, she uses some of her linguistic techniques to render a particularized version of a widespread cultural myth. While readers familiar with Mexican culture would be familiar with *la Llorona*, Cisneros instead titles the story in English. Calling the story "Woman Hollering Creek" connects the setting to its specific geographic location in central Texas. The term "hollering" differs from the more common translations of *la Llorona* as the "wailing" or "weeping" woman. This defamilariazes the name, allowing readers to question the story's possible connection to the myth until the small hints gather into a direct confirmation when Cleófilas wonders, "Perhaps La Llorona is the one they named the creek after" (Cisneros, *Woman Hollering* 51).

Cisneros deploys other linguistic twists of phrase througouth the story. Some of the word choices in the story might seem random to non-bilingual Spanish and English readers. For instance, Cisneros intermixes English with Spanish terms to construct sentences such as the following: "...who doesn't care at all for music or *telenovelas* or romance or roses or the moon floating peraly over the *arroyo*" (*Woman Hollering* 49). Cisneros also uses Spanglish colloquialisms such as "*Bueno* bye" (55), a common, yet humorous, literal translation of "goodbye" that is used casually instead of "adiós." Cisneros uses a particularized mix of Spanglish, Spanish, and English terms to center the experience of her bilingual protagonist struggling to gain power over her life. This bilingual approach pushes against linguistic and literary conventions of mainstream US American literature, reminding readers that a Chicana story taking place in the US Southwest may require a multilingual approach.

Notably, Cleófilas' narrative is one of negotiating differential power not only between women and men, but also between cultures. The story takes place in an area marked by historical layers of colonization, including Spanish colonization of indigenous peoples starting in the 1500s, the wresting of the Texas region from Mexico in 1836, and subsequently fraught racial relations between Anglos and Mexicans (for a history of this region, see David Montejano's

Anglos and Mexicans in the Making of Texas, 1836–1986). Indeed, the region that provides the story's setting can be considered what Mary Louise Pratt has referred to as a "contact zone." Contact zones denote "social spaces where cultures meet, clash, and grapple with each other" (Pratt 24). Contextualized within this historical backdrop of colonization, Cleófilas personal struggle against domestic violence perpetuated by her American husband can be read as a struggle aginst a form of gendered colonization. As Rolando Pérez notes, "[M]any Latino/a writers see the linguistic struggle as inseparable from other social struggles" (95). Mixing languages to account for Chicana/o experience allows Cisneros to participate in "actively creating new forms of American expression" (R. Pérez 96) by using a common bilingual practice and making it her own.

On Cisneros' Novel *Caramelo*

In the novel *Caramelo*, another young Chicana protagonist navigates the competing pulls between cultural gender norms and linguistic conventions. *Caramelo* tells a story made of many stories, told through multiple voices, and woven together as an intertextual epic adventure from one generation to the next, one country to the next. The protagonist and narrator is Celaya Reyes, called "Lala," the only daughter in a family of seven children. Her father is Mexican, and her mother is Mexican American. The family lives in Chicago and travels back and forth each summer to Mexico City, her father's homeland, to visit his mother, "the Awful Grandmother." Lala's character assumes the role of storyteller, recounting the family's history through their travels to and from the US and Mexico and their eventual settling in San Antonio. While Lala tells her stories, she is often interrupted by the grandmother's voice, who critiques Lala's storytelling and sometimes takes over the narration. In the multigenerational saga, the Reyes family's story moves from the young Lala to her grandmother's earlier life, to Lala's parents and her father's siblings. As a *Bildungsroman*, the narrative tells a bicultural coming-of-age story by moving recursively back and forth to Lala's as she grows and serves as a central figure in the family's transnational saga.

Along the way, Lala challenges gendered expecations placed upon her as a young Chicana. For example, Lala disobeys her family when they attempt to forbid her to interact with Candelaria, a peasant girl in Mexico who, Lala eventually learns, is her father's secret "illegitimate" child and, therefore, her sister. Lala's interaction with a darker Mexican girl of a lower socioeconimic class would be considered "unladylike" (Heredia 46) or inappropriate for her supposed middle-class station as compared to Candelaria's status as a member of an underclass. Lala's family's attitudes against consorting with darker, poorer Mexicans highlights the racism within Mexican culture and connects its enforcement to social expectations around gender.

Lala also has to contend with her family's imposition of the virgin/whore dichotomy, which dictates that young women must abide by strict gendered codes of propriety or risk being seen as "whores" or "*putas*." When Lala intends to run off with her boyfriend, her mother lays out the social consequences: "If you leave your father's house without a husband, you are worse than a dog. You aren't my daughter, you aren't a Reyes.... If you leave alone you leave like, and forgive me for saying this but it's true, *como una prostituta*. Is that what you want the world to think?" (Cisneros, *Caramelo* 360). Lala leaves anyway, at least temporarily, but separates from her boyfriend and returns to her family.

The grandmother's storyline exposes another gendered struggle. As "The Awful Grandmother" ages, she notices that "Men no longer looked at her" (Cisneros, *Caramelo* 347). She worries that "society no longer gave her much importance after her role of mothering was over" (347). Feeling her social value wane as her social role as mother is no longer valued, the grandmother's observation reveals the limited options available to Chicanas.

Besides the gendered struggles, the characters also face struggles as Chicanos existing in multiple cultures and geographic spaces. The plot follows the Reyes' family's annual road trip from Chicago to Mexico City, allowing for expression of the multiple cultural geographies inhabited by the Chicana/o characters. The primary geographies in the novel are Chicago as representative of a Chicana/o center within the US and Mexico City as homeland. Later in the novel, the Reyes family moves to San Antonio, which becomes a third home, a convergence in the borderlands. Both of Lala Reyes' parents see each other as from "the other side" or "*el otro lado*." This positioning of the parents as being from or on opposite "sides" creates a space for the dynamics of interpersonal drama, cultural representations, linguistic interplay, and bicultural identity formation by the young protagonist as a Chicana. Lala describes her experience of her two parents as two opposing sides: "For a long time I thought the eagle and the serpent on the Mexican flag were the United States and Mexico fighting. And then, for an even longer time afterward, I thought of the eagle and the serpent as the story of Mother and Father" (Cisneros, *Caramelo* 235). Lala describes her parents as having "lots of fights" that center around issues such as "the Mexicans from this side compared to the Mexicans from that side" (235).

Setting up this construct of the two parents as the bearers of "opposing" geographies and cultures, Cisneros weaves a narrative that engages in what can be described as "simultaneous intra- and intercultural critiques" (Villa 248) of Anglo, Mexicano, and Chicano cultures. The parents as representative of their respective countries is complicated by their shifts in which "side" they identify with and which aspects of each side's culture they are accepting, rejecting, or otherwise critiquing/examining. For example, the Mexican father, Inocencio Reyes, at one point says about the US, "this great country has given me so much" (Cisneros, *Caramelo* 245). The Mexican American mother, Zoila, responds with a less than subtle critique of the US: "Great country, my ass! If they ever get to Toto's number [in the Vietnam draft lottery], I'm taking him personally to Mexico, Mother says, disgusted" (245). The mother goes on to say that "all the brown and black faces are up on the front line," and that the situation seems like "a government conspiracy" (245). At one point, Zoila says that she "can't stand...Mexicans" (353) even though she is married to a Mexican man and is herself of Mexican ethnicity/ origin; at another point, Inocencio is "cursing all Chicanos for acting like Chicanos and giving Mexico a bad name" (379). Through these intra- and intercultural critiques, Cisneros captures the quite complex challenges of negotiating life as an immigrant and as an ethnic "Other" in a hegemonic Anglo-US.

The daughter's history is introduced into the novel in a chapter entitled "All Parts from Mexico, Assembled in the U.S.A., or I am Born," contributing to the positioning of the characters as competing cultural signifiers and Lala as the Chicana hybrid, torn between both of her parent's cultures. As a *Bildungsroman*, the novel portrays the coming of age of Lala in a circular, nonlinear narrative that mimics a sense of ping-pong, a push-pull, bouncing from one culture and geographical center to another; it also creates an expanding sense of a complex cultural identity through Lala's development as a Chicana who is bicultural/bilingual.

Many of the chapters in *Caramelo* have footnotes, in which the narrator provides either commentary on narrative or authorial intentions, translations of Spanish idioms, or historical or geographical references. For example, in the chapter called "Neither with Your Nor Without You" (Cisneros, *Caramelo* 222), a chapter barely over six pages is followed by a three-page footnote. The footnote gives historical context for characters based on actual lives, a lengthy example to explain an idiom, and a history of Carranza's Grocery and Market, presumably an actual San Antonio locale, which the narrator, blurring the lines between Lala the narrator and Cisneros the author, says she "recommended highly until a fire snuffed them out of business" (230). This type of aside acknowledges the reader's presence, as well as the author's, and it creates an oral storytelling quality as part of the intertextual conversations and weavings. This same footnote contains comments on the questionable veracity of the stories in the chapter: "My friend's mother, who still lives in the Colonia Roma and was neighbors with the Vasconcelos family in the forties and fifties, told me this story but made me promise never to tell anyone, which is why I am certain it must be true, or, at the very least, somewhat true" (Mermann-Jozwiak 230).

Drawing on Mexican and Chicano cultures, the text also includes lyrics from popular songs as part of its intertextual construction. The opening chapter begins with an epigraph with song lyrics that set the stage for the initial story of the Reyes family's visit to Acapulco. Another chapter contains the entire lyrics of a song in Spanish and in English; the lyrics to "Júrame" ("Promise Me") are followed by a note that the chapter is "To be accompanied by the scratchy 1927 version of 'Júrame,' as recorded by José Mojica, the Mexican Valentino" and includes a description of the singer: "[I]magine a voice like Caruso, a voice like purple velvet with gold satin tassels, a voice like a bullfighter's bloody jacket, a voice like a water-stained pillow bought at the Lagunilla flea market embroidered with '*No Me Olvides*'" (Cisneros, *Caramelo* 183). Some chapters simply have references to song titles, such as "*Por un amor*," or to other popular singers, such as Lola Beltrán. Other "texts," symbols of pop culture, and iconic figures embedded in the text include references to Pedro Infante movies, Buster Keaton movies, and many references to Mexican *fotonovelas* (serial cartoons, commonly referred to as graphic novels or comic books in the US), such as *La familia Burrón*. One very brief (one paragraph) chapter, entitled "*Fotonovelas*" (63) includes a lengthy footnote consisting entirely of a list of the *fotonovelas* that "The Awful Grandmother" has saved for her son.

As in *Woman Hollering Creek*, Cisneros engages in an interplay of multiple languages in *Caramelo*. One prevalent example of linguistic experimentation involves literal translations from Spanish to English. For example, characters that would be called "tía Güera" or "tío Gordo" in Chicano or Mexicano circles are called "Aunty Light-Skin" and "Uncle Fat-Face." Another example occurs in the direct translation of common phrases and idioms, such as the title of a popular Spanish song sung at birthday celebrations: instead of "Las Mañanitas," Cisneros uses "The Little Mornings." Reviewer Margaret Randall says of this strategy: "[T]he meaning beneath the meaning rises up, grabs the reader and shakes her or him into awareness." On the other hand, the literal translations provided in English without being accompanied by the original phrase in Spanish seems to privilege one language over the other by not acknowledging, and thereby erasing in a sense, the cultural root of the idiom. Additionally, the nuances and layered meanings may be lost on a non-Spanish-speaking readership. Yet, by using these literal translations, the author provides character names and expressions that can be experienced as "universal" signifiers by a broad readership. For example, the grandmother is not "*abuela*" but "The Awful Grandmother," representing any awful grandmother figure, perhaps regardless of geography or culture. While humorous, constructions such as "The Awful Grandmother" also serve as a form of truth-telling, allowing the young protagonist to subvert codes of propriety that demand nothing but "repectful" language from a young woman. Valerie Sayers also observes in *Caramelo* a blending of languages as it relates to the cultural combinations and geographic shifts in the novel's setting: "As they cross the border, Lala also crosses languages: '*Toc*, says the light switch in this country, at home it says *click*. *Honk*, say the cars at home, here they say *tán-tán-tán*'" (Sayers 7). Some of the linguistic border-crossings exemplify the unique, often humorous, language that can occur. For example, the speech of the father character is sometimes expressed as phonetic spellings of English terms as spoken by a Spanish-dominant speaker, such as "*Más-güel*" for "Maxwell" (Cisneros, *Caramelo* 295). The father also takes delight in making linguistic jokes, such as mixing English and Spanish words into intentionally comedic constructions.

According to Claire Joysmith, "Chicana/o texts that use these strategies create a poetics and politics that privileges bicultural and bilingual practices" (149). Joysmith notes, "We could say that "attentive outside readers" are, in a sense, acknowledged through the use of intratextual translational strategies" (150). In *Caramelo*, similar "intratextual translational strategies" can be found. Spanish phrases are sometimes explained in context or translated into English the first time they are used in the novel and then used without contextual or translational clues thereafter. The contextual clues are sometimes actual translations, as in the following example: [E]veryone knows Uncle Fat-Face by his Italian nickname, Rico, instead of Fat-Face or Federico, even though "*rico*" means "rich" in Spanish, and Uncle is always complaining that he is *pobre, pobre*" (Cisneros, *Caramelo* 10). Cisneros follows this up with a punchline:

"It is no disgrace to be poor, Uncle says, citing the Mexican saying,— but it is very inconvenient" (10).

In some instances, the translations are accompanied by cross-cultural explanations: When "The Awful Grandmother" calls the Reyes kids "a bunch of *malcriadas*," Lala the narrator explains that "She means 'badly raised'" (Cisneros, *Caramelo* 70). After the grandmother has a stroke, Zoila (the mother, who has never gotten along with the grandmother, her mother-in-law) "finally dares to address her the way she feels fit. She calls her "*tú*," the familiar "*you*, " not "*usted*," which is "like bowing" (342). In this way, the reader is provided not only a translation, but also an explanation and context for understanding the nature of authority and power relations as expressed through language within this Spanish-speaking family.

These intratextual translations make the text accessible to a monolingual English-speaking readership, while also allowing a bilingual readership to experience the layered nuances on a different level. Through these linguistic experimentations, as well as through the representations of the complex dynamics of culture and gender, *Caramelo* weaves a densely constructed narrative that makes a significant contribution to the body of southwestern Chicana/o literature.

Conclusion

In *Woman Hollering Creek* and *Caramelo*, Cisneros employs the tensions of biculturality to convey the gendered and racialized challenges of Chicana experience in the Southwest borderlands. Indeed, race and gender struggles are intertwined for Cisneros. Describing her own "feminist architecture," the author says, "I guess my feminism and my race are the same thing to me. They're tied in one to another" (Jussawalla & Dasenbrock 298). Through her feminist Chicana narratives with signature linguistic wordplay, Cisneros articules in her fiction what she describes elsewhere as a a kind of cultural bifurcation: "We're always straddling two countries, and we're always living in that kind of schizophrenia that I call, being a Mexican woman living in an American society, but not belonging to either culture." (Madsen 108). In her narratives,

Cisneros explores and expands what it means to be Mexican in and beyond the US Southwest.

Works Cited

Anzaldúa, Gloria. *Borderlands / La Frontera: The New Mestiza*. 3rd ed. San Francisco: Aunt Lute, 2007.

Bruce-Novoa, Juan. *Chicano Authors: Inquiry by Interview*. Austin: U of Texas P, 1980.

Busby, Mark. *The Southwest*. Westport, CT: Greenwood, 2004.

Cisneros, Sandra. *Caramelo*. New York: Knopf, 2002.

_____. *Woman Hollering Creek and Other Stories*. New York: Random House, 1991.

Dunaway, David King. *Writing the Southwest*. Albuquerque: U of New Mexico P, 2003.

Joysmith, Claire. "Response: (Re)Mapping *mexicanidades*: (Re)Locating Chicana Writings and Translation Politics." *Chicana Feminisms: A Critical Reader*. Ed. Gabriela F. Arredondo, et al. Durham: Duke UP, 2003. 146–154.

Jussawalla, Feroza F. & Reed Way Dasenbrock. *Interviews with Writers of the Post-Colonial World*. Jackson: UP of Mississippi, 1992.

Madsen, Deborah L. *Understanding Contemporary Chicana Literature*. Columbia, SC: U of South Carolina P, 2000.

Mermann-Jozwiak, Elisabeth. "Gritos desde la frontera: Ana Castillo, Sandra Cisneros, and Postmodernism." *MELUS* 25.2 (Summer 2000): 101–118.

Montejano, David. *Anglos and Mexicans in the Making of Texas, 1836–1986*. Austin: U of Texas P, 1987.

Perez, Domino Renee. *There Was a Woman: La Llorona from Folklore to Popular Culture*. Austin: U of Texas P, 2008.

Pérez, Rolando. "What Is 'Minor' in Latino Literature." *MELUS* 30.4 (2005): 89–108.

Pratt, Mary Louise. "Arts of the Contact Zone." *Profession* (1991): 33–40.

Rivera, Carmen Haydée. *Border Crossings and Beyond: The Life and Works of Sandra Cisneros*. Santa Barbara: Macmillan, 2009.

Randall, Margaret. "Weaving a Spell. Rev. of *Caramelo*, by Sandra Cisneros." *Women's Review of Books* 20.1 (Oct. 2002): 1–3.

Saldívar-Hull, Sonia. *Feminism on the Border: Chicana Gender Politics and Literature*. Berkeley: U of California P, 2000.

Sayers, Valerie. "Traveling with Cousin Elvis. Rev. of *Caramelo*, by Sandra Cisneros." *New York Times* 29 Sept. 2002: 7+.

Villa, Raúl Homero. *Barrio-Logos: Space and Place in Urban Chicano Literature and Culture*. U of Texas P: Austin, 2000.

Wrede, Theda. *Myth and Environment in Recent Southwestern Literature: Healing Narratives*. Lanham, MD: Lexington Books, 2014.

Writing (and Righting) the Desert Southwest: Literary Legacies and the Restoration of Glen Canyon_____

Laura Smith

> Hell of a place to lose a cow. Hell of a place to lose your heart. Hell of a place, thought Seldom Seen, to lose. Period.
>
> (Abbey, *The Monkey Wrench Gang* 310)

"There is something about the desert," Edward Abbey (*Desert Solitaire* 242) once remarked, and across the American Southwest, indeed throughout southwestern literature, there are few desert landscapes that provoke and stir the imagination more than the canyon landscapes of Glen Canyon in southern Utah. When Glen Canyon was flooded and replaced by Glen Canyon Dam and Lake Powell in the late-1950s and early-1960s, southwestern writers Katie Lee (1919–); Edward Abbey (1927–1989); and, later, Ellen Meloy (1946–2004) and Terry Tempest Williams (1955–) sought, to borrow Henry David Thoreau's proclamation, to "speak a word for Nature, for absolute freedom and wildness, as contrasted with a freedom and culture merely civil" (Thoreau, "Walking" 225). What these writers of the Desert Southwest sought was the restoration of Glen Canyon and a free-flowing Colorado River. This essay tells of the cautionary tales of Katie Lee, Edward Abbey, Ellen Meloy, and Terry Tempest Williams and examines the "ecology of influence" (Philippon) and lasting legacy of these Glen Canyon writers.

Alongside this literary legacy in Glen Canyon sits a political legacy, one that remains as contested and vehemently defended as its literary sibling. And so, whilst Glen Canyon's literary history is echoed in the fortieth anniversary on August 1, 2015 of the publication of Edward Abbey's *The Monkey Wrench Gang*, its political history is also galvanized by the fiftieth anniversary on September 27, 2014 of power generation at Glen Canyon Dam. It is the ensuing politicization of the literary imaginary that frames discussion here—how, through *writing*, one can begin to (attempt to) *right* this landscape of the Desert Southwest. This provides a unique opportunity to bring into relief tensions between the particularities of a literary Glen Canyon and the revalorization (revaluing) of the political landscape of Glen Canyon, taking forward Sara L. Spurgeon's claim that "the increasingly insistent calls to restore Glen Canyon, demonstrates that *literary texts are intrinsically part of the public discourse* surrounding water policy in the West" (754, emphasis added). It is, as David N. Cassuto proposes, pitting *mythology* against *hydrology* in Glen Canyon.

Glen Canyon's Literary Places and Literary Traces

The use of a literary imaginary to defend landscapes of the Desert Southwest did not begin with Glen Canyon; indeed (and, perhaps, somewhat ironically), it was the success of a campaign less than 500 miles north of Glen Canyon that eventually condemned this canyon landscape, and triggered the subsequent literary battle cry in Glen Canyon. Wallace Stegner's *This Is Dinosaur: Echo Park Country and Its Magic Rivers* provided part of the armory of conservation groups opposing the construction of a dam within the boundary of Dinosaur National Monument in the mid-1950s—a collection of essays and photographs, it documented what would be lost to the dam construction. A hard-fought battle by conservationists eventually saw the dam site relocated elsewhere on the Green River, but also saw them concede the development of Glen Canyon Dam on the Colorado River, as part of the wider Colorado River Storage Project. The difference at Glen Canyon, however, is that its literary legacy is one that emerged *post*-dam construction, beginning with Eliot Porter's *The Place No One Knew: Glen Canyon on the Colorado*.

It is a literary legacy informed and molded not just by literary *places*, but also by literary *traces*, those "marks, residues or remnants left in place" (Anderson, *Understanding Cultural* 5) by the literary imaginary. At Glen Canyon, such literary traces, although latent, are manifested through the residual emotion, memory, and myth attached to what Wallace Stegner identifies as "Glen Canyon Submersus" (they are, to echo Jon Anderson, non-material traces).

Yet these traces endure precisely because "they may leave indelible marks on our memory or mind" (Anderson, *Understanding Cultural* 5). As Katie Lee admits, "We are the lucky ones—we didn't just see it with our eyes. I feel its presence all the while I'm gone, an empathy with rock and river that's forever mine" (*Glen Canyon Betrayed* 228). It is through literary traces, imprints, and vestiges that this literature can serve as a custodian of memory, emotion, ideals, and values in Glen Canyon.

Revealed in this literature of the Colorado Plateau is a "desert imagination," where a desert motif provides a backdrop for literary expectation, engagement, and experience with the land: "Since you cannot get the desert into a book any more than a fisherman can haul up the sea with his nets, I have tried to create a world of words in which the desert figures more as medium than as material. Not imitation but evocation has been the goal" (Abbey, *Desert Solitaire* xii). This desert motif, Ellen Meloy argues, might best be understood through "words tethered to its heart: *Sun, stone, sierra, saltbush. Arroyo. Acrophobia. Desire* and *desolation. Dust* and *imagination. Absolute clarity, extreme blue*" (*Eating Stone* 87). For these writers, Glen Canyon lay at the very heart of this desert imagination, and as Edward Abbey remembers, "The canyonlands did have a heart, a living heart, and that heart was Glen Canyon and the golden, flowing Colorado River" (*Beyond* 95)—it is a desert imaginary grounded in a Once and Future Glen (Lee, *Sandstone Seduction*). This fantasy desert, to adopt Peter Wild's phrase, thus becomes "a vehicle for the exercise of the imagination's most colorful wishes" (162). It is through the literary imaginary that the desert's many guises emerge: "Desert as teacher. Desert as mirage. Desert as illusion, largely our own" (Williams, *Red* 5). The desert imagination is not simply *storing* narratives, but offers a way of also *conveying* narratives.

There is also an invention and reinvention of tradition, of mediation and negotiation in the desert imagination. As Terry Tempest Williams recognizes, "This territory is not neutral. The redrock desert and canyon country of southern Utah provokes powerful and divisive opinions" (*Red* 3)—not least between the literary imaginaries of the Glen-Canyon-that-was and the

Lake-Powell-that-is. The naming (and renaming) of places and organizations further reveals literary traces that criss-cross the Colorado Plateau—building on "The folk poetry of the pioneers" (Abbey, *Desert Solitaire* 226)—and points to the question of place-making, as well as authorship, narration, and curation. Glen Canyon was named by Major John Wesley Powell's 1869 survey expedition, after noting "So we have a curious *ensemble* of wonderful features—carved walls, royal arches, glens, alcove gulches, mounds, and monuments. From which of these features shall we select a name? We decide to call it Glen Canyon" (145), with Lake Powell later named after the explorer. More recent (literary) renamings reveal the contested and politicized rights-claims in Glen Canyon—of the canyonlands of the Colorado Plateau as Abbey's Country; of Lake Powell as Lake Foul (Abbey, *Down, Hayduke*; Farmer, *Glen Canyon Dammed*), also Floyd's Void (Farmer, *Glen Canyon Dammed*), or Lake Dominy (McPhee) (after Floyd Dominy [1909–2010], the Bureau of Reclamation Commissioner who oversaw construction of Glen Canyon Dam); of Lake Mead as Lake Merde (Abbey, *Down, Hayduke*); and the Bureau of Reclamation as the Bureau of Wreck-the-Nation (Lee, *Glen Canyon Betrayed*) or Wrecklamation (Abbey, *Monkey Wrench*). Such naming has "anthologized local history, anecdote and myth, binding story to place" (Macfarlane 20).

36.9375° N, 111.4844° W: Where Literature and Environmental Politics Meet in the Desert

> Ah yes, that dam. That Glen Canyon Dam and the 180-mile lake behind it that boatmen call Lake Foul. In all of the Rocky Mountain, Inter-Mountain West, no man-made object has been hated so much, by so many, for so long, with such good reason, as that 700,000-ton plug of gray concrete, blocking our river.
>
> (Abbey, *Down the River* 186)

The flooding of Glen Canyon saw it become "the anti-symbol of the emerging environmental movement, the epitome of human arrogance and destructiveness" (Farmer, *Glen Canyon Dammed* xv). The biography of place that emerged alongside the construction of Glen Canyon Dam and Lake Powell is a mnemonic, marking, claiming, and reclaiming the Glen Canyon landscape. As Bruce Berger acknowledges, "One phenomenon is its literature" (49), a sentiment echoed by John McPhee, as desert writers "capitalized on literary hyperbole and the mystic name of the canyon" (166). And so I wish to pose the question: *What place is there for Southwestern Literature in Glen Canyon debates?*

The stories and literary narratives at Glen Canyon are troubling the distinction between real and imagined landscapes—as Jon Anderson contends, "the distinctions between the fictional and the real often become entangled when we *cross the breach between page and place* (*Page and Place* 11, emphasis added; cf. Jared Farmer's "literary memory of an imagined place"). A tension surrounds the place of the desert imagination in environmental politics and political discourse at Glen Canyon, not least because of the provocative literary war cry to "keep it like it was" (Abbey, *Monkey Wrench* 20) that is echoed across this biography of place. This combined literary canon embodies what Scott Slovic terms a literature of hope, that is, the "assumption that the elevation of consciousness may lead to wholesome political change" (18).

Edward Abbey's and Katie Lee's best known writings on Glen Canyon are personal narratives and reflections of float trips through the Glen prior to and during construction of the dam. "Down the River," a chapter in *Desert Solitaire*, vividly and emotively recounts Edward Abbey's sole float trip through the Glen in 1959, a record "of a last voyage through a place we knew, even then, was doomed" (152). He goes on to note, "Once it was different there. I know, for I was one of the lucky few (there could have been thousands more) who saw Glen Canyon before it was drowned. In fact I saw only a part of it but enough to realize that here was an Eden, a portion of the earth's original paradise" (152). In *Glen Canyon Betrayed*, Katie Lee journals her explorations and adventures amidst the canyons of the Glen and along the Colorado River between 1954 and 1957 and the looming presence of Glen Canyon Dam. For Katie Lee, "Witnessing the asphyxiation of Glen Canyon—slowly, inch by inch—acted like a brand on my soul, burning in my anger, my contempt for those who killed it" (*Glen Canyon Betrayed* 246).

Clear in both Abbey's and Lee's memoirs (as well as in several subsequent essays) is a polemic for the restoration of the Glen, making a case for environmental (and political) reform—firmly embedding the desert imagination in public discourse on "Glen Canyon restoration." The writing is often deliberately provocative, but it is also an eloquent lament to a disappearing canyon landscape; offering solace for the impending deluge. Edward Abbey makes this point when he acknowledges, "Lots of people give a shit about Glen because they never saw it. They're beginning to know what they missed" (Lee, *Sandstone Seduction* 100). And as Katie Lee argues, "The point is to *have the place*; to know it's here when I need it; to regroup and take a fresh outlook to the *other* reality—the one where I make the bucks to get here so I can forget the place where I make the bucks" (Lee, *Glen Canyon Betrayed* 215).

The message of revolt and rebellion present in much of Abbey's and Lee's Glen Canyon writings is tempered by the more philosophical and spiritual writings of Ellen Meloy and Terry Tempest Williams. Writing after the construction of Glen Canyon Dam and the creation of Lake Powell, both Meloy and Williams frequently expand their focus beyond Glen Canyon to the deserts of southern Utah, placing a particular emphasis on the purposes and processes of seeking awareness and paying attention (Slovic) through the desert imagination. For Terry Tempest Williams, there is a mythology imbued in the desert imagination, a mythology rooted in the allegory of Coyote—both as Coyote's country and a Coyote Clan (*Red*)—which is used to understand and respond to ecological upheaval in the desert. Agency in the desert is placed center-stage, for "As if by instinct I had long ago embraced the desert with the full knowledge that neither passion nor beauty comes without risk and that these conditions of being might well burn me right up" (Meloy, *Last Cheater's Waltz* 5). Indeed Meloy, in *The Anthropology of Turquoise*, uses turquoise (both the gemstone and the color) as a medium for unpacking and exploring human attachment to the plateaus and canyons of the American Southwest and beyond. Such a focus allows for "literary investigations of awakening" (Slovic

18), echoing Henry David Thoreau's desire that, "We must learn to reawaken and keep ourselves awake" (*Walden* 90).

But this biography of place is not simply restricted to the Glen-Canyon-that-was, but has also turned to the Lake-Powell-that-is to further bolster a reformist position. As examples of this, one need only look to Edward Abbey's essays "Lake Powell by Houseboat" (*One Life*), and "The Damnation of a Canyon" (*Beyond*), or Ellen Meloy's chapter "Travels with Seldom" (*Raven's Exile*), amongst many others.

What is particularly compelling about the literature of Glen Canyon is a confidence in individual interference. What emerges is a moral argument—a moral obligation—in defence of the Desert Southwest. Inspired by Edward Abbey, there is a belief that "Somebody had to do it" (*Monkey Wrench* 44)—with the justification that "and if you don't attack it, it strip-mines the mountains, dams all the rivers, paves over the desert and puts you in jail anyway" (112). No one encapsulates this better than Katie Lee, when she reflects on the personal compact she has with the Colorado River:

> Then I thought … Hey, I have a compact of *my very own*, made on a personal level, having nothing to do with those people, with politics, with greed or manipulation. *I* have a compact with the Colorado River and its canyons. Furthermore, I hadn't made it on any goddamned piece of paper and sent it up for approval past a row of upright, uptight, know-nothings, some of whom had never seen or heard of a place called Glen Canyon.
>
> The compact asked that I not forget the river-that-was; that I go to canyons that drained into the once-and-future Glen and find whatever solace they might offer, thus easing the pain of the big canyon's loss. […]
>
> Yet, let me urge you (no matter the odds) to seek out such a place. Why? Because *you need it*, whether you know it or not. If and when you find it, tell no one else where it is. Keep it as long as possible and, like a loved one, cherish it, being aware that love is also pain, discovery, joy unrealized and—sooner or later—loss.
>
> (*Glen Canyon Betrayed* 251–252)

One way of understanding how the desert imagination intersects, conflicts, and supplements the political landscape at Glen Canyon is through what Daniel J. Philippon defines as an "ecology of influence." This ecology of influence extends beyond "how nature writing has influenced people's attitudes and behavior, [...] to consider the wide range of connections that exist between particular authors, readers, and texts at particular times and—most importantly—in particular places" (4). The ecology of influence and lasting legacy of these Glen Canyon writers is such that, as Bruce Berger contends, "Glen Canyon became more famous in death than it ever had been in life" (48). Moreover, through "participation in the Thoreauvian tradition of consciousness-raising" (Slovic 100), of seeking awareness and paying attention through the desert imagination, this ecology of influence is realized in the fact that, "Each time we say "the River" we seem to resurrect the lost wild country" (Meloy, *Raven's Exile* 93).

"You're holding a tombstone in your hands:" Rhetoric and Responses to 'Righting' Glen Canyon

The above quote is the concluding remark from Edward Abbey's "Author's Introduction" to *Desert Solitaire*, and the sentiment deserves further elaboration, not least because it serves to set up well the discussion that now follows in this essay: "most of what I write about in this book is already gone or going under fast. This is not a travel guide but an elegy. A memorial. You're holding a tombstone in your hands. A bloody rock. Don't drop it on your foot—throw it at something big and glassy. What do you have to lose?" (xiv). The narrative of *loss* is one that is pronounced across much of the Glen Canyon literary canon—what Wallace Stegner terms a "consciousness of loss" ("Submersus")—and serves as the touch-paper for many conservation and restoration sensibilities.

Although the writings of Edward Abbey and Katie Lee (and to a lesser extent, those of Ellen Meloy and Terry Tempest Williams) might be read as eulogizing Glen Canyon, they also underscore "the power of literature to keep the light of battle burning, even after a dam was constructed" (Spurgeon 746). This biography of place has extended the afterlife of this labyrinthine canyon country of southern Utah.

Through the desert imagination of Edward Abbey and Katie Lee, the demolition of Glen Canyon Dam becomes the ultimate act of restoration. Abbey first recommends blowing up the dam in his nonfiction writing *Desert Solitaire*, noting:

> Some unknown hero with a rucksack full of dynamite strapped to his back will descend into the bowels of the dam; there he will hide his high explosives where they'll do the most good, attach blasting caps to the lot and with angelic ingenuity link the caps to the official dam wiring system in such a way that when the time comes for the grand opening ceremony, when the President and the Secretary of the Interior and the governors of the Four-Corner states are all in full regalia assembled, the button which the President pushes will ignite the loveliest explosion ever seen by man, reducing the great dam to a heap of rubble in the path of the river. (165)

A similar sentiment is later expressed by Katie Lee, "Well, I *don't* want it to be a stinking puddle, and I have as much right to it as they do, more actually; I know and love it. My very soul is in this canyon, so ... I think I'll spend the rest of my days figuring a way to blow up their damn dam" (*Glen Canyon Betrayed* 121).

But it is through Edward Abbey's later fiction—the comic novels *The Monkey Wrench Gang* and *Hayduke Lives!*—that this idea further evolves, becoming the elusive grail of Abbey's quartet of ecodefenders:

> The Baron circled again for one more viewing, pleased with what he saw, what all the tourists on the highway and in the visitor center saw: a huge black spattered "X" upon the dam's massive face, the "X" of condemnation, of doom implacable, inescapable, complete and certain.
>
> (*Hayduke* 184)

A less incendiary proposal from the literary imaginary calls for the decommissioning and bypassing of Glen Canyon Dam. As Edward Abbey submits in his essay "The Damnation of a Canyon,"

We can shut down the Glen Canyon power plant, open the diversion tunnels, and drain the reservoir. This will no doubt expose a drear and hideous scene: immense mud flats and whole plateaus of sodden garbage strewn with dead trees, sunken boats, the skeletons of long-forgotten, decomposing water-skiers. But to those who find the prospect too appalling, I say give nature a little time".

(*Beyond* 103)

This sentiment recurs elsewhere in the literature, with Katie Lee arguing, "Tear the dam down? No. That's expensive and unnecessary. Time, and the river flowing, will take it away. Floyd Dominy wants it left there as his monument. So do I—a monument to his and the bureau's arrogance and stupidity" (*Glen Canyon Betrayed* 254), while Terry Tempest Williams suggests, "let us take down with humility what we once built with pride" (*Red* 181).

The consequences of the worsening drought and the highly charged debates currently being waged over water scarcity in the American Southwest, the work of the Glen Canyon Institute and its Fill Mead First campaign, and the recent publication by former Bureau of Reclamation Commissioner Daniel P. Beard entitled *Deadbeat Dams: Why We Should Abolish the U.S. Bureau of Reclamation and Tear Down Glen Canyon Dam* all offer ready examples of a reinvigoration and revalorization of a political (and politicized) Glen Canyon (cf. Spurgeon). Moreover, Glen Canyon has also featured in two recent documentary films, and these serve as a further barometer of the ecology of influence of desert writers: *DamNation* (2014) spotlights the increasing call to decommission and remove redundant dams, while *Wrenched* (2014) revisits Edward Abbey's legacy at the start of the twenty-first century. Archive footage and interviews with Edward Abbey, Katie Lee, and Terry Tempest Williams, as well as other writers, commentators, and activists, appear across both documentaries. This political reframing points to the beginnings of a paradigm shift in water storage and resource management along the Colorado River, as well as in the restoration of Colorado River ecosystems—for Ellen Meloy, "The stories of how to 'do' the dam are, like the sheer catharsis they serve, epic and legendary" (*Raven's Exile* 95).

The desert imagination also introduces the possibility of the restoration of the Glen *by nature*, when Seldom Seen Smith calls for "a little old *pre*-cision-type earthquake right under this dam" (Abbey, *Monkey Wrench* 34). Another reimagining of this is expressed by Katie Lee when she muses, "But, oh boy, I'd like to see a storm that would blow out every dam on this river, and a few more besides" (Lee, *Glen Canyon Betrayed* 222). The *agency of the river* to bring about ecological restoration is also explored in the literary imaginary, with Katie Lee positing, "No matter how much water drowns my river's home, I'll know he's here, quietly...patiently... working his way to freedom...once again!" (*Glen Canyon Betrayed* 228). Revealed through this desert motif, then, is the promise of a *desert justice*.

Such rhetoric and responses to *righting* Glen Canyon reveals how the desert imagination can be used to make environmental politics subversive. An environmental politics at Glen Canyon is not only influenced by the literature, but in some sense is also produced by the literature. As further illustration of this, Edward Abbey proposes "a few tips on desert etiquette" in his essay "The Great American Desert," advocating,

> Always remove and destroy survey stakes, flagging, advertising signboards, mining claim markers, animal traps, poisoned bait, seismic exploration geophones, and other such artifacts of industrialism. The men who put those things there are up to no good and it is our duty to confound them. Keep America Beautiful. Grow a Beard. Take a Bath. Burn a Billboard.
>
> (*Journey* 19)

Certainly, it is through the fantasy desert (Wild) that these writers have created new environments and evoked a sense of wonder, leading to the re-enchantment of nature.

Terry Tempest Williams' claim that, "We can try and kill all that is native, string it up by its hind legs for all to see, but spirit howls and wildness endures. Anticipate resurrection" (*Unspoken* 144), might serve as the perfect allegory for this essay. *We can try and kill Glen Canyon, flood the gulches and canyons for all to see, but its literary legacy howls and the desert imagination endures. Anticipate the restoration of Glen Canyon and a free-flowing Colorado River.* For it is through the desert imagination that these desert writers—Terry Tempest Williams, Edward Abbey, Katie Lee, and Ellen Meloy— are driving environmental activism and reform. Although written for Edward Abbey, Terry Tempest Williams' message is true of all those writing in defense of Glen Canyon: "His words reverberate on canyon walls, his voice being carried by desert winds on the open skies of the American West. He is Coyote, a dance upon the desert" (*Unspoken* 73).

The fervor of these Glen Canyon writers in reacting to the inundation of this canyon country illustrates the importance of the environment—and particularly the desert imagination—in southwestern literature. A desert imaginary not only serves as a thematic concern, but also as a genesis for actions intended to preserve the natural world for subsequent generations. This literature reveals stories about, and journeys through, an historical place and historical experiences in that place. The literary history and legacy of Glen Canyon—the biography of place—is at least as influential as the political history of Glen Canyon in shaping understanding of this southern Utah landscape.

Works Cited

Abbey, Edward. *Beyond the Wall: Essays from the Outside*. New York: Holt, Rinehart & Winston, 1984.

_____. *Desert Solitaire: A Season in the Wilderness*. 1968. New York: Touchstone, 1990.

_____. *Down the River*. 1982. New York: Plume, 1991.

_____. *Hayduke Lives!: A Novel*. Boston: Little, Brown, 1990.

_____. *The Journey Home: Some Words in Defense of the American West*. 1977. New York: Plume, 1991.

_____. *The Monkey Wrench Gang*. 1975. London: Penguin, 2004.

_____. *One Life at a Time, Please*. New York: Henry Holt & Company, 1988.

Anderson, Jon. *Page and Place: Ongoing Compositions of Plot.* Amsterdam: Rodopi, 2014.

_____. *Understanding Cultural Geography: Places and Traces.* London: Routledge, 2010.

Beard, Daniel P. *Deadbeat Dams: Why We Should Abolish the U.S. Bureau of Reclamation and Tear Down Glen Canyon Dam.* Boulder, CO: Johnson, 2015.

Berger, Bruce. *There Was a River: Essays on the Southwest.* Tucson: U of Arizona P, 1994.

Cassuto, David N. *Dripping Dry: Literature, Politics, and Water in the Desert Southwest.* Ann Arbor: U of Michigan P, 2001.

Farmer, Jared. *Glen Canyon Dammed: Inventing Lake Powell and the Canyon Country.* Tucson: U of Arizona P, 2004.

_____. "*Desert Solitaire* and the Literary Memory of an Imagined Place." *Western American Literature* 38.2 (2003): 155–70.

Lee, Katie. *Glen Canyon Betrayed: A Sensuous Elegy.* Flagstaff, AZ: Fretwater, 2006.

_____. *Sandstone Seduction: Rivers and Lovers, Canyons and Friends.* Boulder, CO: Johnson, 2004.

Macfarlane, Robert. *Landmarks.* London: Hamish Hamilton, 2015.

McPhee, John. *Encounters with the Archdruid.* 1971. New York: Farrar, Straus & Giroux, 1977.

Meloy, Ellen. *The Anthropology of Turquoise: Reflections on Desert, Sea, Stone, and Sky.* New York: Vintage Books, 2003.

_____. *Eating Stone: Imagination and the Loss of the Wild.* New York: Vintage Books, 2006.

_____. *The Last Cheater's Waltz: Beauty and Violence in the Desert Southwest.* Tucson: U of Arizona P, 1999.

_____. *Raven's Exile: A Season on the Green River.* Tucson: U of Arizona P, 1994.

Philippon, Daniel J. *Conserving Words: How American Nature Writers Shaped the Environmental Movement.* Athens: U of Georgia P, 2004.

Porter, Eliot & David Brower. *The Place No One Knew: Glen Canyon on the Colorado.* San Francisco: Sierra Club, 1963.

Powell, John Wesley. *The Exploration of the Colorado River and Its Canyons*. 1895. Washington, DC: National Geographic Society, 2002.

Slovic, Scott. *Seeking Awareness in American Nature Writing: Henry Thoreau, Annie Dillard, Edward Abbey, Wendell Berry, Barry Lopez*. Salt Lake City: U of Utah P, 1992.

Spurgeon, Sara L. "Miracles in the Desert: Literature, Water, and Public Discourse in the American West." *Interdisciplinary Studies in Literature and Environment* 16.4 (2009): 743–59.

Stegner, Wallace. "Glen Canyon Submersus." *The Glen Canyon Reader*. Ed. Mathew Barrett Gross. Tucson: U of Arizona P, 2003. 138–48.

_____. *This Is Dinosaur: Echo Park Country and Its Magic Rivers*. New York: Knopf, 1956.

Thoreau, Henry David. *Walden*. 1854. 150th anniversary ed. Ed. J. Lyndon Shanley. Princeton, NJ: Princeton UP, 2004.

_____. "Walking." *Thoreau: Collected Essays and Poems*. Ed. Elizabeth Hall Witherell. New York: Library of America, 2001. 225–55.

Wild, Peter. *The Opal Desert: Explorations of Fantasy and Reality in the American Southwest*. Austin: U of Texas P, 1999.

Williams, Terry Tempest. *Red: Passion and Patience in the Desert*. New York: Vintage Books, 2002.

_____. *An Unspoken Hunger: Stories from the Field*. New York: Vintage Books, 1995.

CRITICAL
READINGS

The Indian Captivity Narrative: A Genre of the Southwest

Randi Lynn Tanglen

From a literary perspective, captivity narratives traditionally have been understood as the published, first-person accounts of white women taken captive by American Indians. This genre and its conventions eventually became part of the literary tradition of the United States, and over time, the captivity plot became a literary trope that represented assumptions of white cultural superiority and the perceived rightness of usually white-provoked wars. Some captivity narratives were put back into print dozens of times over hundreds of years to exacerbate military and political campaigns against American Indians, an indication of the enduring nature of the captivity narrative and its cultural significance. In the typical understanding of American literary history, the captivity narrative tradition began with the publication of Puritan Mary Rowlandson's 1682 *The Sovereignty and Goodness of God*. But although the Puritan Indian captivity narrative of New England is often assumed to be the first uniquely form of American literature, the first published account of Indian captivity in the Americas actually took place in the Southwest. Indeed, Indian captivity narratives by authors of the Southwest have had a major influence on the development of the captivity narrative form and the scholarship surrounding the genre. The Indian captivity narrative of the Southwest calls attention to the Spanish influence upon American and southwestern literary history and well as the role of the US-Mexican War (1846–1848) in the cultural work of the captivity narrative form as well as American audiences. Written portrayals of Indian captivity set in the Southwest reveal the complex network of intertribal captivity in the Southwest and complicate the traditional understanding of the Indian captivity narrative as a Protestant white woman's genre by including a diverse set of captors and captives—such as conquistadors, tattooed women,

Native American women kidnapped by whites, and Mormon women escaping polygamy.

In 1542, almost one hundred-fifty years before the publication of the first New England Indian captivity narrative, Spanish nobleman and conquistador Álvar Núñez Cabeza de Vaca published his *La Relación*, which told of the failed Narváez Expedition and his captivity with the Karankawa and Coahuiltecan people in what is now Texas. Cabeza de Vaca and three of his men were taken captive after they were shipwrecked and separated from the rest of the expedition party. His captivity narrative recounts his experiences with and customs of many of the tribes of Texas, Arizona, New Mexico, and parts of northern Mexico, including the Capoque, Han, Avavare, and Arbadao people. As an Indian captive, he initially lived in abject poverty and slavery. Over his eight years as a captive, he developed a reputation as a healer and trader and was able to move freely among the tribes. Written as a report to the Spanish crown to defend the failure of the Navráez Expedition, his captivity narrative is a hybrid text—part anthropological report, part adventure story, and part Christian conversion narrative. Cabeza de Vaca argues that though the expedition was a failure, it can still bring glory and profit to Spanish nobility through the exploitation of the lands and goods of the Americas and the Christian conversion of Native peoples. With this argument, he simultaneously positions himself, due to his exposure to and experience with Native people and cultures, to become an invaluable resource in the continued exploration and colonization of the Americas by the Spanish. After writing *La Relación*, he went on to become a colonial governor in Argentina, but was eventually removed from his position and forced to return to Spain due, perhaps in part, to his sympathetic policies toward indigenous peoples.

Although Cabeza de Vaca offers a more nuanced portrayal of indigenous people than subsequent Puritan Indian captivity narratives would, he still maintains that the Native peoples of the Americas were in need of European civilization and Christian conversion. In spite of his own assimilation into the religion and cultures of several tribes, his *La Relación* emphasizes his commitment to the Christian conversion of the Indians: "We commanded them to build churches with crosses; up to that time none had been erected. We also bade them bring their principal men to be baptized" (Cabeza de Vaca 132). In this sense, as one of the earliest published accounts of the Americas and American Indians, Cabeza de Vaca's Indian captivity narrative participates in the cultural work of the captivity trope by maintaining European cultural superiority. Throughout his narrative Cabeza de Vaca has to downplay acceptance into and out of Native cultures by keeping the Christian/heathen dichotomy securely in place in order to justify further Spanish exploration of the New World.

Published accounts of Indian captivity set in what would become the American Southwest did not appear again until the nineteenth century, as the frontier of the United States was pushed west and Mexico invited American settlers to immigrate to Texas and Coahuila as a means to prevent Comanche raids. In 1838, Rachel Plummer wrote the first captivity narrative published in Texas, entitled *Rachael Plummer's Narrative of Twenty One Months' Servitude as a Prisoner Among the Commanchee Indians*. Written with and edited by her father, James W. Parker, her account went through several editions and is the only published captivity narrative from the famous 1836 Fort Parker raid near present day Groesbeck, Texas. Several members of the Parker family, including Plummer's cousin Cynthia Ann Parker, were taken captive by the Comanche and Kiowa people. Plummer was the only captive taken from the raid to both survive and write about her experience. Like Cabeza de Vaca, she began her captivity as a slave, but eventually earned the respect of her captors and successfully advocated for herself with the tribal elders after a physical confrontation with her mistress. This represents a departure from the typical depiction of the female Indian captive as passive victim and even hints at Plummer's partial acceptance into the tribe. In the Southwest, the intertribal taking and exchange of captives was so common that many of the tribes had "multiple social locations into which captives could be incorporated" into the tribe—ranging from slave to adopted son or daughter (Brooks, *Captives and Cousins* 6). The experiences of Plummer and her cousin Cynthia Ann Parker reflect the poles of this spectrum. Cynthia Ann was adopted and eventually married Comanche chief Peta Nocona and had four children with him, including Quanah Parker, the last chief of the Comanche people. By contrast, Plummer was a slave for her tribe, skinning buffalo and working on hides, but, at the same time, advancing her status within the tribe.

Plummer's is the first Indian captivity narrative by a white woman to address the sexual assault and rape of Indian captives when she states, "[t]o undertake to narrate their barbarous treatment would only add to my present distress, for it is with feelings of deepest mortification that I think of it, much less to speak or write of it" (Plummer, *Narrative* 4). When Puritan Mary Rowlandson wrote in 1682 that in spite of "sleeping all sorts together…not one of them ever offered me the least abuse of unchastity to me, in word or action" (107), she was not only speaking to expected standards for female sexual purity, but also most likely telling the truth. Rape was a European, not an American Indian, war practice, and was not practiced among the Algonquian and Iroquoian tribes encountered by the English in the northeast in the seventeenth and eighteenth centuries. But "several instances of white women raped by their Indian captors were reported, especially among the Plains tribes west of the Mississippi" in the nineteenth century, as sexual assault of captives was possibly more common among tribes of the Southwest; however, it is not clear how common, sanctioned, or condemned the practice was in the nineteenth century, when Plummer wrote her narrative (Kolodny, "Among the Indians," 192). Nevertheless, Plummer's honesty about her sexual assault still stands out among other captivity narratives from this period, especially considering that one purpose of the Indian captivity narrative was to "shap[e] recognizable social identities" and based on gender insist upon the sexual, cultural, and religious purity of the white female captive (Castiglia 5).

Plummer's narrative was republished in 1844 with her father's account of his attempts to rescue her and the other Fort Parker captives. Over one-hundred years after its initial publication, Plummer's captivity narrative became the basis for John Ford's iconic western *The Searchers* (1956), indicating the ongoing significance of the Indian captivity narrative of the Southwest in the national cultural imagination. Critics note that John Wayne's character Ethan Edwards was possibly based on Plummer's father, James W. Parker, and Natalie Wood's character of the white captive Debbie Edwards was most likely based on Cynthia Ann Parker. While Cynthia Ann Parker's story would become most remembered, Rachel Plummer's captivity narrative would fall by the wayside and eventually out of print—as it still is today. Nevertheless, it is still a significant influence the captivity narrative tradition of the Southwest.

One of the most popular nineteenth-century captivity narratives in the United States was *The Captivity of the Oatman Girls*, published in 1857. Olive Oatman and her younger sister Mary Ann were taken captive by the Yavapai Apache in New Mexico Territory when Olive was thirteen. After spending one year with the Apaches as slaves, Olive and Mary Ann were eventually traded to the Mohave people in California, after which they both received the ritual tattoo markings of the tribe on their chins and arms. The tattoos had a religious meaning to the Mohave and were an indication of the girls' adoption and assimilation into the tribe. Mary Ann did not survive captivity, but Olive was later ransomed and reunited with her brother Lorenzo. She wrote an account of her ordeal with her brother under the guidance of a heavy-handed ghost-writer, a Methodist minister named Royal B. Stratton. Like most captivity narratives by women (including Rowlandson and Plummer), Oatman's is mediated by a male voice, and it is hard to tell where her story ends and Stratton's narrative intrusion begins. Discursive slippage, the difference between the captive's actual experiences and her interlocutor's interpretive agenda, is perhaps exemplified when Olive describes the sorrow of the girls' Mohave mother at Mary Ann's deathbed:

> I ought to say here that neither that woman nor her daughter ever gave us any unkind treatment. She came up one day, hearing Mary sing, and bent for some time silently over her. She looked in her face, felt of her, and suddenly broke out in a most piteous lamentation. She wept, and wept from the heart and aloud. I never saw a parent seem to feel more keenly over a dying child. (Oatman 142)

Oatman's description of Mohave kindness and humanity is constantly interrupted by Stratton's conventional use of the captivity trope with his depictions of "the degradation, the barbarity, the superstition, the squalidness, that curse the uncounted thousands who people the caverns and wilds that divide the Eastern from the Western inheritance of our mother Republic" (205). Written just nine years after Mexico ceded one-third of its territory to the United States in the aftermath of the US-Mexican War, *The Captivity of the Oatman Girls* reveals anxieties about the acquisitions of new territories in the Southwest after the 1848 Treaty of Guadalupe Hidalgo. In the aftermath of the US-Mexican War, Mexicans living in the lands ceded to the United States became US citizens, and indigenous people in what had become US territories fell under the jurisdiction of the US government. The accumulation of new lands and populations after the US-Mexican War revived nativist anxieties about what it meant to be an American as the nation had to integrate into its body politic peoples representing a variety of racial, ethnic, religious, and national identities. In spite of what was undoubtedly Oatman's acculturation into and acceptance of Mohave culture, Stratton used the captivity narrative format to portray Olive Oatman as a pure and untainted specimen of white cultural superiority.

However, Oatman did not shy away from discussing her Mohave tattoos in her captivity narrative or displaying them in the narrative's frontispiece and promotional materials, which might explain her narrative's immense popularity. When the first edition of *The Captivity of the Oatman Girls* was published in San Francisco in April 1857, it sold out within three weeks. When the second edition of the captivity narrative came out later in the year, half of the six thousand copies had already been pre-purchased by subscription. A third edition soon followed in 1858, along with a nationwide promotional lecture tour, a simultaneous print run in Chicago, and even a play reenacting the Oatman captivity, in which Olive's supposed Mohave husband was played by Junius Brutus Booth, Jr., a famous actor and the brother of John Wilkes Booth. Multiple plays, poems, and novels based on *The Captivity of the Oatman Girls* were produced in her own time and in the present day including the short story "Tonto Woman" (1998) by Leonard Elmore. Olive Oatman's history as an Indian captive and images of her tattoo markings most likely served as the basis for the character of Eva—a white prostitute and former Indian captive—on the recent AMC series *Hell on Wheels*, another indication of the tenacious cultural resonance of the southwestern Indian captivity narrative. Literary critics in the twentieth century, such as Richard Slotkin and Annette Kolodny, theorized that the popularity and endurance of the Indian captivity narrative form can tell us much about the development of a distinctively American psyche, a psychology that often led to violence against racial and ethnic Others and the destruction of the natural environment—even in the present day. In the twenty-first century, Susan Faludi has speculated the Indian captivity narrative "holds a key to our own experience, shedding light on not only the trauma…but our response" to the terrorist attacks of September 11, 2001 ("America's Guardian").

Along with promoting white racial superiority and the justifying white wars, the captivity narrative was appropriated to justify violence against white religious and ethnic minorities, like the Latter-Day Saints of Utah Territory. Ann Eliza Young's *Wife No. 19* (1876) propagates assumptions of Protestant cultural authority onto the nation's frontiers at the same time that several of the western territories—including the heavily Mormon Utah Territory—were being legislated into statehood. When she wrote her narrative, Ann Eliza Young was seeking divorce from her polygamous husband, Brigham Young, President of the Mormon Church, and a major political and financial force in the American West. Young and her non-Mormon supporters hoped that her escape and precedent-setting divorce case would destroy not only the institution of polygamy, but also Mormonism itself. Protestant clergymen were troubled by the ascendancy of this younger religion and were concerned that it would displace the older and more established Protestant sects.

In order to make herself and the Mormon women for whom she was advocating seem sympathetic to her Protestant audience, she, like previous Indian captives, defends the sexual purity of the Mormon captives of polygamy. According to Young, Mormon women, like their Protestant counterparts, are pious and pure women who like Indian captives, these women retain their purity in spite of contact with an inferior culture. Further appropriating the conventions of the white woman's narrative of Indian captivity, Young argues that Mormons are white savages who prevent the enlightened settlement of the West. Anti-Indian and anti-Mormon rhetoric were often conflated, since both Native Americans and Mormons were seen as obstacles to the settlement of the West by white Protestants. Because Mormons viewed Native Americans as remnants of the lost tribes of Israel, Mormon opponents were concerned about a "Mormon-Indian conspiracy," an accusation that became more prevalent in the years following the notorious Mountain Meadows Massacre— an 1857 Mormon attack on an Arkansas emigrant party on its way to California. Rumors circulated of Mormons conspiring with and dressing as Paiutes during the five-day siege. Young spends more time in her 605-page "Mormon captivity narrative" describing the Mountains Meadow Massacre than she does her marriage to Brigham Young, indicating her narrative's appropriation of the anti-Indian rhetoric of the captivity narrative genre. According to Young's narrative, both Mormons and Native Americans need to be eradicated in order for Protestant civilization to thrive as the nation continued to expand its boundaries across the continent.

Andele: The Mexican-Kiowa Captive (1899) continues the tradition of Hispanic captivity accounts set in the Southwest, telling the story of ten-year-old José Andrés Martínez who was taken captive by the Mescalaro Apache outside Las Vegas, New Mexico in 1866. He was eventually traded to the Kiowa and became the adopted son of the chief, Many Bears, who renamed him Andele. As a Kiowa, Andele experienced another type of captivity when the tribe was removed to a reservation in Oklahoma after 1875. He attempted to return to his previous life and family in New Mexico, but eventually came back to the Kiowa to teach at an agency school. Andele's is not a typical captivity narrative, yet his amanuensis, a Methodist missionary named J. J. Methvin, told his story to fit the literary conventions and ideological agenda of the Indian captivity narrative format. For example, Methvin describes Andele's Kiowa captors as "wild, nomadic, barbarous, savage, their glory the glory war and plunder, their religion that of blood revenge, the conscience and moral instinct dead" (25). Andele's rescue is cast in terms of his Christian redemption, as, in the climactic closing chapter, he answers a Methodist altar call and expresses "his disappointment in the Indian religion" (Methvin 121). As historian James F. Brooks observes, "Perhaps the most remarkable element of Andele's text is that the intelligence, humor, affection, and honor of the Kiowa people survive Methkin's condescending and moralizing interjection" (Brooks, "Introduction" 15).

Literary critics have recently provided some new critical approaches to the Indian captivity narrative of the Southwest. Andrea Tinnemeyer, in *Identity Politics of the Captivity Narrative after 1848* (2006), uses published, first-person captivity narratives such as Oatman's as well as novels, song lyrics, and legal cases dealing with Indian captivity to show how the captivity trope was used to incorporate new citizens and lands into the national imaginary after the US-Mexican War. Although *The War in Words: Reading the Dakota Conflict Through the Captivity Literature* (2009) is not about southwestern texts or authors, Kathryn Zabelle Derounian-Stodola's methodology broadens the conventional understanding of the captivity narrative as a white woman's literary genre by defining "captivity literature" as any account that "illustrate[s] variations of the basic captivity, or confinement, narrative" (3). To this end, Victoria Smith, in *Captive Arizona, 1851–1900* (2009), uses the historical archive to recover the captivity experiences of over twenty American, Mexican, Mexican American, and American Indian men and women in territorial Arizona. She incorporates the captivity experiences of Yavapai, Mohave, Tohono O'odham, Yaqui, Chiricahua, and Western Apaches, whose stories she found in "the manuscript collections and other archival sources housed in research libraries across Arizona" (Smith xxvi). For example, Nah-thle-tla, a Chiricahua woman, was captured by Mexicans in 1855. She was sold as a slave and taken to Santa Fe, but she eventually escaped and returned to her family by walking over 250 miles. Nah-thle-tla's captivity experience "lived only in Apache oral tradition" until her son published an account of the incident decades later (Smith 36). The scholarly work of Derounian-Stodola and Smith both regard accounts of Indian captives among the whites as captivity narratives. Accordingly, Apache chief Geronimo's time in US prisons as depicted in *Geronimo: His Own Story* (1906) is an inverse captivity narrative. Written from the Apache tradition of narrating one's oral history, Geronimo's autobiography turns the traditional captivity plot on its head, thereby diminishing—textually at least—the captivity trope's insistence on white cultural superiority.

Indigenous uses of "captivity" are explored by Enrique R. Lamadrid in *Hermanitos and Comanchitos: Indo-Hispano Rituals of Captivity and Redemption* (2003). Lamadrid's work highlights the significance of captive redemption rituals in New Mexico, where the "Moros y Cristianos" ("Moors and Christians") folk dramas have been performed for centuries, well before the publication of the first Indian captivity narrative in seventeenth-century New England. Although they are not published literary texts, these representations of captivity are nonetheless a form of southwestern cultural production and document how European captivity stories were integrated into existing indigenous cultural understandings of captivity and subsequently imbued with a whole different set of meanings. Laguna Pueblo author Leslie Marmon Silko's short story "Yellow Woman" (1981) is about a modern-day Pueblo woman kidnapped by a man named Silva who claims to be a *ka'tsina* mountain spirit. The Yellow Woman stories comes from a Pueblo oral tradition story cycle in which Yellow Woman is led away from the pueblo to live with Whirlwind Man. Silko creates a contemporary context for an ancient story about Yellow Woman's captivity and kidnapping, but also complicates the different degrees of power and agency possessed by the captive woman. Silko's story is a reminder that the tribes of the Southwest participated in the tradition of captivity well before colonial/settler contact and that Native cultural understandings and uses of intertribal captivity differ greatly from the cultural work of the captivity trope that emerged out of the European tradition.

The captivity narrative is still influential in shaping the contemporary literature of the Southwest, particularly evident in Philipp Meyer's 2013 *The Son*. Like previous captivity narratives of the Southwest, *The Son* was extremely popular and even spent several weeks on the *New York Times* bestseller list. A historical novel with an Indian captivity narrative folded into its plot, *The Son* tells the story of Colonel Eli McCullough, the first male born in the Texas Republic. Eli is raised as a Comanche captive after his family is killed in a raid. The tribe eventually adopts him, and he proves himself as a respected warrior. He later becomes a Texas Ranger and the progenitor of a Texas political and oil dynasty, not in spite of, but precisely because of, his Indian captivity experience. But because Eli is an emotional failure and ineffectual Texas patriarch, *The Son* undermines and exposes the myth of American cultural superiority at the heart of the captivity trope. As a form of literary and cultural production, the Indian captivity narrative of the Southwest has been a critical part of the literary history of the region and of the United States.

Works Cited

Brooks, James F. *Captives and Cousins: Kinship, Slavery, and Community in the Southwest Borderlands*. Chapel Hill: U of North Carolina P, 2001.

_____. "Introduction." *Andele: The Mexican-Kiowa Captive*. 1899. Albuquerque: U of New Mexico P, 1996. 1–21.

Cabeza de Vaca, Álvar Núñez. *Adventures into the Unknown Interior of America*. 1542. Trans. & Ed. Cyclone Covey. Albuquerque: U of New Mexico P, 1961.

Castiglia, Christopher. *Bound and Determined: Captivity, Culture-Crossing, and White Womanhood from Mary Rowlandson to Patty Hearst*. Chicago: U of Chicago P, 1996.

Derounian-Stodola, Kathryn Zabelle. *The War in Words: Reading the Dakota Conflict Through the Captivity Literature*. Lincoln: U of Nebraska P, 2009.

_____. & James Arthur Levernier. *The Indian Captivity Narrative, 1550–1900*. New York: Twayne Publishers. 1993.

Faludi, Susan. "America's Guardian Myths." *New York Times*. The New York Times Company, 7 Sept. 2007. Web. 11 Aug. 2015.

Frankel, Glenn. *The Searchers: The Making of an American Legend*. New York: Bloomsbury, 2013.

Geronimo & S. M. Barrett. *Geronimo: His Own Story: The Autobiography of a Great Patriot Warrior*. 1906. Ed. Frederick Jackson Turner. New York: Penguin, 1996.

Kolodny, Annette. "Among the Indians: The Uses of Captivity." *Women's Studies Quarterly* 21 (1993): 184–195.

_____. *The Land Before Her: Fantasy and Experience of the American Frontiers, 1630–1860*. Chapel Hill: U of North Carolina P, 1984.

Hell on Wheels. Created by Joe Gayton & Tony Gayton. AMC. 2011–present. Television series.

Lamadrid, Enrique R. *Hermanitos Comanchitos: Indo-Hispano Rituals of Captivity and Redemption*. Albuquerque: U of New Mexico P, 2003.

Leonard, Elmore. "The Tonto Woman." *The Tonto Woman and Other Western Stories*. New York: Delacorte Press, 1998.

McGinty, Brian. *The Oatman Massacre: A Tale of Desert Captivity and Survival*. Norman: U Oklahoma P, 2005.

Methvin, J. J. *Andele: The Mexican-Kiowa Captive*. 1899. Albuquerque: U of New Mexico P, 1996.

Meyer, Phillip. *The Son*. New York: Harper Collins, 2013.

Mifflin, Margot. *The Blue Tattoo: The Life of Olive Oatman*. Lincoln: U Nebraska P, 2009.

Namias, June. *White Captives: Gender and Ethnicity on the American Frontier*. Chapel Hill: U of North Carolina P, 1993.

Oatman, Lorenzo D. & Olive A. Oatman. *The Captivity of the Oatman Girls Among the Apache and Mohave Indians*. 1858, 1935. New York: Dover, 1994.

Pearce, Roy Harvey. "The Significances of the Captivity Narrative." *American Literature* 19 (1947): 1–20.

Plummer, Rachael. *Rachael Plummer's Narrative of twenty-one months servitude as a prisoner among the Commanchee Indians*. Jenkins Publishing Co, 1977.

_____. *Narrative of the Capture Subsequent Sufferings of Mrs. Rachel Plummer*, 2nd ed. 1828.

Rowlandson, Mary. *The Sovereignty and Goodness of God.* 1682. Ed. Neal Salisbury. Boston: Bedford, 1997.

The Searchers. Dir. John Ford. Perf. John Wayne & Natalie Wood. Warner Bros. Pictures, 1956. Film.

Silko, Leslie Marmon. "Yellow Woman." *Storyteller.* New York: Arcade Publishing, 1981. 54–62.

Slotkin, Richard. *Regeneration Through Violence: The Mythology of the American Frontier 1600–1860.* Norman: U of Oklahoma P, 1973.

Smith, Victoria. *Captive Arizona, 1851–1900.* Lincoln: U of Nebraska P, 2009.

Tinnemeyer, Andrea. *Identity Politics of the Captivity Narrative after 1848.* Lincoln: U Nebraska P, 2006.

Young, Ann Eliza. *Wife No. 19, Or, The Story of a Life in Bondage, Being a Complete Exposé of Mormonism, and Revealing the Sorrows, Sacrifices and Sufferings of Women in Polygamy.* Hartford, CT: Dustin, Gilman, & Co, 1875.

"Balances and Harmonies Always Shifting": An Ecopostcolonial Borderlands Reading of Silko's *Ceremony*

Wilma Shires

In Leslie Marmon Silko's *Ceremony*, the medicine man Betonie remarks, "[B]alances and harmonies always shifting, always necessary to maintain" (130), observing the reality of life's fluctuations. For example, when new elements are introduced into a system, whether a natural or a governmental one, that system is likely to change. Upon the landing of the white Europeans on the North American continent, life for American Indians changed. The changes brought by the Europeans caused a great shift in perceptions and actions in American Indian life. In *Ceremony*, the land, for example, becomes a resource to be used for profit instead of the Sacred Mother to be respected by her children. As a result of this shift in use, the land and its inhabitants become unbalanced and inharmonious (Silko, *Ceremony* 186); therefore, the people experience drought, poverty, physical and mental illness, and problems in their personal relationships. To restore the balance, Tayo must complete the ceremony, or sacred ritual, begun by Betonie. Tayo must work closely with nature, with medicine men, and with a nature goddess from one or all of the previous four worlds, all while grappling with the constraints and racist attitudes that come with living in a colonized nation.

Ceremony tells the story of Tayo, a World War II combat veteran who returns to the US with battle fatigue (now known as PTSD) after having been captured by the Japanese and held in a prison camp. Tayo, unsuccessfully treated by conventional doctors and medicines (Silko, *Ceremony* 15), visits with two medicine men. Both tell him that he is a part of a supernatural process that has been going on for a long time: the attempt to restore the balance and harmony disrupted by American Indian witches when they created white people (135). Although the medicine men help him to an extent, Tayo has to bring about his own cure by completing the ceremony (36, 124). The deeper concern of the story, then, is the actual restoration of balance and harmony so that Tayo, his people, and the land can heal. The themes harmony, balance, and returning home—three common themes in American Indian literatures—involve the relationships among people and their relationship with the land. When examining these ideas, it is useful to apply a critical approach that focuses on nature, lost land, and multicultural communities: an ecopostcolonial-borderlands approach. It is also useful to consider other approaches critics have applied to *Ceremony.*

Selected Critical Approaches

Paula Gunn Allen in "The Psychological Landscape of *Ceremony*" uses elements of ecocriticism combined with Laguna Pueblo cultural facts to argue that "Tayo's illness is a result of separation from the ancient unity of person with land, and his healing is a result of his recognition of this oneness" (7). Holly E. Martin, in "Hybrid Landscapes as Catalysts for Cultural Reconciliation in Leslie Marmon Silko's *Ceremony* and Rudolfo Anaya's *Bless Me, Ultima*," argues that because Tayo is bicultural, he needs the landscape to help him recognize his "cultural hybridity" (131). "The 'Lie' of the Land: Native Sovereignty, Indian Literary Nationalism, and Early Indigenism in Leslie Marmon Silko's *Ceremony*" by Sharon Holm uses poststructuralism, colonialism, and semiotics to argue that even though Tayo may need his home, or a sense of belonging, to heal his "internalized colonization" (261), the Laguna Pueblo have a stronger connection to their land than other tribes have because Laguna Pueblo were never forced to relocate (244). Therefore, all of their stories are directly tied to the landscape they have always seen. For American Indian people forced to relocate, their landscape changes, so the stories become disconnected, sometimes resulting in a shift in the people's cosmology.

According to Monica Avila, in "Leslie Marmon Silko's *Ceremony*: Witchery and Sacrifice of Self," Nelson and Saylor define "internalized colonization" as acceptance of the myth that American Indians and their culture will die (53). Using New

Criticism, Avila argues that Silko develops Tayo as a man who must "sacrifice his individual selfish behavior to complete his ceremony" (53). Carol Mitchell, in an ethnographic reading titled "*Ceremony* as Ritual," details how traditional Laguna Pueblo people took their sacred implements when they separated themselves from the more modern Laguna people. Without the implements, the more modern people, such as Tayo's family, could not fulfill their spiritual needs because they had only "Anglo-American" practices in which to participate (Mitchell 27). Robert C. Bell's article "Circular Design in *Ceremony*," examines theme and structure through structural analysis. He asserts that Silko's "intentional 'disjointed' quality of the plot" is lessened by the "force of the connectedness of the past with the present and to the future" (55). Bell notes that Tayo's story is similar to a hero quest; Tayo's reward is healing if he can find and return his uncle's cattle.

As an example of a novel that is both popular and important literary fiction, *Ceremony* has gained significant critical attention. As previously mentioned, applying an ecopostcolonial borderlands reading to *Ceremony* yields additional understanding of Silko's themes. A good place to start an ecopostcolonial borderlands reading is the setting of the novel.

Natural Setting

Ceremony is set New Mexico, a southwestern state often thought of as mysterious, mystical, or even magical. Its nickname, the Land of Enchantment, can conjure ideas of magic or, perhaps, the supernatural. Indeed, Silko's three destroyers, created by witchery, live in New Laguna, Tayo's village. The goddess Ts'eh visits, loves, and guides Tayo as he struggles to complete the ceremony. New Mexico, steeped in ancient Aztec history, has mountains, canyons, valleys, caves, rivers, and *arroyos* (a dry creek or gulch, which fills seasonally). Varieties of trees, grasses, flowers, and wildlife manage to survive in Gallup, near Tayo's home, with very little rainfall. All parts of nature are necessary to maintain the ecosystem. If any part is disrupted, then many other parts could suffer. This does not mean that the environment is static, however. Tayo wears a jacket at night, one of many realistic elements in the novel because though the temperatures are mild in the daytime, the night air is often chilly, thus illustrating the shifting nature of Tayo's physical environment (Silko, *Ceremony* 242, 248, 250).

The landscape in *Ceremony* is so important that it could be considered a character itself (Martin 131). Nature is made up of all life forms, even when those forms are no longer living (Silko, "Landscape, History" 265). Silko does not privilege humans over ants or uranium over pollen—all are to be respected ("Landscape, History" 265). Paula Gunn Allen asserts that in Native American tradition,

> The tendency to equal distribution of value among all elements in a field, whether the field is social, spiritual, or aesthetic (and the distinction is moot when tribal materials are under discussion), is an integral part of tribal consciousness and is reflected in tribal social and aesthetic systems all over the Americas. In this structural framework, no single element is foregrounded, leaving the others to supply "background." (*The Sacred Hoop* 241)

Silko makes a similar comment: "Each ant, each lizard, each lark is imbued with great value simply because the creature is there, simply because the creature is alive in a place where any life at all is precious" ("Landscape, History" 275). The setting of *Ceremony* is more than just the "time and place of the story"; the landscape is necessary to move the plot forward. For example, the severe drought causes the characters in the novel to think about traditional stories that explain causes and remedies, thus setting into motion Tayo's drive to heal his land, his people, and himself.

According to Silko, the word "landscape" suggests a separation between humans and their surroundings; however, Silko and the Laguna Pueblo maintain, "Viewers are as much a part of the landscape as the boulders they stand on" ("Landscape, History" 264–65). Silko further argues, "Survival [for ancient Pueblo people] depended upon harmony and cooperation not only among human beings, but among all things—the animate and the less animate, since rocks and mountains were known to move, to travel occasionally" ("Landscape, History" 267). Tayo is not separate from his environment; he has to work with it and allow it to help him, such as when he reads the constellation showing him the path and end of his mission. He is successful because he comes to realize the landscape has consciousness even though it is different from human consciousness. Dreams and the landscape, two differing types of consciousness, can be alike: a terrifying experience can be equally terrifying in dreams (273). Tayo has "dreams of black night and loud voices rolling him over and over again like debris caught in a flood" (Silko, *Ceremony* 5). During the war and in his dreams of it, Tayo is at the mercy of the environment. His recurring dream ties him to the Philippine landscape even after World War II has ended.

The Philippine landscape, though mentioned only in flashbacks, is important in *Ceremony* because it is where Tayo is overcome by mental illness. He is in an unfamiliar environment where the goal is destruction. From his traditional viewpoint, Tayo sees the killing of humans and other creatures as well as damaging the earth as unacceptable because it will cause an imbalance in nature; therefore, he cannot make himself shoot the Japanese (Silko, *Ceremony* 7). Betonie explains Tayo's inability to shoot: "'You saw who they were. Thirty thousand years ago they were not strangers. You saw what the evil had done: you saw the witchery ranging as wide as this world'" (124). In war, the created beings, all made by one creator, attempt to destroy one another, thus disrupting balance and harmony.

During his deployment to the Philippine Islands, Tayo loathes the unfamiliar tropical rainfall because it keeps the ground slick and muddy. The rain also causes Tayo and the corporal to drop the blanket in which they have been carrying mortally wounded Rocky (Silko, *Ceremony* 11). Here, Tayo curses the rain: "He damned the rain until the words were a chant, and he sang it while he crawled through the mud . . ." (12). His cursing does not stop the rain in the Philippines, but Tayo believes it brings severe drought to his home in northwestern New Mexico. Tayo sees the rain as an enemy that he cannot defeat, making his conflict with nature more like a conflict with a sentient being. In the novel, the landscape becomes a force that causes human characters to act and to react.

The Land

For nature to maintain balance, all of nature must care for itself. As the novel begins, Tayo's village and the surrounding areas are experiencing a multi-year drought for which Tayo blames himself (Silko, *Ceremony* 11, 12, 14). He knows that individual actions have direct effects on nature (38). Silko enhances this idea by incorporating, bit by bit, a myth that teaches the consequences of not respecting nature (13). In the myth, presented in verse form with varied line spacing to establish a storytelling rhythm, the watchers guarding the Corn Mother's altar are distracted from their duty by a magician. The Corn Mother, offended by the lack of respect, withholds the rain. When all of nature's creatures begin to starve, a healthy hummingbird flies through the area. The green hummingbird explains that he has been visiting, four worlds down, at Earth Mother's house, eating delicious food (54).

Silko, with this myth, begins pointing toward the eternity and connectedness of nature, further illustrated by Tayo's belief that people can move back and forth through time (Silko, *Ceremony* 18). Although living in the fifth world, during which the Europeans arrive, the Laguna Pueblo traditionally believe that the other four worlds still exist and function (68). According to Silko, "All the human beings, animals, and life which have been created emerged from the four worlds below when the earth became habitable" (Silko, "Landscape, History" 271). Ts'eh is most likely from one of these worlds. In the myth, Hummingbird and his newly hatched helper, Fly, complete a series of difficult tasks required by their mother to prove their respect to her so that she will send the much-needed rain. Once respect has been restored, healing occurs in the land. Similarly, Tayo has to complete a series of tasks to restore balance so that he and New Laguna can heal, demonstrating a repeated human mistake that requires ancient belief to correct. Throughout the novel, the characters are depicted as tied to nature: when they abuse nature, they generally suffer as a result. However, not all characters appreciate nature.

For example, Emo, a destroyer, is particularly concerned about gaining profit from the land. He feels he has been cheated out of material wealth by the whites who reap profit from the uranium mines, poisoning the people and the land, while some American Indians starve. Emo says the government has taken all the good land and left the Laguna Pueblo with a "dried up" mother earth (Silko, *Ceremony* 25). Tayo is angered by Emo's comment though Tayo knows that Emo can no longer understand nature as a part of himself. Instead, like much of mainstream culture, Emo sees the land as something to use for personal gain. He shows disrespect to the land by leaving garbage almost everywhere he goes. For example, he leaves broken glass liquor bottles near the ashes of the fire that consumes Harley's clothes and boots (Silko, *Ceremony* 254). Emo and many other American Indians want to emulate the mainstream government's example of extracting wealth from the earth even though such practice can result in destruction. The US government, for instance, damages nature by mining uranium, making bombs, and exploding them in the desert (Silko, *Ceremony* 245). Making the bombs from a natural element and exploding them is an example of using nature to destroy itself, a practice that increases the imbalance. Tayo recognizes that the government's experimental explosions in areas populated by minorities suggest a racist lack of respect for the people. For Tayo, and for traditional Laguna Pueblo—and many other American Indian tribes—all of nature is important. Allen states that in American Indian cultures, the land and the people are one; all creatures are sacred and, therefore, worthy of respect ("Psychological Landscape" 7). All creatures are sacred and, therefore, worthy of respect. Tayo embodies this traditional belief, but Emo, a tool of the ancient witchery, eschews it.

However, throughout the novel, other characters are shown taking care of the land. Tayo, though he is ill, feels more relaxed in the mornings after he turns the goats loose to graze and gives the yellow cat her milk (Silko, *Ceremony* 18). From Josiah, Tayo learns that houseflies, deemed nasty creatures by his school teacher, have a purpose and should be shown respect (Silko, *Ceremony* 101). Ts'eh, a nature goddess, is careful not to disturb any ants as she opens her blue shawl full of plants, flowers, and roots that she intends to transplant (Silko, *Ceremony* 224). When Josiah decides to go into the cattle business, he buys spotted Mexican cattle that can withstand the harsh drought more easily than can the Hereford cattle that are not genetically suited to dry weather and will die of thirst because they do not know to look for water (79). Caring for all of nature results in balance and harmony.

Tayo's Illness

Tayo's sickness and health are tied to the land and to the cultural values and stories related to the land. Because "the land" is not limited to his village or even to New Mexico, Tayo honors his values when he enlists in the US Army and leaves his familiar surroundings. When Tayo is unable to shoot the enemy, he is overcome by battle fatigue (Silko, *Ceremony* 7, 8). Although Rocky tries to reason with him, Tayo thinks the dead Japanese soldier is his uncle, Josiah, Tayo's source of love, knowledge, and strength. After his terrifying war experiences, Tayo blames himself for Rocky's death and for the drought in his village. He cannot correct his perceived errors, and he cannot forgive himself. He is, within himself, unbalanced.

Another cause for Tayo's sickness is the condition of social behavior in New Laguna. Tayo's mother has brought shame upon the family by having a sexual relationship with a white man, which has resulted in the birth of Tayo, a mixed-race child (Silko, *Ceremony* 65). Racial inequality is an indicator of societal illness: if all life is equally worthy of respect, then this race-based shame is contradictory to tribal values. Tayo wonders if his mother's activities have caused the imbalance, but Betonie, the medicine man, squelches the suggestion: "Nothing is that simple . . . you don't write off all the white people, just like you don't trust all the Indians" (128). Here, Betonie offers the correct attitude toward people, based on traditional teachings.

Certainly, the reader cannot "write off" mixed race characters: the healers in the novel are of mixed race. Tayo, Ts'eh, Betonie, and Night Swan are all described with different or unusual eye colors, such as hazel, green, and ochre. Further, Ts'eh is a supernatural being from a previous world. The different eye colors and lighter skin tones of these characters arouse distrust (Silko, *Ceremony* 99).

These different characters must negotiate the borders, the perceived social lines, that separate pure-blood American Indians, mainstream culture, and their own mixed races. They have formed a "vernacular cosmopolitanism," in which they will work together to achieve "shared goals of democratic rule" rather than acknowledge and conform to the current political situation (Bhabha xviii).

Their difference is their strength. The four characters form a kind of family unit based on their differences, need for each other, and common interest in healing their society. As these characters stick together, their "solidarity," as Chandra Talpade Mohanty would call it, allows them to recognize the borders that exist among the groups and realize that they must work together across these lines to effect change (ix, 2). Families such as this are common in colonized nations where death and abandonment are not unusual. These characters, the "Others," understand the changes necessary to defeat the witches' plot to destroy society.

Along with racist attitudes, more evidence that Tayo's society is ailing is that Rocky, a full-blood Laguna Pueblo, volunteers to go to war so that he can escape from his family and, hopefully, begin a new life. He does not like the traditional ways and is embarrassed of his family (Silko, *Ceremony* 73). He would rather deny his background than be denied success in the mainstream culture. The war itself exemplifies societal breakdown as humans destroy each other and their home. The imbalance and lack of harmony among humans cause all of nature to suffer because everything is connected. According to Silko, "Life on the high arid plateau became viable when the human beings were able to imagine themselves as sisters and brothers to the badger, antelope, clay, yucca, and sun" ("Landscape, History" 273). Allen argues, ". . . the land and the people are the same" ("Psychological Landscape" 7). In *Ceremony*, humans have lost the ability to imagine their connectedness; therefore, as previously stated, Tayo is ill because the land is ill.

Tayo's Healing

To heal Tayo and to restore balance, a powerful ceremony involving much of nature is necessary. Betonie begins the cure with a Scalp

Ceremony, using a white corn sand painting, hoops, a knife, and a painting of crossed rainbows (Silko, *Ceremony* 141). During this part of the ceremony, for Tayo, all boundaries disappear, and all of nature comes together (145), showing Tayo that divisions within nature are detrimental. "Scalp Ceremony" is an ironic name because throughout American history, cutting scalps has been a way to kill people. In *Ceremony*, cutting the patient's scalp is necessary to heal the people; the ceremony is not a sacrificial one: the scalp is only cut, not removed.

The stars play a role in Tayo's cure: "[Betonie] was drawing in the dirt with his finger. 'Remember these stars,' he said. 'I've seen them and I've seen the spotted cattle; I've seen a mountain and I've seen a woman'" (Silko, *Ceremony* 152). Tayo sees the star pattern in the September sky and, later, finds the mountain and the woman, Ts'eh. When Tayo hides from the destroyers in the uranium mine,

> he saw the constellation in the north sky, and the fourth star was directly above him; the pattern of the ceremony was in the stars, and the constellation formed a map of the mountains in the directions he had gone for the ceremony. For each star there was a night and a place; this was the last night and the last place, when the darkness of night and the light of day were balanced. (Silko, *Ceremony* 247)

Clearly, even the stars have been watching Tayo. Silko is not anthropomorphizing the stars; instead, she is allowing the stars to be stars, to move around the sky as they always do. In this case, their natural movement provides Tayo with the information he needs to retrieve the spotted cattle. Tayo has seen fate in the stars and understands the connections among all the stories and the one he is living: "he had never been crazy. He had only seen and heard the world as it always was: no boundaries, only transitions through all distances and time" (Silko, *Ceremony* 246).

Invisible Boundaries

Because of the ceremony, Tayo is able to determine that in its natural state, the world has no boundaries. However, the novel shows the types of boundaries, or limens, which develop when humans stake claims on the earth. The demarcations drawn by those in power create borders between groups of people. Gloria Anzaldúa argues, "Borderlands are physically present wherever two or more cultures edge each other, where people of different races occupy the same territory, where under, lower, middle and upper classes touch, where the space between two individuals shrinks with intimacy" (19). In the *arroyo* in Gallup, where Tayo and his mother live, there is little space among the homeless people. American Indians, African Americans, and Mexicans dwell together in Little Africa, a space considered to be unsafe by white people (Silko, *Ceremony* 108). The people in Little Africa usually get along well. When officials come to tear down the tin and cardboard dwellings, Tayo hides in a separate area of the *arroyo* most often used for toilet purposes (112). In the *arroyo*, invisible but tangible borderlines exist and are observed and, sometimes, smelled.

Borders in *Ceremony* are racial and socioeconomic thresholds that separate the white people from the American Indians, blacks, and Mexicans. According to Betonie, the white people exist and practice racial bias because of witchery, or evilness. Betonie makes himself more of an outcast by living in a cave on the north side of Gallup because, he says, that's where Gallup "keeps Indians until Ceremonial time" (Silko, *Ceremony* 117). All of the characters in Silko's novel who live in Gallup will, at some point, come in contact with people of other races and socioeconomic backgrounds. The area where the cultures come together and mix, even if only for a few minutes, is called a "borderland," and it can be a social dead end or a beginning, depending on society's goals.

As the US government has tried to acculturate American Indians into mainstream society, some people living in borderlands have seen the necessity for change and growth. Change and growth are what the healers in *Ceremony* say are necessary for survival. As previously noted, the four healers are mixed race, representing change and growth. In borderlands areas, it might seem safer or more productive for cultures, genders, age groups, and races to compromise on some traditions to allow for the maintenance of beliefs considered more important. Mohanty argues that if people respect each other and tend to their responsibilities, then strong communities can be formed (7). Mohanty's suggestion describes the way American Indians had lived for centuries before the arrival of Europeans on the North America continent.

A good example of a borderland community that creates balance and harmony in *Ceremony* is the US Army. People of different races, socioeconomic backgrounds, and beliefs peacefully coexist, even if only by command, because they all have one main goal: to serve their country. Because of this common goal, soldiers are often shown respect and privilege and, therefore, develop a sense of belonging. Emo, Leroy, Pinkie, Harley, and Rocky all seem to enjoy serving in the Army. Rocky tries to soothe Tayo by telling him the two are where they belong (Silko, *Ceremony* 8). Tayo, however, does not feel that he belongs. As a more traditional American Indian, he senses that the world is out of balance. The soldiers' peaceful coexistence lasts until the war is over and they are discharged. When the American Indian men leave the Army, the common interests among races evaporate, and racist attitudes return, reemphasizing the separation between mainstream culture and American Indian cultures.

The United States and the sovereign nations within it have many borderland areas. To grow and change in borderlands, people have to be able to practice hybridity, described by Anzaldúa as a sort of "fluidity" that allows people to move easily, though not always painlessly, among others. She suggests an answer for healing the wounds that prevent people from living in harmony: "The answer to the problem between the white race and the colored, between males and females, lies in healing the split that originates in the very foundation of our lives, our culture, our languages, our thoughts" (Anzaldúa 102).

Auntie is possessed of dualistic, or split, thinking that includes part of the shared consciousness of her tribe, when "[t]he people had known, with the simple certainty of the world they saw, how everything should be" (Silko, *Ceremony* 68). Auntie knows how she would mend her family's relationship with others who disapprove of mixed-race relationships: she would collect all of the opinions, "tie them into a single prayer bundle that would bring peace to all of them. But now the feelings were twisted, tangled roots, and all the names for the source of this growth were buried under English words, out of reach" (Silko, *Ceremony* 69). Auntie has been forced to change, but she has not been allowed to grow. Over time, she has lost valuable elements of her cultural traditions instead of adding to them elements from different cultures. She cannot shift easily between her culture and the mainstream culture, or even within her own acclimating culture.

In *Ceremony*, Silko shows a culture suffering because the people have lost their connection with nature. The lost connection is the result of the white European culture taking over and imposing its will and lifestyle on the land and the people, forcing them to lose much of their traditional way of life. Though "balances and harmonies always shift," Silko's novel shows that they can be maintained through societal acceptance of all people and respect for nature. An ecopostcolonial borderlands reading of *Ceremony* further emphasizes the importance of the unity of humans with nature and the detrimental effects of racist attitudes among and within cultures.

Works Cited

Allen, Paula Gunn. "The Psychological Landscape of *Ceremony.*" *American Indian Quarterly*. A Special Symposium Issue on Leslie Marmon Silko's *Ceremony* 5.1 (Feb. 1979): 7–12. Web. 16 May 2015.

_____. *The Sacred Hoop: Recovering the Feminine in American Indian Traditions*. Boston: Beacon, 1992.

Anzaldúa, Gloria. *Borderlands/La Frontera: The New Mestiza*. 2nd ed. San Francisco: Aunt Lute Books, 1999.

Avila, Monica. "Leslie Marmon Silko's *Ceremony*: Witchery and Sacrifice of Self." *Explicator* 67.1 (Fall 2008): 53–55. Web. 16 May 2015.

Bell, Robert C. "Circular Design in *Ceremony.*" *American Indian Quarterly*. A Special Symposium Issue on Leslie Marmon Silko's *Ceremony* 5.1 (Feb. 1979): 47–62. Web. 16 May 2015.

Holm, Sharon. "The 'Lie' of the Land: Native Sovereignty, Indian Literary Nationalism, and Early Indigenism in Leslie Marmon Silko's *Ceremony.*" *American Indian Quarterly* 32.3 (2008): 243–74. Web. 16 May 2015.

Martin, Holly E. "Hybrid Landscapes as Catalysts for Cultural Reconciliation in Leslie Marmon Silko's *Ceremony* and Rudolfo Anaya's *Bless Me, Ultima.*" *Atenea* 26.1 (June 2006): 131–49. Web. 16 May 2015.

Mohanty, Chandra Talpade. *Feminism without Borders: Decolonizing Theory, Practicing Solidarity.* Durham, NC: Duke UP, 2003.

Silko, Leslie Marmon. *Ceremony.* New York: Penguin, 1977.

_____. "Landscape, History, and the Pueblo Imagination." *The Ecocriticism Reader: Landmarks in Literary Ecology*. Ed. Cheryll Glotfelty & Harold Fromm. Athens: U of Georgia P, 1996. 264–75.

Mapping the Territory: Mexican American Memoir_____

Paul Guajardo

If Facebook is any indication, we are either a society of solipsistic narcissists or the impulse toward self-disclosure and memoir is inexorably ingrained in the human psyche. Daily, we are subject to the postings of our Internet friends. We see pictures of cats, manicures, meals, vacations, and while most of this is mundane, the autobiographical impulse can have more meaningful impetus—like preserving the past, social and political activism, artistic and aesthetic proclivities, and of course the cathartic liberation of confession.

Paul de Mann argued that any book with a readable title page is somewhat autobiographical, but the converse is also partly true: many memoirs are somewhat fictional, of which James Frey's *A Million Little Pieces* (2003) is an egregious example. Thus, verisimilitude, exaggeration, embellishment, and omission are concepts that recur in discussions of memoir as we consider the role of faulty memory, recreated dialogue, composite characters, and the compression of time. We should also consider writer's motives, agendas, and political leanings, and how these shape our interpretation.

In a *New Yorker* essay, Daniel Mendelsohn humorously discusses negative portrayals of the genre:

> Unseemly self-exposure, unpalatable betrayals, unavoidable mendacity, a soupçon of meretriciousness: memoir [...] has been the black sheep of the literary family. Like a drunken guest at a wedding, it is constantly mortifying its soberer relatives (philosophy, history, literary fiction)—spilling family secrets, embarrassing old friends—motivated [...] by an overpowering need to be the center of attention. (n.p.)

Background

The Southwest is undergoing a marked demographic shift because of immigration from Latin America. As of 2013, according to the US Census Bureau, there were fifty-four million Hispanics in the US, comprising America's largest minority, and of this number, Mexican Americans comprise around 65 percent of the US Hispanic population (the next largest group, Puerto Ricans, comprise slightly less than 10 percent). Latinos are the majority population in California; New Mexico; and, soon, in Texas, too. Mexican American memoirs are vibrant and important because they attempt to establish the identity, place, and purpose of Latinos/as by grappling with the questions of who we are and what our place in society is. Too often immigrants feel left in limbo: Are we Mexican? Are we American? Are we both? Are we neither?

Latino memoirs overlap themes with southwestern literature: the usual coming-of-age experiences, rites-of-passage, focus on family life, the role of women, family fragmentation, social justice and political activism, prejudice, discrimination, racism, poverty, economics, and employment. However, there is some departure with ideas of migrant work: the Catholic Church, folklore, legends, superstitions, cultural traditions, *curanderismo* (folk healing), *machista* attitudes, alienation, displacement, assimilation, acculturation, and notions of *Aztlán* or a homeland where there is a sense of acceptance and belonging.

Early Memoirs

Spanish exploration narratives provide insight into our diverse Southwest history, such as Bartolomé De Las Casas' *A Short Account of the Destruction of the Indies* (1552), and Bernal Diaz's *The Conquest of New Spain* (c.1568). More traditional examples set in the nineteenth and early twentieth century include: *Personal Memoirs of John N. Seguin* (1858), Elena Zamora O'Shea's *El Mesquite* (1935), Miguel Otero's *My Life on the Frontier* (1935), Luis Perez's *El Coyote: The Rebel* (1947), Fabiola Cabeza de Baca Gilbert's *We Fed Them Cactus* (1954), Cleofas M. Jaramillo's

Romance of a Little Village Girl (1955), and Leonor Villegas de Magnón's *The Rebel* (1961).

Later texts that helped map the terrain of contemporary Mexican American autobiography and, by extension, literature of the Southwest, include José Antonio Villarreal's seminal *Pocho* (1959), his autobiographical novel; along with John Rechy's *City of Night* (1963); Tomás Rivera's *...y no se lo trago la tierra* (1971); Rudolfo Anaya's *Bless Me, Ultima* (1972); Ernesto Galarza's *Barrio Boy* (1971); Oscar Zeta Acosta's *The Autobiography of a Brown Buffalo* (1972); and Anthony Quinn's *The Original Sin* (1972).

Immigrant Narratives

Numerous sub-categories exist within the genre of Mexican American autobiographies, and the most fascinating and arguably important, are the first-generation immigrant narratives like Francisco Jiménez's series, which details his life from childhood through graduate school: *The Circuit* (1997), *Breaking Through* (2002), *Reaching Out* (2009), and *Taking Hold* (2015). His stories focus on his family's immigration, sacrifices, hard work, education, and ultimate success. As in other narratives, there is the quick-tempered father who rules with borderline abusive force. Realizing that education is his ticket out of the dusty cycle of migrant work, "Pancho" excels in school.

Elva Treviño Hart's *Barefoot Heart* (1999) is a classic chronicle of migrant work, culminating in Hart's academic and corporate success, but despite her accomplishments (a six-figure salary and a Mercedes), she writes "I was disconnected and distant from my culture, my family, and from my heart and soul" (233). Her book's prologue begins: "I am nobody. And my story is the same as a million others. Poor Mexican American. Female child. We all look alike: dirty feet, brown skin, downcast eyes" (Hart n.p.). She also states that throughout her childhood, she never had a bed, drawing a contrast to her Anglo friend, Kit, who enjoys a two-story house and a personal pony.

Rose Castillo Guilbault's *Farmworker's Daughter: Growing up Mexican in America* (2005) is an assimilation narrative about coming-of-age while juggling two cultures. Guilbault becomes a journalist, which lends her story literary qualities; she provides a nice balance between narration, description, and dialog. Describing her step-father's difficulty with the English language, Guilbault writes: "Americans winced and grew impatient with his heavily accented English, often responding curtly and turning quickly away so as not to encourage further conversation [...] He didn't articulate properly and he stammered, hemmed and hawed, grasping for the right words" (134). But in contrast, she observes, "Of course, that's not how he sounded in Spanish. He was not only articulate, he could be downright eloquent. But over time, I had seen him retreat. He anticipated Americans' response to his speech, his dark skin, and his Indian features. I saw it in the slump of his shoulders, in the downward cast of his eyes, in the downward curve of his mouth" (Guilbault 134).

Similarly, *Journey of Hope: Memoirs of a Mexican Girl* (2007) by Rosalina Rosay recounts growing up in Mexico and immigrating as a child. Despite having an illiterate father, she graduates from college—obtaining a degree in accounting. In her conclusion, she addresses the immigration debate by uniquely criticizing Mexican activists who fault American trade policies, "If anyone is to blame, it is the elite class and the politicians of Mexico. The rich people in Mexico would have been happy to keep us as poor ignorant peasants [...] And the government was—and still is—too corrupt and inefficient to help us" (Rosay 170).

Reyna Grande's *The Distance Between Us* (2012), also details her journey to the US at the age of nine. As a child, she and her two siblings are left behind in Mexico, with a semi-sadistic grandmother, while her parents go to the United States to work in an attempt to save money for a house. She works hard, excels in school, enduring parental and social abuse before graduating from college. After eight years in the United States, at age seventeen, Reyna returns to her former home in Mexico for a visit:

I was afraid to admit that perhaps I might not be the same little girl who used to make mud tortillas [...] I realized that there was something else I had lost the day I left my hometown. Even though my umbilical cord was buried in Iguala, I was no longer considered Mexican enough. To the people there, who had seen me grow up, I was no longer one of them. (Grande 281)

Ramón "Tianguis" Pérez's *Diary of an Undocumented Immigrant* (1991) provides a distinctive Mexican perspective of our country, from someone who comes here to work for a few years and then returns to his Zapotec village. His book begins with his hiring a coyote (human trafficker) to cross the border, but he is apprehended and sent back. Eventually, he makes it to Houston and later to California. Making the decision to leave Mexico was easy, he says, because most of the men from his village had already taken part in the migrant cycle.

One could even say that we're a village of wetbacks. A lot of people, nearly the majority, have gone, come back, and returned to the country to the north; almost all of them have held in their finger the famous green bills that have jokingly been called 'green cards'— immigration cards—for generations […] My people have had to emigrate to survive. (R. Pérez 12)

Likewise, *Illegal: Reflections of an Undocumented Immigrant* by José Ángel N. is an extraordinary narrative that depicts the sad struggles of someone forced to live in the shadows without documentation, almost without an identity. José initially aspires to restaurant work, but he applies himself to learning English and obtains a GED (after three tries). Yet, despite eventually graduating from college, obtaining a graduate degree, becoming a professional translator, and buying a luxury high-rise condo, he cannot visit family in Mexico for fear of not being able to return. José N.'s formal education in Guadalajara, Mexico, ended at age thirteen, but he eventually earns a degree in philosophy, so, in some ways, he attains the American Dream (education, career, home). But because of his (il)legal status, he lives in perpetual fear of deportation. An example of this is his unwillingness, as an author, to use his surname. His eloquent memoir is erudite and philosophical and reflects his wide reading and deep thinking. Ultimately, José marries a "white" woman, who perhaps represents acceptance into mainstream society. Like so many other immigrant narratives, José N.'s story is about flux. As he ponders his new life and the changes that have occurred, he reflects:

> [...] the person I was has been completely transformed. Now when I contemplate the adventure of the young immigrant breaking through the border almost two decades ago, he is almost unrecognizable. Such boldness, such confidence in the face of uncertainty. I think of him now and can't help but feel nostalgic—he is as ambitious as he is naïve[....] (N. 109)

Accomplished Voices

Poet Gary Soto has more than forty books to his credit and has segued into short stories, children's fiction, and young adult fiction. Much of his writing includes his wry observations and recollections about growing up in California's Central Valley. Some of his autobiographical story collections include *Living Up the Street* (1985), *Small Faces* (1986), *Lesser Evils: Ten Quartets* (1988), *A Summer Life* (1990), and *The Effects of Knut Hamsun on a Fresno Boy* (2000).

Victor Villaseñor has kept the autobiographical genre vibrant with his numerous works of memoir, autobiography, and family biographies, most notably: *Rain of Gold* (1991), *Wild Steps of Heaven* (1996), *Burro Genius* (2004), and *Crazy Loco Love* (2008). These two latter works relate his struggles in school as someone severely dyslexic. In addition to learning disabilities, he struggles with the institutional racism so prevalent at the time. Ultimately, in *Crazy Loco Love*, he vows: "I, VICTOR EDMUNDO VILLASEÑOR, TAKE THIS HOLY OATH BEFORE YOU, GOD ALMIGHTY, as your son, to write my people's story WITH ALL MY HEART AND SOUL! I'll write! I'll do my part with all the power and intensity ..." (375).

After a generation or two, as Hispanics become more assimilated in mainstream culture, they sometimes embody the "I'm having an identity-crisis" syndrome; for example, Oscar Zeta Acosta's *The Autobiography of a Brown Buffalo* (1972) presents his unease as a minority, which results in a three-part quest: a search for his past, his roots and identity, combined with a physical road-trip (to visit Hemingway's grave in Idaho and then to visit Hunter S. Thompson in Colorado, ultimately ending up in Juárez, Mexico, the place of his birth. Thrown in for good measure are several drug trips. In the segregated town of Riverbank, California, society is stratified into three classes: Protestants, Holy Rollers, and Catholics; Anglos, Okies, and Mexicans; clerks, cannery workers, and field hands. Acosta assimilates as an attempt to compensate for his marginalized status. He plays football, is in band, serves as student body president, joins the Air Force, becomes a Baptist missionary, receives a law degree, and runs for sheriff of Los Angeles County. Despite such accomplishments, Acosta is at odds with his ethnicity and continually hides behind masks; he pretends to be a Samoan, an Indian chief, Filipino, Hawaiian, Arabian, and Spanish. But ultimately, he concludes: "I am neither a Mexican nor an American. I am neither a Catholic nor a Protestant. I am a Chicano by ancestry and a Brown Buffalo by choice" (Acosta 199).

Another accomplished writer with an uneasy relationship to his roots is Richard Rodriguez whose unique contribution to American letters includes four collections: *Hunger of Memory: The Education of Richard Rodriguez* (1982), *Days of Obligation: An Argument with my Mexican Father* (1992), *Brown: The Last Discovery of America* (2003), and *Darling: A Spiritual Autobiography* (2014). Initially disparaged for his views against affirmative action and bilingual education, during the last thirty years, he has subsequently redeemed himself by writing provocative, profound, and poignant essays about ethnicity, class, and sexuality. In his first literary foray, he irritated minority scholars by writing that he felt alienated from his roots. Rodriguez asserted that his parents were no longer his parents in a cultural sense. Presciently, he acknowledged that he was considered "…a dupe, an ass, the fool—Tom Brown, the brown Uncle Tom" (Rodriguez 4) and that he was "…a comic victim of two cultures" (5). But his thesis is that education transformed him and allowed him entry into mainstream, middle-class America, a story that is increasingly common in the Southwest.

In one scene of Rick P. Rivera's *A Fabricated Mexican* (1995), an autobiographical novel, the protagonist is mistaken for a *gabacho* (derogatory term for Anglos):

> "I'm a Chicano too. I just don't look like it." …But I want to tell the paisano that my parents were born in Mexico […] That I didn't have an accent […] probably because I watched too much television […] I picked grapes […] I knew how to cook menudo. I wanted him to hear me sing songs by Javier Solis […] But somehow I couldn't say anything more. (81)

But these sorts of observations are not always so simple, "I thought about how at one time I had tried to deny all of this. I tried not to be Mexican. Not to speak a Mexican's language and sing Mexican songs. Not to eat Mexican food" (Rivera 131). Again, the "culprit" is education, "There was irony in my education as it had changed me, maybe even improved; but it also separated me from family, language, and culture, making me a stranger to those with whom I had once been familiar" (138). These sentiments about one's place in society, about assimilation, echo those of Richard Rodriguez.

Female Narratives

Numerous Chicanas have contributed unique narratives to Mexican American literature including Cherríe Moraga, *Loving in the War Years* (1983), and Gloria Anzaldúa's boundary-crossing works, along with Denise Chavez's *A Taco Testimony: Meditations on Family, Food and Culture* (2006), Pat Mora's *House of Houses* (1997), also Norma Elia Cantú's *Canícula: Snapshots of a Girlhood En La Frontera* (1995). Contemporary memoirs by Chicanas are often nonlinear and sometimes contain snippets of poetry, essays, anecdotes, *dichos* (aphorisms), feminist or lesbian politics, letters, recipes, and family photos. Scholars continue to discuss the different ways in which women approach the genre.

As with their male counterparts, there is sometimes an awkward relationship to the dominant culture. Stephanie Elizondo Griest's travel memoir, *Mexican Enough: My Life Between the Borderlines* (2008) is the account of a young woman who is half Mexican, but who makes "a conscious choice to be white" (4). At the University of Texas at Austin, she learns that there are scholarships for minorities, so she decides to "Mexify" herself by decorating her dorm with posters of Frida Kahlo and the Virgin of Guadalupe, drinking margaritas, reading Sandra Cisneros, and hyphenating her last name with her mother's maiden name. Later, feeling guilty and alienated from her culture, she decides to travel throughout Mexico learning about her roots and striving to become, "Mexican Enough." Like other minorities growing up in the United States, she learns about discrimination. In Griest's first travel memoir, *Around the Bloc: My Life in Moscow, Beijing, and Havana* (2004), she notes that:

> Sounding *pachuco* and "acting Mexican" were considered insults [...] conjuring images of an uneducated someone whose jeans hung around their ankles and who had slicked-back, greasy hair. Spanish for me was a language of hushed whispers followed by laughter [...] of rosaries and funerals and *quinceaneras* and weddings [...] and my *abuelita* in an apron feeding me beans. (xiii)

All of this represents what Stephanie wishes to leave behind.

Mary Helen Ponce's *Hoyt Street* (1993), is an endearing example of the coming-of-age memoir by someone who grew up in the San Fernando Valley. Born in 1938, the youngest of ten children, she adeptly captures not only the nuances of childhood, but also the social and, to some extent, communal history of a particular time and place. Describing an early experience at school, she writes,

> The other students were all blond Anglo's, the children of growers [...] They looked at us with childlike curiosity. Josey and I felt ill at ease. Our stained hands betrayed us as migratory workers; our imperfect English told of a lack of education. It was only when we read aloud that I felt I was as smart as the regular students. (Ponce 180)

Cultural Conflict

Domingo Martinez is another memoirist who has an uneasy relationship to his heritage in *The Boy Kings of Texas* (2012) as a result of growing up amidst prejudice in the Southwest. Acknowledging the privilege of social class, Martinez doesn't want to identify with his Mexican roots, "I did my best to forget Spanish from the start" (*Boy Kings* 29). He longs to leave his hometown, Brownsville: "I want out of this [...] hole of a border town at the bottom of Texas, out of this racist, ignorant, locus-eating, lower Texas toxic hell pit. I've endured my father, my grandmother, years of pathetic education, beatings, berations, concentrations of shame, and this heat most hellish" (197). Despite this depressing view of home, there is some redemption toward the end of his second memoir, *My Heart is a Drunken Compass* (2014). He wants to play "a song about cowboys and border bandits" for his girlfriend Sarah: "It's about where I'm from [...] It's my people, from the border. This is who I am" (Martinez, *My Heart* 248).

Because of inequities and cultural conflict (among other complex reasons), a growing subcategory for memoirs is the depiction of drugs, gangs, and prison life including Floyd Salas' impressive *Buffalo Nickel* (1992)—the account of his brother's heroin addiction, incarcerations, and the tragic suicide of four children; Miguel Duran's *Don't Spit on My Corner* (1992) narrates his years as a "teenage pachuco." Also noteworthy is Reymundo Sanchez's *My Bloody Life: The Making of a Latin King* (2000), which was followed up with *Lady Q: The Rise and Fall of a Latin Queen* (2008). Also in this group is Mona Ruiz's *Two Badges: The Lives of Mona Ruiz* (1997). She was both a gang member and a police officer.

Luis Rodriguez's *Always Running* (1993), is a popular account of someone who grow up in East Los Angeles and drifted into drugs, gangs, and prison. Rodriguez narrates how one day, "...a caravan of low-scraping cars slow-dragged in front of the school. A crew of mean-looking vatos piled out, armed with chains, bats, metal pipes and zip guns" (42). While these gang members terrorize the school, Rodriguez is intrigued, "I wanted this power. I wanted to be able to bring a whole school to its knees and even make teachers squirm [...] I was a broken boy, shy and fearful. I wanted what Thee Mystics [sic] had; I wanted the power to hurt somebody" (42).

Jimmy Santiago Baca brings poetic sensibilities to his award-winning *A Place to Stand* (2001), which details his abandonment as a child, life in an orphanage, life on the streets, and ultimately, five years in prison all because he continually felt like an outsider, an immigrant in his own land. He landed in prison "…by being a poor kid with too much anger and the wrong skin color" (Baca 4). He blames his poor choices in life on the feeling that,

> I didn't belong, I didn't fit in, I was a deviant. Security guards and managers followed me in store aisles; Anglo housewives […] clutched their purses as I passed. I felt socially censured […] prohibited from entering certain neighborhoods or restaurants, mistrusted by government officials, treated as a flunky by schoolteachers, profiled by counselors as a troublemaker, taunted by police, and disdained by judges. (Bacca 4)

According to Baca, this is a result of his having a Mexican accent and brown skin. "Feeling inferior in a white world, alien and ashamed, I longed for another place to live, outside of society" (4).

Academic Voices
Predictably, many Hispanics intellectuals and academics have penned their literary self-portraits: for example: David Maldonado's *Crossing Guadalupe Street* (2001) recounts his migration from Seguin, Texas, to president of the Iliff School of Theology in Denver. Journalist John Philip Santos wrote *Places Left Unfished in the Time of Creation* (1999), which he followed up with *The Farthest Home is in an Empire of Fire: A Tejano Elegy* (2010). Poet and prose writer Luis Alberto Urrea (who is half Mexican) penned *Nobody's Son: Notes from an American Life*, in which he observes, "I, the son of the border, had a barb-wire fence neatly bisecting my heart. The border, in other words, ran through me" (11). Another "half-Mexican" who grows up in El Paso is Gloria López-Stafford whose memoir is titled *A Place in El Paso: A Mexican American Childhood* (1996).

Luis Leal a distinguished and revered professor tells his story in *An Auto/Biography* (2000), which was compiled by Mario T. Garcia. *Julian Nava: My Mexican American Journey* (2002) relates

Nava's journey from East Los Angeles to Harvard, from School Board President to Ambassador of Mexico. He was even a pall-bearer to Cesar Chavez. History professor Ramón Eduardo Ruiz Urueta's *Memories of a Hyphenated Man* (2003) tells of a history professor who grew up middle class, but not necessarily privileged. Another faculty memoir is Texas A&M professor Marco Portales' *Latino Sun, Rising: Our Spanish Speaking U.S. World* (2005). Ignacio Garcia, a Texas native who holds an endowed chair and teaches western and Latino history at Brigham Young University, has produced a memoir of his childhood and the awakening of his political conscience: *Chicano While Mormon: Activism, War, and Keeping the Faith* (2015).

Some Hispanic "celebrities" have also penned their stories, notably actor Anthony Quinn, who was born in Mexico, detailed in *Original Sin* (1972). In Joan Baez's *Daybreak* (1966), she essentially disavows ethnic solidarity. Linda Chavez's *An Unlikely Conservative* (2002) depicts her political shift from liberal to conservative, predictably not making her popular with minorities. NPR personality, Maria Hinojosa's *Raising Raul* (1999) chronicles motherhood and Hinojosa's rise in the radio world. One notable autobiography of a sports figure's hard-scrabble life is Olympic Gold medalist Henry Cejudo's *American Victory: Wrestling, Dreams and a Journey Toward Home* (2011). Linda Ronstadt, who (like Joan Baez) has oblique Hispanic origins, titled her autobiography, *Simple Dreams: A Musical Memoir* (2013).

José Antonio Burciaga, born in El Paso, Texas, adeptly combines comedy and prose. As a founding member of the Chicano comedy troupe *Culture Clash*, his books, *Drink Cultura: Chicanismo* (1993) and *Spilling the Beans: Loteria Chicana* (1995) are collections of creative non-fiction: essays on Chicano history and culture as well as personal reflections. Acknowledging his often unrecognized bicultural status, he writes, "*Yo soy Mexicano*! [...] And I am a *gabacho*! Culturally, I have as much of the Mexicano as I do of the gringo. I am as comfortable with the Mexican as I am with the Anglo-American culture" (Burciaga 62). He continues, "I am tortillas and frijoles, but

I am also hamburgers and hot dogs [...] I'm Mexican by nature and American by nurture" (63).

Critical Reception

Surprisingly, despite the prevalence of memoir within Mexican American literature, there has been scant critical focus on these narratives aside from a few obligatory book reviews. As Hispanic populations continue to grow—in the Southwest especially—there will be a corresponding increase in scholarly essays about individual writers and works, but currently, few full-length books address this genre. Genaro Padilla's *My History, Not Yours: The Formation of Mexican American Autobiography* (1993) is one notable exception along with Ramón Saldívar's *Chicano Narrative: The Dialectics of Difference* (1990), which devotes a few chapters to autobiographies. John Alba Cutler is another significant scholar who peripherally addresses memoirs in *Ends of Assimilation: The Formation of Chicano Literature* (2015).

Political and economic refugees from Mexico vote resoundingly and unequivocally with their feet, while risking everything, including their lives, to cross hostile borders and enter the US. As Hispanics continue immigrating and writing their recollections, our history will expand and our Southwest culture will change. As Mexico (and Latin America) evolves as a result of drug and political cartels, the immigration phenomenon will remain a constant, and while policy wonks debate whether immigrants enrich or impoverish our country, we have more to learn by reading these poignant personal descriptions than by listening to the double-speak of those insulated inside Washington. Minority memoirs are not just immigrant stories, but universal narratives about life and the human condition. These autobiographies currently chronicle the rapid changes occurring in the Southwest and throughout the US. Ultimately, we are more alike than we are different—as the study of our rich multicultural history makes clear.

Works Cited

Acosta, Oscar Zeta. *The Autobiography of a Brown Buffalo*. New York: Vintage, 1989.

Anaya, Rudolfo A. *Bless Me, Ultima*. New York: Warner, 1994.

Anzaldúa, Gloria. *Borderlands/La Frontera: The New Mestiza*. San Francisco: Spinsters/Aunt Lute, 1987.

Baca, Jimmy Santiago. *A Place to Stand: The Making of a Poet*. New York: Grove, 2001.

Baez, Joan. *Daybreak*. New York: Avon Books, 1966.

Burciaga. José Antonio. *Drink Cultura: Chicanismo*. Santa Barbara: Joshua Odell Editions, 1993.

_____. *Spilling the Beans: Loteria Chicana*. Santa Barbara: Joshua Odell Editions, 1995.

Cantú, Norma E. *Canícula: Snapshots of a Girlhood En La Frontera*. Albuquerque: U of New Mexico P, 1995.

Cejudo, Henry & Bill Plaschke. *American Victory: Wrestling, Dreams and a Journey Toward Home*. New York: Celebra, 2011.

Centers for Disease Control and Prevention. "Hispanic or Latino Populations." *Minority Health*. CDC, 5 May 2015. Web. 14 Nov. 2015.<http://www.cdc.gov/minorityhealth/populations/REMP/hispanic.html>.

Chavez, Linda. *An Unlikely Conservative: The Transformation of an Ex-liberal, Or, How I Became the Most Hated Hispanic in America*. New York: Basic Books, 2002.

Cutler, John Alba. *Ends of Assimilation: The Formation of Chicano Literature*. Oxford, UK: Oxford UP, 2015.

De Las Casas, Bartolomé. *A Short Account of the Destruction of the Indies*. London: Penguin Books, 1992.

Diaz, Bernal. *The Conquest of New Spain*. London: Penguin Books, 1963.

Durán, Miguel. *Don't Spit on My Corner*. Houston: Arte Público Press, 1992.

Frey, James. *A Million Little Pieces*. New York: Nan Talese/Doubleday, 2003.

Galarza, Ernesto. *Barrio Boy*. Notre Dame, NC: U of Notre Dame P, 1971.

García, Ignacio M. *Chicano While Mormon: Activism, War, and Keeping the Faith*. Lantham, MD: Fairleigh Dickinson UP, 2015.

García, Mario T. *Luis Leal: An Auto/biography*. Austin: U of Texas P, 2000.

Gilbert, Fabiola Cabeza De Baca. *We Fed Them Cactus*. Albuquerque: U of New Mexico P, 1954.

Grande, Reyna. *The Distance Between Us: A Memoir*. New York: Atria, 2012.

Griest, Stephanie Elizondo. *Around the Bloc: My Life in Moscow, Beijing, and Havana*. New York: Villard, 2004.

_____. *Mexican Enough: My Life Between the Borderlines*. New York: Atria, 2008.

Guilbault, Rose Castillo. *Farmworker's Daughter: Growing up Mexican in America*. Berkeley, CA: Heyday, 2006.

Hart, Elva Treviño. *Barefoot Heart: Stories of a Migrant Child*. Tempe, AZ: Bilingual/Editorial Bilingüe, 1999.

Hinojosa, Maria. *Raising Raul: Adventures Raising Myself and My Son*. New York: Penguin Books, 1999.

Jaramillo, Cleo. *Romance of a Little Village Girl*. San Antonio: The Naylor Company, 1955.

Jiménez, Francisco. *Breaking Through*. Boston: Houghton Mifflin, 2001.

_____. *The Circuit: Stories from the Life of a Migrant Child*. Albuquerque: U of New Mexico P, 1997.

_____. *Reaching out*. Boston: Houghton Mifflin, 2008.

_____. *Taking Hold: From Migrant Childhood to Columbia University*. Boston: Houghton Mifflin, 2015.

López-Stafford, Gloria. *A Place in El Paso: A Mexican American Childhood*. Albuquerque: U of New Mexico P, 1996.

Magnón, Leonor Villegas de. *The Rebel*. Houston, TX: Arte Público Press, 1994.

Maldonado, David. *Crossing Guadalupe Street: Growing up Hispanic and Protestant*. Albuquerque: U of New Mexico P, 2001.

Martinez, Domingo. *The Boy Kings of Texas: A Memoir*. Guilford, CT: Lyons Press, 2012.

_____. *My Heart Is a Drunken Compass: A Memoir*. Guilford, CT: Lyons Press, 2014.

Mendelsohn, Daniel. "But Enough About Me." *New Yorker.* Condé Nast, 25 Jan. 2010. Web. 14 Nov. 2015. <http://www.newyorker.com/magazine/2010/01/25/but-enough-about-me-2>.

Mora, Pat. *House of Houses.* Boston: Beacon, 1997.

Moraga, Cherríe. *Loving in the War Years: Lo Que Nunca Pasó Por Sus Labios.* Boston: South End Press, 1983.

Morales, Dionicio. *Dionicio Morales: A Life in Two Cultures.* Houston, TX: Piñata Books, 1997.

N., José Ángel. *Illegal: Reflections of an Undocumented Immigrant.* Urbana: U of Illinois P, 2014.

Nava, Julian. *Julian Nava: My Mexican American Journey.* Houston, TX: Arte Público Press, 2002.

O'Shea, Elena Zamora. *El Mesquite: A Story of the Early Spanish Settlements.* College Station: Texas A & M UP, 2000.

Otero, Miguel. *My Life on the Frontier, 1864–1882.* Albuquerque: U of New Mexico P, 1987.

Pérez, Luis. *El Coyote, the Rebel.* Houston, TX: Arte Público Press, 2000.

Pérez, Ramón. *Diary of an Undocumented Immigrant.* Houston, TX: Arte Público Press, 1991.

Ponce, Mary Helen. *Hoyt Street: An Autobiography.* Albuquerque: U of New Mexico P, 1993.

Portales, Marco. *Latino Sun, Rising: Our Spanish-speaking U.S. World.* College Station: Texas A & M UP, 2005.

Quinn, Anthony. *The Original Sin: A Self-Portrait.* Boston: Little, Brown, 1972.

Rechy, John. *City of Night.* New York: Grove, 1963.

Rivera, Tomás. *…y no se lo tragó la tierra.* Houston: Arte Público Press, 1987.

Rodríguez, Luis J. *Always Running: La Vida Loca, Gang Days in L.A.* Willimantic, CT: Curbstone, 1993.

Rodríguez, Richard. *Brown: The Last Discovery of America.* New York: Penguin, 2003.

_____. *Darling: A Spiritual Autobiography.* New York: Penguin, 2014.

_____. *Days of Obligation: An Argument with My Mexican Father.* New York: Viking, 1992.

_____. *Hunger of Memory: The Education of Richard Rodriguez: An Autobiography*. Boston: David Godine, 1982.

Ronstadt, Linda. *Simple Dreams: A Musical Memoir*. New York: Simon & Schuster, 2013.

Rosay, Rosalina. *Journey of Hope: Memoirs of a Mexican Girl*. Los Angeles: AR Publishing, 2007.

Ruiz, Mona & Geoff Boucher. *Two Badges: The Lives of Mona Ruiz*. Houston: Arte Público Press, 1997.

Ruiz, Ramón Eduardo. *Memories of a Hyphenated Man*. Tucson: U of Arizona P, 2003.

Salas, Floyd. *Buffalo Nickel: A Memoir*. Houston, TX: Arte Público Press, 1992.

Sanchez, Reymundo & Sonia Rodriguez. *Lady Q: The Rise and Fall of a Latin Queen*. Chicago: Chicago Review Press, 2008.

Sanchez, Reymundo. *My Bloody Life: The Making of a Latin King*. Chicago: Chicago Review Press, 2000.

Santos, John Phillip. *Places Left Unfinished at the Time of Creation*. New York: Viking, 1999.

_____. *The Farthest Home Is in an Empire of Fire: A Tejano Elegy*. New York: Viking, 2010.

Seguín, Juan N. *A Revolution Remembered: The Memoirs and Selected Correspondence of Juan N. Seguín*. Austin: Texas State Historical Association, 2002.

Soto, Gary. *The Effects of Knut Hamsun on a Fresno Boy: Recollections and Short Essays*. New York: Persea, 2000.

_____. *Lesser Evils: Ten Quartets*. Houston, TX: Arte Público Press, 1988.

_____. *Living up the Street: Narrative Recollections*. San Francisco: Strawberry Hill, 1985.

_____. *Small Faces*. Houston, TX: Arte Público Press, 1986.

_____. *A Summer Life*. Hanover, NH: U of New England P, 1990.

Urrea, Luis Alberto. *Nobody's Son: Notes from an American Life*. Tucson: U of Arizona P, 1998.

Villarreal, José Antonio. *Pocho*. New York: Anchor, 1989.

Villaseñor, Victor. *Burro Genius: A Memoir*. New York: Rayo, 2004.

_____. *Crazy Loco Love*. Houston, TX: Arte Público Press, 2008.

_____. *Rain of Gold*. Houston, TX: Arte Público Press, 1991.

_____. *Wild Steps of Heaven.* New York: A Delta Book, 1996.

Resisting Dominant National Narratives: Recovering María Amparo Ruiz de Burton's *Squatter and the Don* and (Re)writing Mexican American History[1]

Annette Portillo

As a result of the "U.S. Hispanic Literary Heritage Project," which seeks to republish works that have been confined to libraries and archival collections, the traditional American literary canon and Chican@ canon alike have been transformed.[2] It is through such projects that we have been reintroduced to such authors as María Amparo Ruiz de Burton, whose novels counter stereotypical images of Mexican Americans/*Californios*. Through a (re)reading of southwestern literature, this essay seeks to counter the notion of America's "eastern-centered" historical origins and the myth of a cohesive, self-contained "American" national narrative. In addition, this essay examines "regional consciousness" and formations of "regional identities" as an integral component to redefining the dominant narrative as it allows for a more comprehensive examination of how specific locations contributed and countered the notion of a unified Americanism. Ruiz de Burton's *The Squatter and the Don*, a "recovered" novel, originally published in 1885, not only critiques the hypocrisy of a "democratic" America, but also portrays instances of assimilation and integration. Thus, although Ruiz de Burton utilizes a popular literary form, she subversively resists the dominant national narrative by writing her community back into history through "fictional" characters. Her novel recalls the systematic relocation and socioeconomic destruction of a conquered Mexican population in the late nineteenth century. And typical of sentimental literature, she calls on her readers to sympathize with the then dispossessed Mexican population. In addition to its significance in aiding our understanding of regional identities, Ruiz de Burton's novel is also noteworthy because of its depiction of the larger national project of the elite Californios' desire to assimilate. In her study that seeks to "write Chicanas into history," Emma Pérez suggests that "Chicana history has been a conscious effort to retool, to shift meanings and read against the grain, to negotiate Eurocentricity whether within European historical models or within the paradigms of United States historiography" (xvii). Thus, given the context of Ruiz de Burton's novel, her work serves to better our understanding of the multi-perspective narratives of history. While, on one level, she uses the historical romance genre that was popular in the mid- to late nineteenth century, on another level, she is manipulating this form in order to counter the dominant history that has stereotyped and, in some instances, erased her people's story from the national narrative. Similar to other early Chicana writers, Ruiz de Burton's historical romance novels can assist in the overall project to reconceptualize our preconceived notions of Chicana/o and American history. Pérez states that since "[t]hey are restricted to the boundaries of arguments that came before, Chicano/a historians have tended to build a discipline that mimics the making of the frontier, or 'American West,' while at the same time opposing the ideological making of the 'West' (Pérez 4). Thus, I argue that, in order to complicate the very tenets of American literary history, we must re-read and critique such authors as Ruiz de Burton, who complicate our understanding of not only Chican@ history and literature, but dominant narratives of southwestern American literature and culture.

The Myth of "Southwestern" Literature and History

There have been a large number of essays written by historians and literary critics alike regarding the West, including harsh critiques of traditional historians who disregard the West as a region and, therefore, relegate it to the "margins" of US historical and literary narratives.[3] In particular, historian, Patricia Limerick argues for the necessity to incorporate the "West" into discussions surrounding American history (83–104). She states that traditionally Western historians have favored the western movement narrative and the story of "eastern-centered" historical origins of America that inevitably perpetuate the myth of a cohesive, self-contained "American" national narrative. Therefore, the incorporation of the West as a concept within historiography would fragment the notion of national synthesis. Although critiques exist of Limerick's attempts to define and somehow solidify the West as a region worth studying in relation to national history, she maintains that "Western regional history has been a construction of hindsight and on that count it is remarkably similar to the constructions governing the rest of American history (92)." Limerick notes that, in the past, it was "reasonable" to use the concept of regionalism, that is, the study of the West, to somehow synthesize American history by taking various stories from different communities and pull them into one story "as these various groups interacted in the big process of the invasion and conquest of the region" (94). But now, there exist different narrative origins of, for example, colonial history where there are stories from Spanish colonial New Mexico, Spanish colonial Texas, in addition to British colonial Virginia and Massachusetts.[4] This argument for a "multi-origin" story is useful as it allows for a multitude of perspectives regarding American history and literature, but it also becomes problematic given that the objective is for a possible "union," "reconciliation" or "common story" between opposing groups. The "West" connotes specific images and stereotypes that problematize one's perception about this region. Limerick also concedes that this essentialist definition of the West may have various meanings depending on the historian.

How then does "regionalism" function to revise the dominant national narrative of the westward movement that erases and negates specific populations who have now become marginalized within literary history? In her essay, "'Not in the Least American': Nineteenth-Century Literary Regionalism as UnAmerican Literature," Judith Fetterly argues for the reclamation of the term "regionalism" and the title "un-American" to describe formerly marginalized works. Fetterly also acknowledges that the term "un-American" is problematic as it is associated with the term it opposes, but she seeks "to expose how the term 'American' has been used to create a literary canon so hegemonic in the privilege of certain subjectivities as to make the term un-American not simply politically useful but actually meaningful" (Fetterley 16–17). I agree, that (re)claiming such terms as "region" the "West" and "American" are useful for engaging in the necessary critical dialogue regarding cultural and ethnic studies, but there is still the danger of affirming a unified and coherent notion of American literary history. In fact, these very concepts that we wish to (re)claim can marginalize further and hinder us from recovering alternative narratives. For example, Leticia M. Garza-Falcon argues that historian Walter Prescott Webb perpetuated stereotypes about the Mexican population and this "dominative" history was characterized by the concept of progress and a unified, cohesive American nation. Similarly, later narratives by Frederick Jackson Turner, reinforced the concept of the West as a "national identity associated with a people struggling against odds which are eventually overcome" (22–23). As a result, the national narrative inevitably erases or negates the Native American and Mexican American populations. Thus, it is only through a distorted perception of the West that we come to view the identity and culture of these "marginal" groups. In his discussion of "regional consciousness" Reed Way Dasenbrock asks: "What is Southwest literature? What is the Southwest? For whom is the Southwest? What is Southwest southwest of?" (123). He explains that American regionalism is distinctly literature by those authors, such as Sarah Orne Jewett and Hamlin Garland, who celebrate the local as they relate an "insiders" view of their own region. But in contrast, traditional southwestern literature by authors such as Willa Cather, Mary Austin, and Charles Fletcher Lummis celebrate the exotic as they are "outsiders" to the regions and groups of people they are discussing (Dasenbrock 123). It is this very notion of the "southwest" that marginalizes the various colonized groups in this region, such as Mexican-Americans and American Indians who consider the West as their center (123).

The Squatter and the Don Counters Dominant National Narratives

Ruiz de Burton was the granddaughter of Don José Manuel Ruiz, commandant of the presidio in the Mexican state of Baja California and owner of the Rancho Ensenada de Todos Santos, which spanned

48,884 acres. According to Kathleen Crawford in her article "María Amparo Ruiz de Burton: The General's Lady," this land was conferred upon Lieutenant José Manuel Ruiz of the Spanish Army who had provided assistance in founding missions in Lower California (199). In the introduction to the republished edition of *The Squatter and the Don*, Sanchez and Pita note that Ruiz de Burton was born in either La Paz or Loreto, Baja California, between 1832 and 1835 (8, fn 13). During the takeover of La Paz by American troops in 1848, she met her future husband, Lieutenant Colonel Henry Stanton Burton, who served on the First Regiment of New York Volunteers. After resistance by the Mexican citizens, America took control of Baja California, and the Treaty of Guadalupe was signed in 1848. The treaty did not include Baja California as part of the newly acquired land by America. Therefore, residents of Baja were given a choice to either stay or be taken as refugees to Alta California (Ruiz de Burton 9). Ruiz de Burton, along with her mother and brother, were among those who accepted passage to Monterey on the war transport, Lexington. It was here as the daughter of a "prominent Spanish family" that she "enjoyed the privileges of a private professor from Spain" (Crawford 200). Her romance with Henry Burton met with opposition, as she was the daughter of a Spanish Catholic family and he a Protestant and national figure. Their public romance was the topic of various articles in local newspapers and reported on by historian Herbert Howe Bancroft. They were eventually married on July 7, 1849 by a Protestant minister. In 1854, Burton homesteaded a large piece of property, Rancho Jamul, where the confusing land title would prove disastrous for Ruiz de Burton after becoming a widow (Crawford 202).

In 1859, Colonel Burton was ordered east to Fort Monroe, Virginia. After returning to California for two years when Burton was placed in command of Alcatraz Island, they moved back to the East, where Burton worked at several posts during the Civil War (Crawford 204). It was in the East where Ruiz de Burton had a wide circle of friends and in a letter to her friend Mariano Guadalupe Vallejo, she describes her attendance at the inauguration for President Abraham Lincoln in 1861. The influential friends she made in Washington would prove to help her as she later fought to retain her land in California (Crawford 205). After the capture of Petersburg, Virginia, in 1865, Colonel Burton contracted malarial fever. He had recurrent attacks of this illness and died five years later of apoplexy. Ruiz de Burton returned home to Rancho Jamul with children Nellie and Henry and, for the next twenty-four years, engaged in numerous battles for the legal ownership of her land both in Jamul and in Ensenada. As a businesswoman, she continued running cattle, growing wheat, barley, and castor beans. And she owned warehouses near her land in Baja California. But it was the publication of her novels, *Who Would Have Thought It* (1872) and *The Squatter and the Don* (1885) that speak to the aftermath of the Mexican-American War, the deterritorialization of Mexican citizens and the issues of American identity and nationhood during the Civil War.

In *The Squatter and the Don*, Ruiz de Burton allegorically represents the deterritorialization of the Californio elite by the colonization of the United States and aftermath of the Treaty of Guadalupe Hidalgo (1848). Her work incites harsh critiques against rising capitalism and monopolies that destroyed the social and economic stability of the Californios. Although the treaty signed after the Mexican-American War promised protection of land grants and full rights as US citizens, the Land Law of 1851 was passed in order to determine the validity of Spanish-Mexican grants that had been issued to the Californio landowners. Since litigation over these land grants was prolonged for many years and the price of lawyers and services was expensive, the result was the "legal" dispossession of the Californios' land by the government and squatters. In California, soon after the Mexican-American war, the free-wage labor dominated over the pre-capitalist economy of the Mexican period (1821–1848). Ruiz de Burton follows the decline of the elite Californio*s*, who suffered displacement by such entrepreneurs as Leland Stanford and Collis P. Huntington. It should be noted that Ruiz de Burton's perspective is from the privileged Californio elite, since she is a prominent Spanish American and inherits land from her grandfather and husband. Thus, her national agenda excludes and even dehumanizes the lower class Mexican *vaqueros* and what she refers to as the *indios*.[5] Nevertheless, at this moment of capitalist transformation, she makes harsh critiques of monopolies and corrupt government officials. The rancho economy that relied on cattle ranching and agriculture gave way to large scale capitalist farmers, who became dominant in the industry. Industrialization grew rapidly in the early 1880s and large corporations began to alienate the small wage earner. According to Robert Wiebe:

> ...the basic distinction lay between individual enterprise and corporate wealth, between the scattered knights of private initiative and the soulless monsters of monopoly. An ingenious, preserving man who had won a personal fortune still belonged among the nation's heroes; sinister corporations that profited at the people's expense were the despoilers. (46)

In addition, more railroad tracks were constructed in 1885 than any other period in American history that allowed small communities to be pulled into this emerging system of transportation (Wiebe 48).

Ruiz de Burton addresses all of these issues in *The Squatter and the Don* as her allegorical representation critiques big business while simultaneously supporting the individual entrepreneur and community of self-determination. Her text serves to reconstruct the image of those who identified as Mexican to her white, middle-class audience, whose perceptions of the Spanish Californios were dehumanizing and stereotypical. These images and ethnic "identities" are also complicated given the internal class divisions between elite *rancheros* and working-class Mexicans. According to Tomas Almaguer, "The introduction of a new, Anglo-dominated class structure led to bitter contention between powerful Mexican rancheros and European-American capitalists for control of the most arable land in the state" (45). Thus, this conflict would overshadow that of the internal ethnic class conflicts. It is clear that, on one level, Ruiz de Burton's national project is assimilationist as she specifically characterizes the Californios as elite, "white," respectable people of "reason." For example, the patriarch of the Alamar family, Don

---

114   Critical Insights

Mariano, is portrayed as a righteous man who believes in the system of American laws that in theory should protect his family's rights and property. Don Mariano does not oppose the ideals of a democratic and free America, but rather the corruption that exists within the government:

> We have had no one speak for us. By the treaty of Guadalupe Hidalgo the American nation pledged its honor to respect our land titles just the same as Mexico would have done. Unfortunately, however, the discovery of gold brought to California the riff-raff of the world, and with it a horde of land sharks... ...They do not want government land. They want the land of the Spanish people, because we 'have too much,' they say. So, to win...the votes of the squatters, our representatives in Congress helped to pass laws declaring all lands in California open to preemption... Then, as a coating of whitewash to the stain on the nation's honor, a 'land commission' was established to examine land titles. (Ruiz de Burton 67)

This passage is characteristic of the many instances that Ruiz de Burton asserts her voice into the novel, critiquing the existing laws and those that have lent to the deterritorialization and consequent economic destruction of her people. She continually addresses the issue of citizen's rights, but problematizes the issue citizenship as she exposes the violation of the treaty. Although her novel follows a romantic plot represented by marriages between Anglos and Californios, her political commentary writes Californios back into history. Her text counters the dominant history that is being written by such figures as Bancroft as she manipulates a specific literary form to reveal the realist conditions of the Californios as a result of the war.

In his review of *The Squatter and the Don*, Manuel M. Martin-Rodriguez criticizes Ruiz de Burton's classist perspective and assimilationist tone. He notes that the conflict the Alamars undergo to retain their land is depicted "as a will to participate in the development and exploitation of the new opportunities for enrichment brought about by the U.S. economy, conscious of the fact that such action will enable them to preserve their social status"

(Martin-Rodriguez 43). He posits that her novel also echoes the "promotional literature" of the time that described or advertised California as the "land of milk and honey" as it encouraged colonization by Anglo-Americans (42). It is true that she dismisses the voices of those working class groups referred to as the "Indians" or "*vaqueros*" and dehumanizes lower-class Anglo squatters, but her work is still politically charged as it exposes the hypocrisy of a country claiming ideologies based on freedom. After living in the East for ten years, Ruiz de Burton would have been familiar with the popular images of California and its "natives" that were portrayed in magazines and newspapers. It is then possible to read her novel as an engagement with these stereotypical and colonialist perceptions of California. She appropriates the romance genre for the purposes of appealing to a white middle-class audience, but manipulates this form to include social and political commentary on issues surrounding class, ethnicity, and gender.

In the same way that African American women writers wrote novels that countered racism, Ruiz de Burton inscribes her own sense of community and citizenship in her novel. While the uplift movement and colored women's clubs of the late nineteenth century worked towards the integration and uplift of African Americans arguing for cultural citizenship, the struggles of the Californios are centered around the issue of land and property. What does it mean to be a citizen of the United States? Is it possible to completely assimilate if the rights agreed to within a treaty are never fulfilled? Although not "representative" of the entire "Mexican" community of the late nineteenth century, Ruiz de Burton's novels can be considered historical references in which to acquire a more complete view of the history that had traditionally erased or marginalized specific minority populations.

In his critique of the introduction by Sanchez and Pita, Martin-Rodriguez argues that this novel is the "ideological construct of the Californio elite" and "an intellectual legitimation of their privileged status." And although it is a "protest novel," it is from the point of view of an aristocratic Mexican American and, therefore, should not "be described as the direct origin of more

Critical Insights

recent contestatory discourses" (Martin-Rodriguez 46). I agree that we must problematize the intended audience and class-oriented position of the novel, but we cannot simply eliminate texts from the canon of "Chicana/o" literature because they are not overtly oppositional. However problematically defined, Sanchez and Pita note the "historical" relevance and importance of this text to a larger literary tradition of Chicanas/os. In their introduction to the novel, they argue "It is the story, in part, of the repercussions of United States expansionism and the rise of corporate monopoly power like that of the railroad trusts; however, it primarily reconstructs the loss of land and power of the conquered population from the perspective of one who although acculturated, had a forceful voice and, more importantly, a clear memory" (Ruiz de Burton 51). We can problematize the defining characteristics of the Chicana/o canon indefinitely, but it is important to note how these earlier writers do in fact counter and rewrite specific dominant histories as they engage and manipulate popular narrative forms that allow for a telling of history from another perspective. For example, Chicana historian Pérez argues that we need to move beyond the limits of assimilation. "What does assimilation mean in cultural and socioeconomic terms? …Isn't there a weaving between cultures, between worlds, between borders? Is there ever a complete process of assimilation? In a capitalist patriarchal society, is it really assimilation that is desired, expected, and striven for from the bottom?" (Pérez 80). Pérez posits "that women's activities, their spoken words, have been overdetermined as assimilationist even when scholars have detected opposition and resistance" and argues for a "differential consciousness" where agency is reinscribed into communities where "transformative identities" (re)create newness (81). This is useful as it allows us to examine such works as Ruiz de Burton's without limiting ourselves to the boundaries of assimilation and instead read her works within the context of capitalist transformation. For example, Ruiz de Burton creates a space and voice of resistance as she inscribes herself into the profession of writing.

Ruiz de Burton began writing *The Squatter and the Don* after her return to San Diego in 1880.[6] Similar to her first novel, she published this text under a pseudonym, C. Loyal, under which this first edition was copyrighted. With only minor changes, the second edition was copyrighted by Samuel Carson & Co. in San Francisco in 1885 (Ruiz de Burton 11). She discusses the publication of her book in a letter to her friend Prof. George Davidson:

> Only two of three friends know I am writing it. I want to publish it this fall, in September. This is an additional reason for my wishing to get my 3 months extra pay, and my pension increased, to have this much to help me with the publication. Will you try to help me? Please do so. If I am able to pay for the stenotype plates I will make something; if not, all the profits will go to the pocket of the publishers and book-sellers.[7]

The publishing industry and access given to Californio/Mexican American writers is significant given the social and political climate of the late nineteenth century. This struggle with publication is similar to African American writers in the first half of the nineteenth century. According to Carla Peterson, writers appropriated novelizing techniques as they adapted "to the economy of the dominant culture in which the novel was fast becoming one of the most popular and lucrative forms of writing…" (150). And similar to Ruiz de Burton, "African American writers often found themselves dependent on a white readership and thus found their freedom of expression constrained by larger socioeconomic issues of commodification, readership, and publication, especially since they ultimately sought to profit from the sale of their books" (Peterson 150). What does it mean for a woman of Mexican origin to "sell" her novel at this particular moment? And how does her novel reveal or problematize our notion of "regional" literature, Southwest literature, and American literary history?

As "historical documentation," *The Squatter and the Don* addresses the issue of "American citizenship" for the Mexican population of California as interpreted through the Treaty of Guadalupe Hidalgo (1848), the Land Act of 1851, and the established monopoly, the "Big Four," who controlled the railroads that provided economic movement into and out of the state. Ruiz de Burton is not only concerned about the loss of land and economic opportunities, but also the diminishing power of the elite Californios. In the words of Don Mariano,

> I shall always lay it at the door of our legislators—that they have not only caused me to suffer many outrages, but, with those same laws, they are sapping the very life essence of public morality. They are teaching the people to lose all respect for the rights of others—to lose all respect for their national honor. Because we, *the natives* of California, the Spano-Americans, were, at the close of the war with Mexico, left in the lap of the American nation, or, rather, huddled at her feet like motherless, helpless children, Congress *thought* we might as well be kicked and cuffed as treated kindly. There was no one to be our champion, no one to take our part and object to our being robbed. It ought to have been sufficient that by the treaty of Guadalupe Hidalgo the national faith, the nation's honor was pledged to respect our property. They never thought of that. With very unbecoming haste, Congress hurried to pass laws to legalize their despoliation of the conquered Californians, forgetting the nation's pledge to protect us. (174–75)

Her political project not only critiques the government, but also strategically embraces other Americans who are "victims" of Congress and California delegation. And within this nationalist agenda, there are specific markers of class, such as the romance plot that embraces a marriage between Don Mariano's daughter, Mercedes, and William Darrel's son, Clarence, which is symbolic of the Californios (un)willingness to engage in a partnership with the United States. The legal complications that occur as a result of marriages between the Alamars and the middle class white families, the Mechlins and Darrells, pose challenges to the process of acculturation.[8] Ruiz de Burton's inability to reconcile the romantic plot is shown through the death and physical disempowerment of various characters. George Mechlin, who is married to Elvira Alamar, is crippled after he is shot in the leg by a squatter, William Mathews, for dismissing an appeal to the title of the Don's land. As a result, George is unable to return to his duties at the bank he had founded in New York. Gabriel Alamar, who is married to Lizzie

Mechlin, is also unable to return to work at the bank in San Francisco because of fraudulent claims and lawsuits brought against the Mechlins by corrupt lawyers Roper and Gasbang. Ruiz de Burton's novel conveys to her readers the hardships endured by the newly disenfranchised Californios who were once prominent members of the ruling class. Thus, her narrative becomes semi-autobiographical as she narrates Gabriel's downfall as a hod carrier, which results in a serious accident that nearly kills him.

> In that hod full of bricks not only his own sad experience was represented, but *the entire history* of the native Californians of Spanish descent was epitomized. Yes, Gabriel carrying his hod full of bricks up a steep ladder, was a symbolic representation of his race. The natives, of Spanish origin, having lost all their property, must henceforth be hod carriers. (Ruiz de Burton 352)

The destruction and downfall of these families is seen further as Mr. Mechlin commits suicide after the death of Don Mariano, who repeated at his death bed, "the sins of our legislators!" Thus, Ruiz de Burton's novel indicts the corrupt officials, corporate monopolies, and legislators for the socio-economic decline of the Californios and other "loyal" American citizens. And it is in her last chapter that she calls for redemption and justice.

Navigating the Culture of Professionalism: Re-Defining Chicana Literature

The Squatter and the Don, a historical romance and protest novel, defies simple categorization within a larger framework of the American literary canon and especially traditional definitions of "southwestern" literature. At this historical moment there was a rise in "professionalism" as organizations such as the American Bar Association (1878), American Historical Association (1884) and Modern Language Association (1883) were founded. There was a shift in how social authority was distributed as "experts" or those with specialized knowledge were given privileged status. According to Wai Chee Dimock, this rise in professionalism was "predicated on a set of reading conventions, on the authority of expert readers, and conversely, on the dependency of the illiterate" (88). Ruiz de Burton's participation in this "culture of professionalism" was apparent more through her business endeavors after her husband's death. On her rancho, she raised cattle and grew wheat, barley, and castor beans that she sold to a paint company. In addition, she irrigated her rancho after she began a water project with the help of Professor George Davidson from Berkeley, who determined how she could supply San Diego with water from the ravines. Although this later plan was never achieved and her legal struggles regarding the legitimacy of her land titles continued until her death in 1895, it is the profession of writing that allows her agency in the form of a protest novel. Her specialized knowledge of her community and the aftermath of the treaty allow for Ruiz de Burton to not only sell her story, but also critique those larger institutions of authority. And ironically it is within this new literary marketplace that Ruiz de Burton acquires a space in which to speak. The difficulty she had in getting her novel published can be attributed to the new publishing industry whose emphasis was on bestsellers and the growth of advertising systems. Therefore, even though it might seem that this commercial enterprise was somehow democratizing authorship as it allowed for stories by and about the common folk, there were still exclusions based on gender and race. In effect, Ruiz de Burton uses this legitimized profession to rupture popular notions of American identity.

Although Ruiz de Burton chooses a popular genre, that is, the romance novel, to tell her story, she subversively gives an authoritative voice to the dispossessed Mexican population critiquing those responsible for the deterritorialization of Californios/as. Her novel in part illustrates a specific "consciousness" that opposed, although not entirely, America's racist practices against the Mexican population. She counters dominant histories and literature that mythologized Mexicans as passive and unwilling to assimilate. And her work contributes to our understanding of a larger Chicana literary heritage and more importantly critiques dominant canons and concepts of Southwestern literature. In her review of "history as narrative," Garza-Falcon argues for a reading of "Chicana" literature as "real" history that stands in opposition to "public history," that perpetuates fictionalized views that become "normalized" and accepted as truth (22–23).

> [Henry] Fielding believed that fiction, through its power of imagination, could achieve a representation of reality unlikely to be conceptualized in any public history. In this way, we see how the defining of reality, or what constitutes the "natural" as defined by those in a position of authority, comes to be resisted as the aesthetic and cultural productions of peoples bereft of a sanctioned history come to the fore. (Garza-Falcon 23)

Thus, if we look at the literature and historical works of Ruiz de Burton, we are informed about another history and alternative national narrative. Through the social-historical analysis of her work, we find that the real "oppositional consciousness" have always existed, although only recently began to complicate dominant national narratives and American literary history.

Notes

1. I am grateful to those who read earlier versions of this essay and provided feedback, Drs. Mary Pat Brady, Helena Maria Viramontes, and Sunn Shelley Wong. I'm especially thankful to my undergraduate mentor Dr. Rosaura Sánchez who introduced me to the work of Ruiz de Burton. And to Dr. Genaro Padilla who furthered my interest in nineteenth-century Mexican American women's literature. Also, thank you to Dr. William Brannon for providing editing suggestions and comments.

2. "Recovering the U.S. Hispanic Literary Heritage Project is an international project to locate, preserve and disseminate Hispanic culture of the United States in its written form since colonial times until 1960. The project has compiled a comprehensive bibliography of books, pamphlets, manuscripts and ephemera produced by Latinos." For further information on the project, see: <https://artepublicopress. com/recovery-project/>. And for a more comprehensive description, see: Ramón Gutiérrez and Genaro Padilla, eds., *Recovering the U.S. Hispanic Literary Heritage* (Houston, TX: Arte Publico Press, 1993).

3.   See, for example, these works on the West without specificity to state, *Reading the West: New Essays on the Literature of the American West*, ed. Michael Kowaleski (Cambridge, UK: Cambridge University Press, 1996); Eric Heyne, *Desert, Garden, Margin, Range: Literature on the American Frontier* (New York: Twayne Publishers, 1992); *Trails Toward a New Western History*, eds. Patricia Nelson Limerick, Clyde Milner Jr., & Charles Rankin (Lawrence: University of Kansas Press, 1991); *Old West—New West: Centennial Essays*, ed. Barbara Meldrum (Moscow, ID: University of Idaho Press, 1993); *Many Wests: Place, Culture, and Regional Identity*, eds. David Wrobel & Michael Steiner (Lawrence: University of Kansas Press, 1997); *Over the Edge: Remapping the American West*, eds. Valerie Matsumoto & Blake Allmendinger (Berkeley: University of California Press, 1999).

4.   Limerick parallels this revised analysis of regions with the "Dickensian narrative" where "a bunch of *very* unrelated people are separately introduced, and then, not necessarily with any great speed, they move toward one another." And they become "all entangled in one another's lives" as they move into a common story (95).

5.   For further discussion on Ruiz De Burton's work as assimilationist and her use of classist and racist portrayals of *mestizos* and *indios* see: Josef Raab, "The Imagined Inter-American Community of María Amparo Ruiz de Burton." *American Studies* 53.1, The Americas in the Nineteenth Century: Inter-American Perspectives on U.S. Literature (2008): 77–95; and Manuel M. Martin-Rodriguez, "Textual and Land Reclamations: The Critical Reception of Early Chicana/o Literature," *Recovering the U.S. Hispanic Literary Heritage*, Vol. II, eds. Erlinda Gonzales-Berry & Chuck Tatum (Houston, TX: Arte Publico Press, 1996), 40–58.

6.   In their introduction, Sanchez and Pita note "All we know for certain is that she published her novels after Burton's death and that her novels and copious correspondence with a wide range of people indicate a strong background in the classics, in English, Spanish and American literature, and in European and American history and other areas. There is no information on her education in La Paz before she sailed for Alta California, but the family's position of prestige would have doubtlessly afforded some privileges for the governor's children and grandchildren, and we know that upon arriving in Monterey with

her mother, she is said to have entered a school where she learned to master the English language" (*The Squatter and the Don*, 10).

7.   Ruiz de Burton, letter to Professor Davidson, dated 6/9/1884. Available at Berkeley, CA: Bancroft Library, quoted in Sanchez and Pita, intro., *The Squatter and the Don*, 12.

8.   "The various antimiscegenation statutes that prohibited intermarriages between white Americans and other racialized groups (blacks, Indians, Asian immigrants) were not enacted against Mexicans. This social tolerance toward Anglo/Mexican amalgamation was, nonetheless, rigidly circumscribed along predictable class lines." For further discussion on the intermarriages between Californio elite and Anglo-Americans, see Almaguer 57–60.

Works Cited

Almaguer, Tomas. *Racial Faultlines: The Historical Origins of White Supremacy in California.* Berkeley: U of California P, 1994.

Crawford, Kathleen. "Maria Amparo Ruiz de Burton: The General's Lady," *Journal of San Diego History* 30 (Summer 84): 198–211.

Dasenbrock, Reed Way. "Southwest of What? Southwestern Literature as a Form of Frontier Literature." *Desert, Garden, Margin, Range: Literature on the American Frontier.* Ed. Eric Heyne. New York: Twayne, 1992. 123–132.

Dimock, Wai Chee. "Feminism, New Historicism, and the Reader." *Readers in History: Nineteenth-Century American Literature and the Contexts of Response.* Ed. James Machor. Baltimore, MD: John Hopkins UP, 1993. 85–106.

Fetterly, Judith. "'Not in the Least American': Nineteenth-Century Literary Regionalism as UnAmerican Literature." *Nineteenth-Century American Women Writers: A Critical Reader.* Ed. Karen Kilcup. Malden, MA: Blackwell Publishers, 1998.

Garza-Falcon, Leticia M. *Gente Decente: A Borderlands Response to the Rhetoric of Dominance.* Austin: U of Texas P, 1998.

Limerick, Patricia Nelson. "Region and Reason." *All Over the Map: Rethinking American Regions.* Ed. Edward Ayers, Patricia N. Limerick, Stephen Nissenbaum, & Peter S. Onuf. Baltimore, MD: John Hopkins UP, 1996.

Martin-Rodriguez, Manuel M. "Textual and Land Reclamations: The Critical Reception of Early Chicana/o Literature." *Recovering the U.S. Hispanic Literary Heritage*, Vol. II, Ed. Erlinda Gonzales-Berry & Chuck Tatum. Houston, TX: Arte Publico Press, 1996. 40–58.

Pérez, Emma. *The Decolonial Imaginary: Writing Chicanas into History*. Bloomington: Indiana UP, 1999.

Peterson, Carla L. *"Doers of the Word:" African-American Women Speakers & Writers in the North (1830–1880)*. New Brunswick, NJ: Rutgers UP, 1998.

Ruiz de Burton, María Amparo. *Squatter and the Don* (1885). Ed. Rosaura Sanchez & Beatrice Pita. Houston, TX: Arte Publico Press, 1992.

Turner, Frederick Jackson. "The Significance of the Frontier in American History." 1947. *The Frontier in American History*. Tucson: U of Arizona P, 1997. 1–38.

Wiebe, Robert H. *The Search For Order 1877–1920*. New York: Hill & Wang, 1967.

Ecological Martyrs: Ecocritical Considerations Beside Spiritual Mestizaje in Ana Castillo's *So Far from God*_____

Mike Lemon

For most readers and theorists, Ana Castillo's *So Far from God* reveals a discernible shift within the text, from magical realist elements to ecocritical and political considerations. However, a transition in terminology here—from magical realism[1] to spiritual imagery—should occur because it allows for a nuanced distinction for the novel's modal shift. In interviews, Castillo argues for this change, insisting that "the 'magic' [in the text] is modeled on religious miracles depicted in the lives of Catholic saints" (Caminero-Santangelo 83; Platt 79). Any consideration of the spiritual encapsulates Catholicism, indigenous beliefs, and syncretic spiritual movements that combine Catholicism with traditional rituals. The mixing of Christianity and native belief systems creates what Gloria Anzaldúa calls spiritual *mestizaje*. Mestizaje is a Spanish word that translates as "miscegenation." Combining this concept with the spiritual allows readers to reassess the novel's presentation of multiple spiritual movements and discuss how the "magical"—now spiritual—influences the environmental concerns.

The combination of spiritual rituals and environmental concerns takes shape as Sofi and her daughters, Esperanza, Caridad, Fe, and La Loca, move within domestic, public, and spiritual spaces in order to enact change for the New Mexico communities of Tomé and Belen. The novel's spiritual *mestizaje* creates a new discourse, in which particular locations and culture meet ecological injustices to form an environmental justice movement. Entering into this discourse requires engaging with ecocritical and Chicana theorists to demonstrate how environmental justice movements of the late twentieth century wrestle with the particulars of place in Castillo's novel. The novel's emphasis on Catholic and syncretic imagery and ritual informs the character's environmental justice movement

126

and represents a move that situates particular cultural and religious practices with specific environmental injustices for New Mexico.

Environmental Justice Movements: An Overview

A quick review of existing research on the novel's environmental concerns positions the novel in historical and theoretical terms. Kamala Platt historicizes the environmental justice movements as emerging from protests against environmental racism in the early 1980s. Esperanza's disappearance in the Persian Gulf situates *So Far from God* in the late 1980s and early '90s. These movements distinguish themselves from national, mainstream environmental agencies because the latter focus on conservation or preservation of natural resources, while the former highlights the intersections between ecological, class, social, and gender politics. In other words, larger environmental agencies mostly protect "nature" at the expense of people, and environmental justice movements include peoples within their agendas. For Platt, there exists "a similar spectrum of environmental oppression... the formula in each context is nearly identical: being poor, a person of color, an indigenous person, and a woman are factors that works against one's chances of having the choice of an economically and ecologically sustainable lifestyle in a relatively unpolluted, noncarcinogenic environment" (75–6). David Harvey agrees, pointing towards "the strong involvement of women," and quotes from Krauss, who notes that "'African American women's narratives strongly link environmental justice to other social justice movements, such as jobs, housing, and crime. ... For Native American women, environmental justice is bound up with the sovereignty of the indigenous peoples'" (qtd. in Harvey 386–7). For the peoples within the novel, the local environmental justice movement creates "alliances between indigenous and other socially marginalized groups" and provides "a means of developing resistance to outside domination" (Platt 77). The novel's ecological concerns mirror organizations from the Southwest. Gwyn Kirk highlights, among other agencies, the Southwest Organizing Project, the Southwest Network for Environmental and Economic Justice, and other agencies who advocate for watersheds and water rights (183–5). For real life and fictionalized environmental justice movements, specific concerns shape how these local groups organize.

The focus on locality poses a problem for moving towards a national agenda. While a web of similar interests join these individual movements under the umbrella term "environmental justice," Harvey notes that although individual movements have collaborated with national or other grassroots groups, "[it] preserves its fiercely independent 'militant particularism[.]" It rejects government and broadly 'bourgeois' attempts at cooptation and absorption into a middle-class and professional-based resistance" (372). The term "militant particularism" becomes important when discussing the novel. Harvey is not stressing particularly militant environmental change, which verges on ecoterrorism. Sofi and her community do not take up arms against the land's polluters. Rather, militant particularism emphasizes the necessity for participants within these local movements to fight for specifics rather than generalizations. Social and ecological concerns connect environmental justice movements to specific places. For Chicana theorists, environmental justice movements link spirituality and politics in interesting ways.

The intersections between spirituality, politics, and the environment appear in [Theresa] Delgadillo's expansion on Anzaldúa's spiritual *mestizaje*. She defines the phenomenon as "the transformative renewal of one's relationship to the sacred through a radical and sustained multimodal and self-reflexive critique of oppression in all its manifestations and a creative and engaged participation in shaping life that honors the sacred" (Delgadillo 1). Delgadillo emphasizes the multimodal within spiritual *mestizaje*. This resists hegemonic structures on several levels, but for this discussion, two levels are equally important. On one level, multimodal spirituality permits Catholicism to coexist alongside earth-based practices, like *curanderismo*.[2] One form of knowledge is not privileged over another, but spiritual mestizaje creates "an ethic of recognizing multiple ways of knowing" (Delgadillo 4). Accepting different ways of knowing and interacting with the world allows for empathy. On another level, the multimodal subverts cultural essentialism. Laura Pulido warns that, "Romanticized cultural heritages are a form of essentialism in that they regard the characteristics of a particular group as unitary and fixed or eternal" (122). In other words, essentialism disregards particulars within a culture and makes everyone the same. Reaffirming particular elements within a culture becomes areas of resistance. This fracturing leads to multimodal and nuanced inspections of how people adapt culture to a region's environmental concerns. As a person—or persons—move towards multimodal representations of spirituality, a "self-reflexive critique of oppression in all its manifestations" becomes part of the transformative moment. The moment also invokes movement between levels of knowledge. Anzaldúa uses the Nahuatl (Aztec language) word *nepantla* to define this liminal space and explains "I associate *nepantla* with states of mind that question old ideas and beliefs, acquire new perspectives, change worldviews, and shift from one world to another" (qtd. in Delgadillo 8). The questioning comes from this self-reflexive moment, when a person confronts his/her worldview. As one critiques oppression in its various manifestations, then that person can become an active participant in shaping the world around them. However, participation comes after the confrontation.

Ana Castillo's novel provides ample examples of how characters enter spiritual *mestizaje* and interconnect spirituality with political and environmental concerns. Although Sofi, Esperanza, and Fe symbolize particular elements that inform the formation of New Mexican environmental discourse, their stories speak against oppressive structures outside of the strictly spiritual. For example, Fe loses her life because of industrial waste, but she is not considered here because she is not a "spiritual" character. Of the daughters, Caridad and La Loca are the most spiritually inclined daughters, and they represent multimodal spirituality. Caridad's journey from a no-good daughter to a *curandera* presents a syncretic spiritual movement that mixes elements from Catholicism with earth-based rituals. She ultimately disappears into the earth, suggesting a return to an indigenous goddess, Tsichtinako. La Loca becomes a character who subverts orthodox Catholic thought through her reclusion, yet her reentrance into the community at the Stations of the Cross becomes a moment that conflates spiritual and environmental concerns.

A Return to Earth: Caridad's Spiritual Journey

Caridad's journey to become a *curandera* begins with a violent confrontation with the land. She has built a reputation for being loose with her love. That is, until one night she returns home bloody and left for dead (Castillo 32–3). Her attack reminds one critic of an early church saint. Alma Alvarez writes, "the physical attack on Caridad's nipples and the scourging of her body, in fact, recalls the fate of Saint Agatha [who] attempted to preserve control of her mind through control of her virginity (body). The consequences of this control were mutilation and death" (88). For Alvarez, Caridad's near death experience retells narratives about mystic Spanish nuns, and the beast Doña Felicia dreams is a representation of the church (88). Nevertheless, another reading can view this beastly perpetrator a different way. For Caridad and Doña Felicia, the monster reads as a force of nature:

> It was not a stray and desperate coyote … but a thing, both tangible and amorphous. A thing that might be described as made of sharp metal and splintered wood, of limestone, gold, and brittle parchment. It held the weight of a continent and was indelible as ink, centuries old and yet as strong as a wolf. It had no shape and was darker than the dark night, and mostly, as Caridad would never forget, it was a pure force.
> That night doña Felicia dreamt of the *malogra*[.] (Castillo 77)

Caridad's description presents fragmented images of the land and its bioregion. While not a coyote (which, in certain Native American tribes, symbolizes a creator/trickster god) the force is composed of materials found within the New Mexican biosphere. Gail Pérez connects Caridad's vision to Felicia's dream involving the *malogra*, an Hispano mythical creature that roams the night and usually manifests as wool that "diminishes and increases in size in the very presence of the unfortunate one who see it" (Cobos 104). Its usual manifestation as wool—either from a sheep or the cottonwood tree—suggest[s] natural images relevant to the New Mexican region. She explains, "Castillo rewrites the creature to represent the conquest, placing Caridad in the place of the raped earth and indigenous woman[.] ... The gold and parchment suggest the bitter struggle over land grants in New Mexico" (Pérez 83). The beast's weight and intangibility suggests a colonial reading; the monster has been colonized by Hispano, then Anglo conquerors. Caridad's encounter with it represents a particularly violent confrontation with one's environment and its heritage.

However, Caridad's attack leads towards a miraculous healing and awareness of the surrounding area's ability to heal. In reasons unexplained within the novel, Caridad is restored. Pérez speculates that Caridad's "Holy Restoration" comes through La Loca's prayers (76), yet Doña Felicia situates the spiritual within Caridad herself. Felicia, a *curandera* and the younger woman's mentor, exclaims, "Look what you did to yourself! ... It was the help of God ... but *you* healed yourself by pure will" (Castillo 55). Through the older woman's guidance, Caridad begins her training to become a *curandera*. Delgadillo connects the *curanderismo* of the border "with growing ecologically driven interests in homeopathy and organic and natural food supplies [making] it especially significant in contemporary Chicana spirituality" (17). Through her training, Caridad learns how to heal with a mixture of natural items and spiritual knowledge. Although it is a syncretic ritual that combines elements of indigenous traditions with Catholic elements, these earth-based practices usually pass from one female generation to the next; the emphasis on the feminine subverts the traditionally patriarchal Catholic system of priests and situates knowledge within the feminine.

Caridad's connections to the earth and feminine spaces ultimately move her away from religion or syncretic tradition towards an indigenous spirituality. She does so through her year-long hermitage in the mountains and her return to Tsichtinako. Caridad's removal from society begins shortly after her pilgrimage with her mentor to Chimayo for Holy Week. Laura Gillman and Stacey Floyd-Thomas view this interest in "pilgrimages inspired by the acts and deeds of indigenous native saints" as a departure from "institutionalized religious customs" (165). She becomes, for these critics, "a redemptive nationalist" who invests her time in learning about Amerindian culture, traditions, and rituals (Gillman & Floyd-Thomas 165). While at Chimayo, Caridad encounters the woman-on-the-wall, who readers later know as Esmeralda. The *curandera*-in-training is struck by this woman's beauty; the narrator tells readers that "In and of herself there was nothing about her that was unusually striking. She was dark. Indian or Mexican. Black, black hair. Big sturdy thigh" (Castillo 79). The narrator's emphasis on the woman's body implies a sexual or erotic attraction towards the woman. On the other hand, the narrator's description suggests a newfound appreciation for indigenous femininity. Pérez synthesizes the two, proclaiming that "redemption, we are to understand, involved loving her indigenous self in the person of Esmeralda" (84). Whichever the case may be, she removes herself into the desert shortly thereafter and is not seen for a year. Alvarez posits that this removal makes Caridad a "desert mother." She explains that when Caridad goes into the mountains, "her characterization as a type of nun, who seems more heroic for having had a sexual past, allows Castillo to acknowledge Caridad's sexuality. This acknowledgment manifests when Caridad retreats to the desert cave to pray and meditate on her love for another woman" (Alvarez 89). Pérez positions Caridad's spirituality within indigenous terms (84). The community's reaction to finding the "little hermit" is a mixture of Catholic Hispanos and Pueblos, as well as Natives who do not practice Christianity. Some believe Caridad is a saint, yet her own contemplations on the woman-on-the-wall suggest a shift from orthodoxy towards meditations on femininity, sexuality, indigeneity, and spiritual world.

Caridad's transition from the syncretic to indigenous based spirituality becomes complete when she returns to Tsichtinako. After establishing a non-sexual, but loving relationship with Esmeralda, Caridad and she visit Esmeralda's grandmother in the Acoma Pueblo's Sky City. Following them is Francisco el Penitente, who has become obsessed with Caridad, to the point of stalking the two women. Francisco represents patriarchal Catholic orthodoxy. He is the most explicitly religious male character in the novel, being introduced to readers as carving *bultos*—wooden saints— and carrying the cross at Chimayo. For Perez, he symbolizes both the church and the Franciscan missionaries who travelled with the conquistadores; he views Caridad "as the feminine has always been throughout history...the whore of his sexual fantasies and the virgin guiding his own personal salvation" (84–5). Conflating the whore/Madonna dichotomy in Caridad, Francisco pursues her and Esmeralda, seeking to maintain oppressive patriarchal structures. The two women, however, opt for another way.

By throwing themselves off the mesa, Caridad and Esmeralda embrace an indigenous spirituality that emphasizes femininity and creation. The narrator informs the reader that no bodies were found, but many heard "the spirit deity Tsichtinako calling loudly with a voice like wind, guiding the two women back, not out toward the sun's rays or up to the clouds but down, deep within the soft, moist earth where Esmeralda and Caridad would be safe and live forever" (Castillo 211).

Tscichtinako, the female Acoma goddess of creation, has called back her children. The movement downward invites several interpretations. One, the earth becomes central to the women's safety and eternal rest. The movement towards the sky—the traditionally heavenly destination for Christianity—becomes subverted by the dark earth. Two, the earthy image suggests the womb. Ralph E. Rodriguez notes, "They have returned to what the Acoma myth of creation refers to as the earth's womb" (qtd. in Caminero-Santangelo 90). There, the two women escape oppression in all its forms; in this case, they have rest from patriarchal, ecclesiastical, and capitalist subjugation. This indigenous, earth-based spirituality reclaims femininity from Catholic revisions that demonized women.

This spirituality, as beautiful, redeeming, and protective as it is for these two women, does present some problems for enacting sustainable social or environmental change. Caridad's spiritual journey, with its emphasis on indigenous practices and earth-based rituals, creates an awareness of one's ethnicity and region. However, it does not transition as easily towards social or environmental activism. In the same breath that she celebrates Caridad and Esmeralda's removal from oppression, one critic curtly notes that "this world cannot be fixed by being good workers and good girls" (Pérez 86). Marta Caminero-Santangelo agrees, noting that Caridad's experience becomes romanticized by both the narrator and the community within the novel. She writes, "Caridad's spiritual connection to the environment—to the land in a pristine, untouched form—translates not into any kind of social consciousness" (91). Nevertheless, Castillo's novel explores New Mexico's spiritual *mestizaje* and shows how other rituals and characters inform ecological awareness towards environmental justice movements.

What Is She Wearing?: The Stations of the Cross and La Loca's Outfit

Castillo connects the spiritual and political characteristics of a New Mexican environmental justice movement throughout the novel, particularly so during the Stations of the Cross scene. As the villages of Tomé and Belen gather for Holy Friday, the ritualistic procession that traditionally helps Catholics and Christians remember the condemnation, crucifixion, and death of Jesus of Nazareth instead becomes something new. The narrator repeatedly affirms, "there had never been no procession like that one before" (Castillo 242, 244). Alvarez discusses the newness of the procession as a connection between the ritual and liberation theology, writing that "… in this practice this profound focus on Christ's suffering, as well as individual's consciousness of his/her position in society, allows the individual to become conscious and empathetic of suffering of others in society" (96). Liberation theology is the concept that Catholics—and ostensibly all Christians—have a moral obligation to help those around them. It is a movement that joins religious faith with ethical and social action.

Instead of being strictly religious, the community gathers and conflates images from the procession with testimonies of environmental and social injustice. The people's witnesses take Jesus' place, because no one "was elected to carry a life-size cross" (Castillo 241). The narrator demonstrates this substitution by juxtaposing the two together; for a brief example, consider the following short passage of the first two stations:

> When Jesus was condemned to death, the spokesperson for the committee working to protest dumping radioactive waste in the sewer addressed the crowd. Jesus bore his cross and a man declared that most of the Native and hispano families throughout the land were living below poverty level, one out of six families collected food stamps. (Castillo 242)

The cited witnesses present two tenets within the community's environmental justice movement, as well as represent what Platt calls "the symbiotic relationship of spirituality with material justice" (88). The first portion juxtaposes Jesus' death sentence with the poisoning of the land through improper radioactive waste disposal. The pairing suggests a clear cut ecological disaster that threatens the entire ecosystem—human and nonhuman, plant and mineral. The second portion connects Jesus's cross with the poverty line. This seemingly suggests a deviation from environmental concerns; however, environmental justice movements do not exclude social concerns. As Taylor notes,

> It is a strange paradox that [established environmental organizations] which [exhort] the harmonious coexistence of people and nature, and [worry] about the continued survival of nature ..., somehow [forget] about the survival of humans, especially those who have lost their "habitats" and "food sources." (qtd. in Harvey 386)

In other words, neglecting how people live creates a paradoxical discourse within environmental organizations because they refuse to acknowledge a species within the environment. Pulido specifies this paradox for the New Mexican region. She presents data from 1990 that "per capita income in Río Arriba county was $11,979 for whites as compared to $7,496 for Hispanics. The result is a highly polarized economy geared towards wildlife and wilderness production for the enjoyment of urban middle-class residents"

(Pulido 125). Pulido's data comes from a county just north of the novel's setting and explicitly ties current conservation trends to economic disparity. The promotion of wilderness tourism comes at the expense of unemployment and wage differences. The financial disadvantages for these native and Hispanic communities hold the same weight as their physical wellbeing within the novel's environmental commentary.

Within this politically charged procession, La Loca, Sofi's fourth daughter, becomes an embodied metaphor because her outfit represents spiritual and environmental elements. The daughter most removed from society, she attends the Holy Friday procession. As the novel's narrator stresses, this represents her first outing from her family's homestead, since her "Holy Resurrection". Considered dead at the age of three, she rose from her casket and "lifted herself up into the air and landed on the church roof" (Castillo 23). From that moment, she becomes a subversive spiritual agent within the community. At first, one scholar writes, "La Loca's resurrection and levitation become a source of devotion for the Rio Abajo inhabitants" (Alvarez 84). She quickly becomes a canonical figure, losing her Christian name for the saintly title, La Loca Santa—"The Crazy Saint."

The loss of her "Christian" name may appear an innocuous detail, but it underscores the subversive nature of La Loca's story because it challenges Catholic theology through presenting a clairvoyant female character outside the church. From the chapel's rooftop, she details her journey into hell, purgatory, and heaven. She rebukes the authority of Father Jerome, who, as a priest, has the responsibility of declaring the young girl's resurrection a miracle or a devilish trick. La Loca's response to the padre reveals her purpose. She says, "God sent me back to help you all, to pray for you all," including Father Jerome (Castillo 24). When the good Father corrects her, she replies "'No, Padre[.] Remember it is *I* who am here to pray for *you*'" (24). Her exchange with the priest highlights an intersection that is at once challenging and supportive. In her rebuke, La Loca refers to Jerome's title, but immediately undercuts his position by emphasizing her role. However, her feelings of revulsion to humans because of their smell leads to Loca becoming a recluse. That is, until the Stations of the Cross.

For this momentous occasion, La Loca chooses to wear a pair of jeans with the label and back pocket removed, a red Pendleton shirt, and a blue chenille robe. As eclectic as they may seem, all the pieces of Loca's outfit have cultural significance within the New Mexican community. The jeans are a form of protest against the treatment of textile workers. Caminero-Santangelo observes that "La Loca's gesture of political resistance, limited though it is, can have effects because it is distinctly different from her general mode of detachment" (88). Although the critic limits the gesture because Loca does not interact with the community, she fails to note that Loca wears the boycott jeans to the procession. This suggests an explicit choice to publically protest the mistreatment of factory workers.

Neither Castillo's narrator nor scholars give the Pendleton shirt significance, but it seemingly suggests Loca's relationship to husbandry and the traditional agriculture of her community. Loca's work around the house connects to a tradition of "Chicanas [working] on family garden plots, planting, harvesting, and processing fruits and vegetables for home use" (Kirk 187). Her involvement with her mother's business extends to caring for the animals. The wool plaid shirt reflects her own life's work caring for the animals that she and her mother process for the *carniceria*. Yet, Loca's relationship with animals is more than slaughter. She represents a compassionate relationship with her animals, which in turn implies an attempt at ecological legitimation. To her, the animals are more than meat and commodity. This ties Loca to Ganados del Valle, a New Mexican cooperative run by Hispanos. Pulido discusses the co-op at length and how it uses culturalism to argue for grazing rights in New Mexico. She notes the organization uses "general exoticization of Hispanos by the dominant society, the regional reification of cultural differences, and the larger swirl of Hispano oppositional discourses [of dispossession and victimization]" as means to promote ecological stewardship (Pulido 133–4). Doing so allows this cooperative to delegitimize cultural stereotypes concerning Hispano agricultural practices and, at the same time, legitimize their ecological stand. Similar to Ganados, Loca's compassion for the animals suggests an ecological rather than economic position. She communicates and relates to them more than human animals.

Lastly, the robe has spiritual significance placed upon it. Her mother Sofi objects to her outfit, but Loca responds by affirming the robe's blueness, which the narrator says, "[is] no naïve remark coming from a young woman who knew that in her land, blue [is] a sacred color and, therefore, appropriate for the occasion" (Castillo 241). The narrator's clarifying comments function on three levels. One, Loca places sacred significance onto the robe because, in her community and its construction of sacredness, blue is a holy color. The narrator tells readers that in a drawing of La Loca, riding her horse Gato Negro "[the robe] flowed and looked more like el San Martin Caballero's Roman robe than a chenille bathrobe" (232). To those citizens who observe La Loca that day, the robe signifies a mission similar to Saint Martin Caballero, who is the patron saint for those in need. Two, the robe becomes a symbol for spiritual *mestizaje* because it represents multiple spiritual traditions. Pérez observes a conflation of religious and spiritual images, writing that "Most beautifully, Loca parades through Tomé wrapped in Esperanza's blue bathrobe, the color of the mantle of Our Lady of Guadalupe, but also of the Aztec creator Ometeotl, 'the mother-father of the Gods and the origin of all the natural forces end of everything that was'" (90). Three and perhaps most importantly, the narrator notes that Loca understands this significance, and this understanding contradicts Caminero-Santangelo's previous observation. La Loca makes conscious decisions that couples clothes with political and spiritual statements. This coupling returns to mind when readers consider for whom the community canonizes her: patron of all of God's creatures, animal and human alike (Castillo 232). The patronage suggests La Loca's guardianship over ecological concerns that extend to nonhuman and human animals alike.

Canonization Practices in M.O.M.A.S.

Nevertheless, La Loca's canonization represents a divergent split within scholarship; focusing on the particulars within the novel's environmental justice movement clarifies why the saints and martyrs matter. Shortly after La Loca's death, Sofi forms M.O.M.A.S, or Mothers of Saints and Martyrs, an organization of mothers who could canonize their daughters—and eventually sons—as saints or martyrs. For critics like Caminero-Santangelo, the canonization and subsequent organization M.O.M.A.S. represent an ideological division. She writes, "In the area of religion ... helpless 'faith' in miracles and magic is ultimately deflated as a route to agency in favor of a liberation theology that combines religious rites with political protest" (Caminero-Santangelo 92). In other words, faith placed in canonized figures like La Loca and their acts does not constitute real political action; this form of Catholic thought cannot promote change. This line of logic also includes Caminero-Santangelo's critique of Caridad's romanticized departure from this earth. Instead, she, along with Alvarez, places emphasis on liberation theory as moments of real political protest. She specifically points to the Stations of the Cross chapter because the juxtaposition joins political and religious thought "as a form of collective protest and agency propelled by the novel's starkest moment of 'realism' rather than its 'magic' or 'miracles'" (Caminero-Santangelo 89). While her emphasis on action over wishful thinking is valid, her logic creates a dichotomy that downplays the uniqueness of saints and martyrs within the novel's environmental movement.

To return to the formation of environmental justice movements, an important distinction between these grassroots political movements and national organizations lies in the movement's particulars. While each justice movement stresses the intersections between ecological and social injustice through some universal channels, how the group addresses these issues depends upon a range of specifics localized to that place. To take away the particular aspects of a movement in favor of a national agenda could potentially derail the local movement. The opposite could occur in similar fashion: the local cannot push its particular agenda onto other movements. Applying this idea to the novel, it seems that liberation theology, with its emphasis on bettering the community, represents an ideological concept that all environment justice movements share, although perhaps without the religious overtones. However, the designation of saints and martyrs represents a particular spiritual aspect of Tomé's movement that cannot be removed, because of what the organization represents. Gillman and Floyd-Thomas observe that "what *la Loca* has always represented [is] a spirit of reflexivity, reliance on internal strength as well as familial solidarity—a solidarity that is rooted in local customs, beliefs, and values" (167–8). Saints and martyrs may not extend to other communities, but this portion of Catholic thought remains important to how Sofi and her community form their co-ops, because it conceptually informs how they enact environmental and social change.

Yet, M.O.M.A.S. is not a strictly Catholic organization. The requirement for membership in the organization is to be the mother of a daughter or son who could be called a saint or martyr. While it appropriates the church's designations, the selection and veneration of saints and martyrs is chosen by mothers. The designation system, however, is loosely described. This leads the narrator to call the organization "a little elitist" (Castillo 247). The difference between a saint or a martyr is given as "Saints had the unquestionable potential of performing miracles while martyrs were simple revered and considered emissaries to the santos" (248). Although the language is overtly religious, the implications are more spiritual. La Loca qualifies as a saint, because she performs miracles, including her resurrection and prayers for families. Caridad qualifies for sainthood, too, even though her spirituality is heresy. She heals herself and others and ultimately achieves a spiritual "death." Although Caridad has returned to an indigenous goddess, M.O.M.A.S venerates her. Additionally, the organization M.O.M.A.S. functions as a celebration of these canonized children, as well as a forum for social and environmental activism on local and federal levels (Castillo 251). This returns readers again to the connection between multimodal spirituality and political, social, and environmental activism. M.O.M.A.S. becomes an organization that sometimes oversteps local particulars, but also links spiritual *mestizaje* with environmental justice movements.

In conclusion, spiritual mestizaje—an awareness of the multiple spiritualties that self-reflexively leads to active participation against oppressive structures—influences the formation of environmental activism through particular environmental justice movements within Ana Castillo's novel. In Caridad, Castillo presents readers with a spiritual journey that promotes an awareness of syncretic spiritual traditions like *curanderismo* along the US/Mexico border. Although she does not participate in environmental protest, Caridad highlights the necessity of self-awareness of one's ethnicity and cultural background, or what Gloria Anzaldúa terms *conocimiento*. In particular for Chicanas, this includes an introduction to indigenous myths that could provide knowledge to stand against oppressive powers. In La Loca, Castillo writes a character whose actions and decisions lead to political and ecological considerations. In particular, La Loca's participation in the Stations of the Cross addresses the symbiosis between spiritual imagery (and clothing) and environmental activism. Within M.O.M.A.S., the canonization of La Loca and Caridad provides an instance of activist organizations being informed by particular local religious structures—"nuevo mejicano-style Spanish Catholics" venerating ecological saints and martyrs (Castillo 87). These religious designations for the sisters are key to the development of the community's conscious environmental action.

Notes

1. Magical realism is a genre in which authors portray supernatural events as if they occur in the day-to-day world.

2. *Curanderismo* (ku-ran-da-reez-mo) is a form of folk healing that emphasizes spirituality and herbal remedies. A male practitioner is called a *curandero*, while a female is a *curandera*.

Works Cited

Alvarez, Alma Rosa. *Liberation Theology in Chicana/o Literature*. New York: Routledge, 2007.

Caminero-Santangelo, Marta. "'The Pleas of the Desperate:' Collective Agency Versus Magical Realism in Ana Castillo's *So Far from God.*" *Tulsa Studies in Women's Literature* 24.1 (Spring 2005): 81–103.

Castillo, Ana. *So Far From God.* New York: W. W. Norton, 1993.

Cobos, Ruben. *A Dictionary of New Mexican and Southern Colorado Spanish.* Santa Fe: Museum of New Mexico Press, 1983.

Delgadillo, Theresa. *Spiritual Mestizaje: Religion, Gender, Race, and Nation in Contemporary Chicana Narrative.* Durham, NC: Duke UP, 2011.

Gillman, Laura & Stacey M. Floyd-Thomas. "Con un pie a cada lado/With a Foot in Each Place: Mestisaje as Transnational Feminisms in Ana Castillo's *So Far from God.*" *Meridians* 2.1 (2001): 158–75.

Harvey, David. "The Environment of Justice." *Justice, Nature, and the Geography of Difference.* Malden, MA: Blackwell, 1996. 366–402.

Kirk, Gwyn. "Ecofeminism and Chicano Environmental Struggles: Bridges Across Gender and Race." *Chicano Culture, Ecology, Politics: Subversive Kin.* Ed. Devon G. Peña. Tuscon: U of Arizona P, 1998. 177–200.

Pérez, Gail. "Ana Castillo as Santera: Reconstructing Popular Religious Praxis." *Voces: A Journal of Chicana/Latina Studies* 2.1 (Spring 1998): 64–101.

Platt, Kamala. "Ecocritical Chicana Literature: Ana Castillo's 'Virtual Realism.'" *ISLE: Interdisciplinary Studies in Literature and Environment* 3.1 (Summer 1996): 67–96.

Pulido, Laura. "Ecological Legitimacy and Cultural Essentialism: Hispano Grazing in New Mexico." *Chicano Culture, Ecology, Politics: Subversive Kin.* Ed. Devon G. Peña. Tuscon: U of Arizona P, 1998. 121–40.

Willa Cather and Southwestern Aesthetics_____

John Samson

In her biography, *Willa Cather: The Emerging Voice*, Sharon O'Brien notes that:

> In later statements, Willa Cather liked to portray her transformation from the author of *Alexander's Bridge* (1912) to the author of *O Pioneers!* (1913) as miraculous... In between her watershed experience, the liberating weeks she spent in the Southwest early in 1912. (381)

Although O'Brien says that this explanation is a bit simplistic, nevertheless "The Southwest trip and its immediate aftermath... constitute the turning point in Willa Cather's life as a writer" (400). Cather will return again and again to the Southwest, to Arizona and New Mexico, especially Santa Fe. O'Brien and Judith Fryer, also in a 1987 essay, provide thorough and convincing discussions of how Cather's experiences in the desert Southwest made for this turning point and this fascination. O'Brien's psychoanalytic reading argues that the Southwest represented to Cather first a balance—of earth and sky, nature and culture, the masculine and the feminine, hidden spaces not isolated and enclosed spaces not closed—and second an "Outland," a place of refuge, of magic, of the energies of forbidden desires. These qualities lead to "a relaxation of ego boundaries," which frees Cather as a woman and writer. Fryer's study discusses Cather's Southwest as enabling the movement from desire to art: the spatial freedom of the landscape leads to acute sensuous perception, and the focus on detail gives form to space. The landscape—for Cather, associated with remembered childhood freedom—is thus recreated as a touchstone for artistic creation.

These are powerful and interesting accounts, but by examining Cather's views of the Southwest evident particularly in *The Song of the Lark*, but also in *The Professor's House* and *Death Comes for the Archbishop*, in light of statements contemporaneous to them, we can understand more fully and precisely how the Southwest is, for Cather, a place of aesthetic development. Novelistic discourse is always vitally connected to the cultural discourses surrounding it, and looking at how America in the second and third decades of the twentieth century conceived of the Southwest aesthetically will also show how Cather's views partake of a wider-ranging perception that might best be labeled an aesthetic discourse of the Southwest as well a discourse closely involved with the advent of modernism in America.

The period of Cather's writings on the Southwest—from *The Song of the Lark* in 1915 to *The Professor's House* in 1925 and *Death Comes for the Archbishop* in 1927—coincides with a virtual explosion of interest in the area. These dates, for example, mirror those of the Taos Society of Artists, chartered in 1915 and dissolved in 1927, and during this time, artists' colonies were developing in Phoenix and Santa Fe as well (Sandzen 350). The numbers of artists and writers, not to mention consumers and promoters of the arts, coming to the Southwest at this time is extensive: D. H. Lawrence, Georgia O'Keeffe, and Mabel Dodge Luhan are merely the most famous of the migration. The year 1915 also saw the Panama-California Exposition in San Diego, devoted to a celebration of American arts— North and South American, ancient and contemporary. Among the exhibits, "It was quite fitting…," writes Paul A. F. Walter, "that New Mexico art and artists be assigned a commanding part in the work of creating" this expo ("New Mexico's Contribution" 3). Art from Taos and Santa Fe, along with Native American art was exhibited in the New Mexico Building, the "Cathedral of the Desert," which was being copied as the Museum of New Mexico in downtown Santa Fe.

The building of the Museum of New Mexico, along with the restoration of the Palace of the Governors, were celebrated at the opening in 1917, billed as the "Congress of Science, Art, and Education." Edgar Hewett, who directed these projects as well as the Panama-California Expo, hoped that the Palace and the Museum of New Mexico "may perhaps set a standard of architectural fitness for the entire State and be a means of establishing eventually a regional type" (325). In his address at the opening ceremonies, Frank Springer, former territorial senator, added, "This building that we have erected expresses something of gratitude for, and appreciation of, their [the Southwestern painters'] works, to bring them to the attention of the world" (Robertson & Nestor 59). The Museum of New Mexico provided not only exhibition space, but also studios that furthered the burgeoning Santa Fe art colony in the early 1920s (Robertson & Nestor 81). In addition, writes Walter, "The establishment of the School for American Archaeology at Santa Fe..., as planned and directed by Dr. Edgar L. Hewett, lifted the Santa Fe-Taos art movement from a mere passing phenomenon into the significance of a creative force of lasting value in American art" ("The Santa Fe-Taos Art Movement" 330). Meanwhile, Mabel Dodge, who had lived in Paris and maintained a salon in Greenwich Village (near where Cather lived) and thus knew all the artistic avant-garde, visited Taos in 1916 and settled there shortly afterward, encouraging interest in Taos by such artists as Andrew Dasburg and Marsden Hartley.

These aesthetic developments were of course influenced by a number of larger social factors. Arizona and New Mexico had just achieved statehood in 1912 and were strongly bent on establishing cultural legitimacy as something beyond the Wild West of forbidding deserts, gunslingers, cowboys, and Indians. The Atchison, Topeka and Santa Fe Railroad in particular did much to "civilize" the area and its image. In an interesting study, *Paintbrushes and Pistols: How the Taos Artists Sold the West,* Sherry Clayton Taggett and Ted Schwarz chronicle how the Santa Fe (as the railroad was called) used the Taos (and Santa Fe) artists' work to illustrate a less wild and a more promotable side to the region. The Santa Fe's Harvey House dining and hotel operation provided excellent accommodations and further collected and exhibited the art of the Southwest. Tourism blossomed, and as Merle Armitage notes,

> It was inevitable that travelers on the Santa Fe would discover the beauty and integrity of the various Indian arts, but the discovery was made possible largely through the discrimination and energy of the

Harvey system which owns one of the finest collections of authentic Southwest Indian crafts in existence. (154)

Harvey's "Indian Detours" motor-coach tours for the well-to-do, not only promoted such art, but also included stops at the studios of Anglo artists in Santa Fe and Taos, whose paintings and sculptures could be purchased (Chauvenet 187–90). As Taggett and Schwarz say (with slight exaggeration), "Together they [the Taos Society of Artists, Fred Harvey, and the Santa Fe] would create the westward migration that has resulted in the vast metropolitan developments that exist today…[and] radically changed styles of both American fine art and commercial illustration" (3). Within this burgeoning interest in the Southwest is a notable consistency of perspective: artists and other observers, and certainly Cather, tended to see the area in similar aesthetic terms. Four aspects of this perception stand out: the landscape itself, the occasion for rehistoricizing, the conjoining of three cultures, and the opportunity for freedom, individualism and feminism.

In *The Song of the Lark*, Cather foreshadows the landscapes of Panther Canyon by describing, early in the novel, one of Thea's trips to the Sand Hills, her favorite place, outside Moonstone (41–50). Ray Kennedy, a railroad man who had led an "adventurous life … in Mexico and the Southwest" (Cather, *Song* 42), takes her to see "the line of many-coloured hills… all the open, pastel colors of the desert"; they stop at Pedro's Cup, "a great ampitheatre, cut out in the hills, its floor smooth and packed hard" (43). Cather stresses here the simplicity and the linearity, as well as the color, of the landscape. These qualities recur when Thea visits Panther Canyon, as Cather notes "perpendicular cliffs, stripped with even-running strata of rocks… and the v-shaped inner gorge" (267). Again and again Cather repeats the imagery of the color yellow or gold (267, 268, 269, 272, 275, 277, 280) saying, for example, that "when Thea dreamed about the canyon… her conception of it was of yellow rocks baking in the sunlight… a voice out of the past, not very loud, that went on saying a few simple things to the solitude eternally" (271). This imagery both stresses the value (gold) or enlightenment that Thea sees in the landscape and indicates that the value is related to is simple aesthetic qualities: the desert, its mesas, canyons, and mountains represent an aesthetics stripped down to the basics of line, form, and color.

In her later novels of the Southwest, Cather will continue to stress the significance of landscape as form and color. In *The Professor's House*, Tom Outland describes his Blue Mesa as "like the profile of a big beast lying down . . . [or] the solid cube . . . [or] a big cheese" (Cather, *The Professor's* 191–92). The colors, too are strikingly simple: "at daybreak . . . the mesa top would be red with sunrise, and all the slim cedars along the rocks would be gold—metallic, like tarnished gold-foil... [At] sunset... the mesa was like one great ink-black rock against a sky on fire" (192-93). In *Death Comes for the Archbishop*, Father Latour first arrives in Santa Fe at sunset and sees "a sweep of red carnelian-colored hills lying at the foot of the mountains...; they curved like two arms about a depression in the plain; and in that depression was Santa Fe at last!" (Cather, *Death* 22). Here, as elsewhere, the simplicity of line and color allow Cather to inject a symbolic value into the landscape, the imagery of jewelry always associated in these novels with the southwestern landscape, whose embrace welcomes Latour.

Others, too, saw the landscape in these terms. Cather's friend Mabel Dodge Luhan in her memoir *Edge of Taos Desert* describes a trip to Santo Domingo Pueblo:

> Out of the level desert over to the left rose a group of little hills like those in the Da Vinci backgrounds, and farther beyond them stretched the distant desert with a high range of purple mountains against the sky... There was no disturbance in the scene, nothing to complicate the forms. (Luhan 59)

Luhan also emphasizes the colors, describing "the shining ether that brought out every height and depth of tone and color in the natural world and enhanced them beyond the ordinary" (32). To the artists, the landscape represented something aesthetically basic or fundamental; as Birger Sandzen says in a 1915 article, "For learning the fundamental principles of design and color treatment, the open and bare scenery offers far greater advantages than the closed-in ground" ("Sketching" 347). For Taos painter Oscar Berninghaus, the striking colors and lines of the area were highly amenable to his work, for "the painter must first see the picture as point, as color, and as form" (Tagett & Schwarz 127).

Also aesthetically significant is the region's light. To Thea, "the desert sunrise [is] a light-hearted affair, where the sun springs out of bed and the world is golden in an instant" (Cather, *Song* 281), while for Latour "There was so much sky, more than at sea, more than anywhere else in the world" (Cather, *Death* 232). For Luhan, like Cather's characters, the quality of light imparts a sense of vibrancy, of intensity: "From the very first day I found that the sunshine in New Mexico could do almost anything with one," she says… "It entered into one's deepest places and melted the thick, slow densities. It made one feel *good*. That is, alive" (Luhan 17). According to Walter, "landscapes that rivaled in… brightness those of Normandy and Brittany" attracted the painters, too. Edna Robertson and Sarah Nestor, in their study of early Santa Fe artists, simply conclude that "It is in the air itself, so clear and sharp in the high altitude, that shapes and colors come through with startling intensity" (3).

The light infuses the landscape not only with intensity, but with mystery as well. Latour explains, "The desert, the mountains and mesas, were continually re-formed and re-colored by the cloud shadows. The whole country seemed fluid to the eye under this ever-varying distribution of light" (Cather, *Death* 96). To Luhan, this is "the strangest landscape I had ever faced" (29): she says, "I have seen the mountains and the hills move from time to time. The rocks vibrate and sway, dancing together" (31). Arthur J. Burdick titles his 1904 book on the deserts of the Southwest *The Mystic Mid-Region* and says, "There is a mystery about the desert which is both fascinating and repellant . . . Strange tales come out of the desert" (5). For Cather's characters, the mystery always has a spiritual dimension. After his first night on the mesa, Outland concludes that "For me the mesa was no longer an adventure, but a religious emotion. I had read of filial piety in the Latin poets, and I know that was what I felt for this place" (Cather, *The Professor's* 251). "In 'The

Ancient People' section of *The Song of the Lark*," Fryer concludes, "the Southwest is literally a sacred space," as it also obviously is for Latour in *Death Comes for the Archbishop* (Fryer 29).

Finally, the one aspect of the landscape most significant to Cather and the others is how humans, the ancient cliff dwellers and the contemporary Pueblo Indians, find a natural home there. Obviously, for Cather, the "Ancient People" (i.e., the Anasazi) and their descendants, the Pueblo Indians, were of great significance aesthetically. In her 1916 essay on Mesa Verde, Cather describes the cliff dwellers' architecture—and lives—as "absolutely harmonious with its site and setting" (Rosowski & Slote 84), for with regard to their natural environment, "They accommodated themselves to it, interpreted it and made it personal; lived in a dignified relation with it" (85). As a result, "their lives were so full of ritual and symbolism that all their common actions were ceremonial" (85). Cather uses the same terms to describe Latour's perception of the Hopis, who "seemed to have none of the European's desire to 'master' nature, to arrange and re-create. They spent their ingenuity in the other direction; in accommodating themselves to the scene in which they found themselves" (Cather, *Death* 234). In *The Song of the Lark*, Cather makes even more explicit the aesthetic significance of the Ancient People's accommodation with the landscape. Early in the novel, Kennedy shows Thea a turquoise he had gotten from the Pueblo Indians and tells Thea of the cliff dwellers, whose "women were their artist . . . . What I like about those old aborigines is, that they got all their ideas from nature" (Cather, *Song* 106). He then concludes, "You feel like it's up to you to do your best... You feel like you owed them something" (107). This is exactly what Thea herself will directly experience in Panther Canyon. She opens herself to the natural landscape, identifies with the cliff dwellers, especially the women, and deepens her sense of their and her artistry. She contemplates the pottery, made by the Anasazi women, and reflects:

> What was any art but an effort to make a sheath, a mould in which to imprison for a moment the shining elusive element which is life itself...The Indian women had held it in their jars... In singing one

made a vessel of one's throat and nostrils and held it on one's breath, caught the stream in a scale of natural intervals. (Cather, *Song* 273)

As a result, "Not only did the world seem older and richer to Thea now, but she herself seemed older" (Cather, *Song* 275). She has matured as an artist, and "Everything seemed suddenly to take the form of a desire for action... [and] she was going to Germany to study without further loss of time" (276).

Again here Cather is representing in Thea—as in Outland and Latour—an attitude typical of the time, which saw a considerable interest in the ancient and contemporary Pueblo culture. In fact, of any aspect of the desert Southwest, this seems to be of the most and most crucial aesthetic interest. Discussing "The Santa Fe-Taos Art Movement," Walter moves from the landscape to its inhabitants:

> It is the historic background, the atmosphere, the environment, the sunshine, the sky, the climate, the people, the mingling of nations and races, and above all, the American Indian, who in this region embodies in himself a long lineage of artistic aspiration, of poetic culture... all combining to make Santa Fe and Taos... an inspiration to the artistic temperament. (333–35)

Walter continues by noting that in the cliff dwellings is "an indigenous American architecture" and "the dawn of graphic art within the present limits of the United States" ("The Santa Fe-Taos" 335) and art spawned by "the prompting of nature" (335). "The artist of today," he concludes, cannot but be similarly inspired by "this surpassing land of contrast, weirdness, beauty, and glory" (335).

The cliff dwellers were more than artistic precursors, though, for since Adolph Bandelier's writings in the 1890s, Pueblo culture, both ancient and contemporary, was the object of considerably study. In the School of American Archaeology, founded in Santa Fe in 1907 (Robertson & Nestor 25), Pueblo pottery artifacts and other art objects were exhibited and studied. Walter notes that "Appreciation is growing with public and critics, as they gain an insight into the thought underlying them and as they grasp the spiritual quality in their execution...the delicacy of the tints, coupled with a broad, free sweep of the brush, make them masterpieces" ("New Mexico's Contribution" 7–9). Others noticed these qualities, too. The nearness to nature of the Pueblo Indians to some observers accounted for their artistry. Taos artist Victor Higgins says, "The Taos Indians are a people living in an absolutely natural state," while Bert Geer Phillips explains that "the rhythm of nature" that is central to the Taos Indians "is coming out in a new expression through the watercolor paintings" of the Taos Society artists (Tagett & Schwarz 77). The perception and adoption of the Pueblos' natural aesthetic also included their architecture, especially the adobe construction and what would come to be called the Santa Fe style of design. Hewett traces the Palace of the Governors and the Museum of Santa Fe back to "the children of its [the Rio Grande's] soil, who for ages have been building their habitations and sanctuaries out of the earth from which they were born" (327). Luhan, observing the construction of an adobe house, concludes that "working with the earth was a noble occupation… a sacred matter, for the wonder of creation is in it, the wonder of transformation which always seems of greatest significance to Indians" (292).

The sense of the Indians' spirituality, recognized here by Luhan, as by Cather, was also of great importance to the artists. Phillips, who of the Taos and Santa Fe artists most deeply knew the Indians and their culture, sees the aesthetic value of spirituality. He says, "The Indians worship all things beautiful…. It is not the passive appreciation that is the reaction to beauty of many white people. It is an integral part of their being. Their religion revolves around the rhythm and life of nature" (Tagett & Schwarz 76–77). Soon after her arrival in Taos, Luhan, who later married a member of Taos Pueblo, was taken by Phillips to observe a ceremony there. She records that her then-husband Maurice Sterne observes, "These Indians have a real Art of their own." Mable replies to him in terms similar to Cather's description of Thea's experience in Panther Canyon: "But it was their life that seemed so real to me every time I got near enough to it to feel it. Real, real, and deep as fate, and full of wonder and experience" (Luhan 101).

Much of this fascination with Pueblo-Anasazi culture involves a movement to rehistoricize the American past, to situate the American present in a new historical context. O'Brien describes Cather's experience in the Southwest as her "being introduced to a native American cultural inheritance preserved in the cliff-dwellers' ruins and living in the dances, rituals, and folk art of the Hopis... a healthy counterpoint to the aggressive individualism, spiritual emptiness, and corrupt materialism of modern American life" (414). In *The Song of the Lark*, Thea identifies with the Ancient People as cultural ancestors distinct from the Eurocentric heritage that is for her overly aggressive, vapid, and patriarchal, as Cather in the previous section of the novel, "Stupid Faces," focuses on Thea's discontent with her Chicago society. In Thea's kinship with the Ancient People, particularly with the women artists, Cather poses an alternative, matrilineal cultural heritage, the sort of true history Kennedy had earlier found there and opposed to the history found in books (Cather, *Song* 107). "Those people had felt the beginnings of what was to come," Thea reflects, thus identifying them with a cultural origin. Again, in *The Professor's House*, Cather presents "Tom Outland's Story" of the Anasazi as a counterpoint to St. Peter's books on the Spanish explorers, as an alternative and true American past.

Many others at this time were engaged in a similar rehistoricizing. The Panama-California Expo was perhaps the most obvious expression of the desire to ground the American present in an exclusively American past, particularly its artistic past. In a 1917 article discussing Taos and Santa Fe in Art, Evelyn Marie Stuart says,

> Here, if anywhere, should the new American school be founded, for it is the oldest seat of art in the country, its ancient basket and pottery patterns, its crude carved stone images and prehistoric pictures executed on the walls of caves representing the earliest beginnings of American art. Here the artist is farthest away from the influence of Europe and under the thrall of native American [sic] primitive vitality and color. (345–47)

Stuart's last line says much. There is, she perceives, a concerted effort to turn away from Europe as cultural progenitor, as Europe at the time is engaged in war and dissolution of monarchies and is thus seen by many Americans as in a state of decay and collapse. Like William Carlos Williams, who was concurrently attempting a poetry in the American grain, Southwestern artists were also seeking a genuinely American foundation for their work. Taos artist Walter Ufer explains:

> I believe that if America gets a National Art it will come more from the Southwest than from the Atlantic Board. Because we are really different from Europeans, and further away from European influence, the better for us. We already have too much of Indian blood within our veins to be classified as Europeans. (Tagett & Schwarz 187)

Higgins agrees, saying that "There is in the mind of every member of the Taos art colony the knowledge that here is the oldest of American civilizations. . . . Their architecture is the only naturally American architecture in the nation today. All other styles were borrowed from Europe" (Tagett & Schwarz 194–95). The artists building on this foundation are, Springer stated at the opening of the Museum, "the most democratic group of painters in America... There is a glorious future for art in the Southwest—for art in America" (Robertson & Nestor 59). Ufer goes further: "Here, some day, will be written the great American epic, the great American opera" (Walter, "Art Movement" 337).

Part of this epitomizing of the Southwest as genuinely American is the perception of it as a multicultural space, whose Anglo, Hispanic, and Native American cultures meet and interact—not a melting-pot, assimilationist America, but an America of cultural dialogue. In *The Song of the Lark*, Kennedy's love of the Southwest is based not only on his imaginative evocation of the cliff dwellers, but on "his love of Mexico and Mexicans" (46). Thea, too, rejects the mainstream of her Moonstone culture, which has assimilated Swedes, Bohemians, and Germans into dull conformity; she prefers instead the culture of Mexican Town, just outside Moonstone. There, she can sing and dance (and scandalize her family and the townspeople), opening herself to the Mexicans, as she later does to the Ancient People, and consequently developing as an artist. The whole of *Death Comes for the Archbishop* is a testament to this pluralistic cultural acceptance, as it is Latour's openness and accommodation—along with his condemnation of any sort of cultural supplantation—that is perhaps most evident in the stories of his interactions with Mexican, Hopi, Zuni, and Navajo cultures.

Hewett sees as a major virtue of Santa Fe that, from the mountains, "One looks down upon three cultures: Indian, Spanish, and American… One thinks of the Eternal City and of looking down from the Capitoline Hill upon the work of the aborigines, kings, emperors, popes—the greatest vista of human history" (324). As a result, state Robertson and Nestor, "the area's long tri-cultural background (Spanish, Indian, and Anglo) contributes to the tolerant atmosphere in which the arts flourish" (3). Perhaps the best symbol of the tri-cultural aesthetic is the Museum of New Mexico in Santa Fe: developed by Hewett and constructed by Jesse Nusbaum—both Anglos—the building, like its predecessor, the New Mexico Building at the San Diego Expo, is perhaps best described as a blending of the three cultures, as, of course, was and is the art inside.

Encounters with these cultures and with the area has, to Cather, a liberating effect. In Mexican Town, Thea feels free of the restrictions, of class and piety, so stifling in Moonstone, a liberation she completes in Panther Canyon. There, she tells Ottenburg, "It's waking up every morning with the feeling that your life is your own, and your strength is your own" (Cather, *Song* 284). The symbol of this is the eagle she sees and salutes after this conversation (287–88), an image Cather introduced in one of Kennedy's stories of the Southwest (49). Obviously, it represents the freedom she has begun to achieve, just as for Outland, the Eagle's Nest, where he keeps the diary that St. Peter will edit, represents more largely the freedom he will find on the mesa and the freedom he represents to St. Peter, who is suffocating among his family and in his room. Yet one must qualify this idea of freedom, which perhaps might better be termed individualism, for Cather presents in the liberation of Thea a strong sense of artistic responsibility, the "Endeavor, achievement, desire, glorious striving of human art!" (*Song* 288) that the eagle makes her think of. As Cather says in an essay-fragment titled "Light on Adobe Walls," "Every artist knows that there is no such thing as 'freedom' in art. The first thing an artist does when he begins a new work is to lay down the barriers and limitations" (*Not Under Forty* 123). Also, one should note that this individualism is, for Cather, highly gendered. As a number of critics have noticed, O'Brien most cogently, Cather presents in Panther Canyon a highly feminine landscape, appropriate for the development of the woman artist.

Appropriately so, too, for the Southwest was historically a place where women, such as Luhan, Mary Austin, and Georgia O'Keeffe played at this time a large role in the development of the arts. Hewett recognizes the influence of women's groups in the construction of the Museum of New Mexico and the Palace of the Governors (319), and he, like Cather, sees an ancient and natural foundation for this role. He says, "For, as they [the cliff dwellers] understood it, it was from the earth-mother that the first people of New Mexico came. She cradled them in cave and cliff while waiting on the ages" (Hewett 327). Upon seeing a ceremony at Taos Pueblo, Luhan notices that "the power of the tribe was invested in the two women who gently danced," and she concludes, "And old—perhaps the oldest—allegory was confronting us there. The feminine principle is the strongest one in nature" (100). Cather would agree, as she presents the matriarchal, natural culture of the Ancient People.

The southwestern aesthetic that I have been describing— its emphasis on the basics of line and color, its insistence on the new and the original American, its individualism—this aesthetic is an instance, if not the epitome, of the modernism developing in American art at this time. There are many connections among the southwestern artists and the modernists centered around New York's Greenwich Village. The year 1913 saw the famous Armory Show in New York, considered by most to mark the advent of the modern in America (it introduced Picasso, Matisse, Duchamp, et al. to the country). Several of the artists who had been spending time in New Mexico attended, as did several who would soon go to the Southwest. Taos artist Ernest Blumenschein wrote an essay on the show for *Century* magazine in 1914. Though there is no evidence that Cather saw the show, she could hardly avoid hearing about it or discussing it, for she was living in Greenwich Village at the time—where the salons of Mabel Dodge (which Cather did attend) and O'Keeffe's husband, Alfred Stieglitz, were the places where the discourse of the modern was disseminated.

This modernist discourse had as its main tenets the same general qualities seen in the aesthetics of the Southwest. It sought a foundation in primitive art, Picasso in African art or Gauguin in Tahitian. It was highly individualistic and highly concerned—especially in cubism and abstraction—with basic forms and lines. To Cather, modernism was embodied in what she theorized as "the novel démeublé," the unfurnished novel. Using a reference to painting, she says,

> There are hopeful signs that some of the younger writers are trying to break away from mere verisimilitude, and, following the development of modern painting, to interpret imaginatively the material and social investiture of their characters; to present their sense by suggestion rather than by enumeration. The higher process of art are all processes of simplification. (Cather, *Not Under Forty* 48–49)

These "higher processes of art" Cather, like many of her contemporaries, experienced and represented in the Southwest. They are at the heart of southwestern aesthetics.

Works Cited

Armitage, Merle. *Operations Santa Fe: Atchison, Topeka & Santa Fe Railway System*. New York: Duell, Sloan & Pearce, 1948.

Burdick, Arthur J. *The Mystic Mid-Region: The Deserts of the Southwest*. New York: G. P. Putnam's Sons, 1904.

Cather, Willa. *Death Comes for the Archbishop*. 1927. New York: Vintage Books, 1971.

_____. *Not Under Forty*. 1936. New York: Alfred A. Knopf, 1967.

_____. *The Professor's House*. 1925. New York: Vintage Books, 1973.

_____. *The Song of the Lark*. 1915. Boston: Houghton Mifflin Co., 1987.

Chauvenet, Beatrice. *Hewett and Friends: A Biography of Santa Fe's Vibrant Era*. Santa Fe: Museum of New Mexico Press, 1983.

Dewitt, Miriam Hapgood. *Taos: A Memory*. Albuquerque: U of New Mexico P, 1992.

Fryer, Judith. "Desert, Rock, Shelter, Legend." *The Desert Is No Lady: Southwestern Landscapes in Women's Writing and Art*. Ed. Vera Norwood & Janice Monk. New Haven: Yale UP, 1987.

Hewett, Edgar L. "The School of American Archaeology." *Art and Archaeology* 4 (December 1916): 317–29.

Luhan, Mabel Dodge. *Edge of Taos Desert: An Escape to Reality*. New York: Harcourt, Brace & Company, 1937.

O'Brien, Sharon. *Willa Cather: The Emerging Voice*. New York: Oxford UP, 1987.

Peixotto, Ernest. "The Taos Society of Artists." *Scribners* 60 (August 1916): 257–60.

Robertson, Edna & Sarah Nestor. *Artists of the Canyons and Caminos*. New York: Peregrine Smith, 1976.

Rosowski, Susan J. & Bernice Slote. "Willa Cather's Mesa Verde Essay: The Genesis of *The Professor's House*." *Prairie Schooner* 58 (1984): 81–92.

Sandzen, Birger. "The Southwest as a Sketching Ground." *Fine Arts Journal* 35 (May 1917): 333–51.

Stuart, Evelyn Marie. "Taos and the Indian in Art." *Fine Arts Journal* 35 (May 1917): 341–48.

Tagett, Sherry Clayton & Ted Schwarz. *Paintbrushes and Pistols: How the Taos Artists Sold the West*. Santa Fe: John Muir Publications, 1990.

Walter, Paul A. F. "New Mexico's Contribution to the Panama-California Exposition." *El Palacio* 3 (October 1915): 3–16.

_____. "The Santa Fe-Taos Art Movement." *Art and Archaeology* 4 (December 1916): 330–38.

Creative Genius: Willa Cather's Characters and the Influence of the American Desert Southwest_____

Max Despain

Cather Visits the Southwest

In 1912, Willa Cather spent several weeks visiting her brother, Douglass, in Winslow, Arizona, marking her first visit to the desert in the Southwest. Soon, the American Southwest would be an important site of creative and artistic growth for characters in three of her novels. The expansive, complex landscape, rich with ancient heritage and massive land formations, was a perfect proving ground for her ideas about how creative genius grows. Cather describes her writing as trying to achieve something that cannot be put into words: "It is the inexplicable presence of the thing not named [. . .] that gives high quality to the novel" ("Novel Démeublé" n.p.). Cather's literary response to the American desert in the Southwest reflects her personal growth as an artist. Cather understands that creating imagined identities from Native American cultural ruins and remains, such as the Panther Canyon cliff dwellings for Thea Kronborg in *The Song of the Lark*, and the Cliff City for Tom Outland in *The Professor's House*, influences these characters' identities. In *Death Comes for the Archbishop*, although the striking formations at Acoma and the "Stone Lips" (127) are compelling to Bishop Jean-Marie Latour, rather than changing his own personality, he expresses his genius by using the landscape to help change his parishioners. Ultimately, Cather uses the southwestern landscape to inspire her characters to their versions of creative genius, be it as an artist, an engineer, or a priest.

The impact of the desert and its influence on Willa Cather's personal creative process cannot be underestimated. Biographer James Woodress centers his prologue on her 1912 visit to Arizona, including outings to the Grand Canyon, Flagstaff, and Walnut Canyon. He notes how she compliments the Grand Canyon but adds that it "had only a geologic history" (8). On the other hand, Cather is "deeply moved by her experience" in Walnut Canyon, where her imagination has an explosion of creativity in the presence of "some three hundred cliff dwellings about one thousand years old" (9). Woodress's pairing of these experiences shows how Cather's notion of artistic growth has a heritage in human experience. Creative inspiration happens chiefly when she can imagine the lives of the ancient inhabitants of the ruins. The ancient societies inspire Cather precisely because of their struggle against the austere environment.

Creative imposition gives people in the Southwest a near-spiritual feeling about the cliff dwellings and the majestic scenes, including the real-life Bishop Lamy's cathedral in Santa Fe, New Mexico, built out of local stone. In juxtaposition with the relics of past civilizations as well as the grandeur of the setting, both Cather and her characters are inspired to individual self-examination. Socially and historically, Cather constructs ways of understanding identity under the pressure of the unique southwestern landscape so that her characters find they have new perspectives on themselves as they undergo important changes in identity.

First Southwest Novel: *The Song of the Lark* (1915)
Cather prepares us to read Thea Kronborg's time in the canyon in *The Song of the Lark* as a process towards artistic genius when the author emphasizes Thea's need for a physical involvement to anchor experiences and remember them as if they had been a part of her "self". Literally, Cather requires Thea to pretend to be a Native American from the past as a new place from which she can look back with new perspective on herself and what she has learned, particularly in her training as a singer. However, this inventive act does not occur on a purely clean slate. Remembering her former mentor and would-be husband, Ray Kennedy, we understand how Thea has been primed for this encounter with Panther Canyon. Not only does Ray plant the idea of cliff dwellers' suffering, he also tells her that the cliff dwellings should inspire her to do her best "on account of those fellows having it so hard" (*The Song* 107). He tells her that the Indian women were their communities' artists, readying Thea for her epiphany in the waters of the canyon about art and her

future singing plans. The railroad man, whose life involved close association with the desert, influences Thea's ability to discover her own identity in a "cleft in the earth" (269) in Arizona.

The singing skill Thea develops during her time in Chicago lacked inspiration, but the quiet hours of repose in Panther Canyon cultivate Thea's artistic imagination. As if she has been waiting for "something to catch up with her" (Cather, *The Song* 269), she fills her leisure with "pleasant and incomplete conceptions in her mind"— not ideas, but fragrances, colors, and sound. Thea becomes "a mere receptacle for heat…a colour [sic]…or a repetition of sound" (270). Those hours prepare her to find artistic inspiration one of the times she bathes in the stream.

The water where Thea washes daily had been the source of nourishment to the ancient dwellers of the canyon; it has "personality" and was "a continuity of life" (Cather, *The Song* 273). She connects how important the water is to the Native American Sinagua Indians (Moseley 216), who had lived in the cliffs, when she realizes that those women had decorated the vessels to carry water as if to honor its essential nature in those people's lives. Considering the arid quality of the southwestern desert and the arduous climb from the cliff dwellings to the stream, water—widely accepted as the most important nutrient for human existence—is a rare and precious commodity for the Sinaguans. This realization gives Thea the inspirational understanding for what it means to be an artist. She asks herself "what was any art but an effort to make a sheath, a mould in which to imprison for a moment the shining, elusive element which is life itself… too sweet to lose?" (*The Song* 273). She thinks of the jars, equating her own body to a "vessel," which captures this quality of life, "[catches] the stream in a scale of natural intervals" (273) that are the notes of her songs. The canyon experience combined with Thea's inspiration in the bathing pool give her both the theory and the method that will make her interpretation of her operatic roles something recognized as artistic genius.

If we jump forward several years, after Thea's training in Germany and her initial success overseas, we can observe her environment and her method. We understand that the lasting influence of Panther Canyon has helped make Thea into an artistic genius as an opera singer. Her childhood friend, Dr. Archie, walks past her New York residence, and we find vestiges of the canyon in the setting he describes, including a river and a fourteen-story apartment hotel that "rose above him like a perpendicular cliff" (Cather, *The Song* 357). We learn that Thea performs Swedish movements, which remind us of the physical exertion that inspired her imagination in the canyon. She never hurries her bath and was "fairly playing in the water," using her brushes and sponges and soap "like toys" (370). Remembering how the running stream water metaphorically transformed into the "elusive element" (273) of life for Thea in Panther Canyon, she revisits this inspirational moment in her memory even if the bath water now runs from a tap in a New York hotel. These rudiments of her long, indolent days in the American Southwest remain a part of her method for remaining a flourishing opera star in a high-paced, urban setting.

The Southwestern landscape, abundant in empty ruins and expansive spaces, makes an ideal location for inspiration: a site where Thea gains a new perspective of herself and develops a new philosophy of artistry through her experiences in Panther Canyon. When she turns these ideas back on herself, Thea sees that she can choose her destiny by focusing on a professional singing career. In the process of working out her ideas in the creatively inspiring space of the canyon, Thea learns a method that enhances her career. By the time we last read about Thea performing on stage, we come to understand that her "body had become an instrument of her ideas" (Cather, *The Song* 410) in a way only possible because of her desert Southwest experience.

Second Southwest Novel: *The Professor's House* (1925)

Cather revisits the creative influence found in the desert Southwest in her already drafted "Tom Outland's Story," until the tale finds a place, ten years later in her new novel, *The Professor's House*. Between the 1915 publication of *The Song of the Lark* and the 1925 appearance of *The Professor's House,* Cather came into her own as an author. She won the Pulitzer Prize for *One of Ours* (1922), but was disillusioned by her award-winning, World War I novel's reception. These experiences solidify the unique presence of her character's autobiographical excerpt in the middle of *The Professor's House*, which shows us the effects of the unique Southwestern landscape on Tom's identity and thought process.

Penning S. S. McClure's autobiography about two years before she began her Southwest novels would have reminded Cather how people's environment and experiences always return to an examination of the self. Cather's ghostwriting of McClure's autobiography may have resulted in her increased interest in examining and inhabiting identities. In the proceedings of the 1925 Bowdoin conference recorded in *An Institute of Modern Literature,* Cather claims the importance of juxtaposition: "the point from which [the author] proposes to look at his subject [is the most important thing] for it looks different from different points of view" (Staples 164). When she claims that she wanted the "fresh air that blew off the Blue Mesa" to be a feeling that came almost through a window, as in a Dutch painting, she recognizes the role of juxtaposition in inspiring creative imagination leading to unique self-reflection (165). The way Cather uses juxtaposition in *The Professor's House* reveals how her imagination comes to life in the face of the austere desert Southwest. While Thea Kronborg takes this imaginative recreation and applies it to her own career, Tom Outland seems to wrestle with the spiritual concepts he discovered after the mesa city becomes emptied of its relics. Cather explores how the nearly mystical experience for young Tom can become scientific discoveries as her character pushes these concepts from his imagination into the real world.

Tom Outland's discovery of Cliff City is full of juxtaposition that we witness secondhand in "Tom Outland's Story." The story is a brief autobiographical account, which includes his time on Blue Mesa and which Tom wrote for his friend and mentor Professor Godfrey St. Peter. The result of Tom's experience with the southwestern landscape is the way that he incorporates his inventiveness into the identity he imagines for the ancient community. In their article on an essay Cather wrote about Mesa Verde, the real-life version of the Blue Mesa, Susan J. Rosowski and Bernice Slote agree when they note that "we glimpse the creative process as Cather described it, that of first withdrawing her ego and experiencing her subject by a sympathetic imagination" (91). In a useful method for his own self-examination, Tom recreates the daily life of the people after "the notion struck [him] like a rifle ball that this mesa had once been like a bee-hive; it was full of cliff-hung villages, it had been the home of a powerful tribe, a particular civilization" (Cather, *The Professor's* 221–22). The recreation of the mesa's past almost assails Tom, much the same as a battle wound. Cather foreshadows Tom's future in this moment when she connects his imaginative spark to the fatal conclusion of his involvement in World War I. The embitterment he will ultimately experience contrasting life in human society with the time he spent on the mesa leads him to fight and die in the war, leaving behind an invention influenced by his relationship to the Blue Mesa.

But well before his disillusioned end, his friend and partner sells the ancient artifacts they discovered on the site, and Tom's self-constructed narrative allows him to search for meaning in his experience with the mesa until he realizes "something had happened in me that made it possible for me to co-ordinate and simplify, and that process, going on in my mind, brought with it great happiness" (Cather, *The Professor's* 254). The disenchanted idealist goes on to describe how the mesa was "no longer an adventure, but a religious emotion" (254). Tom's time on the mesa achieves a spiritual quality in part because the relics he has so treasured are gone. With the artifacts now only in Tom's memory and imagination, the mesa takes on the quality of a reliquary or a shrine for those ancient items. Now Tom can appreciate the mesa and his relationship to the location through memory and imagination about the items because he can no longer see the real things. Cather notes the role of inventiveness in Tom's peace and in his new understanding of his own happiness and identity.

The quality of juxtaposition that brings about Tom's enriched understanding finds its best example when he writes that reading the *Aeneid* in his present time away from the mesa always involved a mental picture of the text alongside a second picture of his readings on the Blue Mesa. Tom writes to St. Peter that "Happiness is something one can't explain" (Cather, *The Professor's* 254), no words can describe this creative growth. Throughout the rest of his short life, Tom carries this summer as a part of his sense of self. Absence becomes the most important element in Tom's development, and now he can see himself differently. He learns that absence can be as important as presence when he remembers the invisible, but pure-seeming, air of the desert.

In school after his time on the mesa, Tom might have been responding to the disillusioning experience of being in a society focused on material gain, but the irony of his success as an engineer is that he perfects a "bulkheaded vacuum" that other people use to revolutionize military aviation after Tom's death. Much as he loved the air on the mesa, he invents a space void of anything, including air. The engine mimics his understanding of the society around him: a place absent of the spiritual quality in the Blue Mesa air. This engine has much commercial potential, but Tom Outland seems to be more interested in the concepts behind it than commercializing his invention.

Scholar Steven Trout acknowledges in his essay "Rebuilding the Outland Engine" that Cather struggled to understand the exact scientific principles behind Tom's engine, but the important point is that her use of the invention requires the absence of atmosphere (1). Cather deals in absence: the sold-off artifacts, the materialistic society, and now the engine's vacuum. When Cather describes the way Tom loved the pure, mesa air (Cather, *The Professor's* 220), she helps readers understand how he could invent an engine that represents the loss and disillusionment he felt about his experience with the ancient community in the mesa. That loss was a void, and the money-hungry society where he builds the "bulkheaded vacuum" takes over the invention after Tom Outland's death so that the disillusionment he poured into the making of the engine becomes the power behind so much military destruction.

Last Southwest Novel: *Death Comes for the Archbishop* (1927)

After finishing *The Professor's House*, Cather traveled two more times to the American Southwest in the summers of 1925 and 1926 (Stout 231–32). There, she envisioned and solidified her conception of her only novel whose primary setting is the desert Southwest, *Death Comes for the Archbishop*. The shifting and related use of the splendid southwestern landscape only makes sense in the perspective of her journeys. Christopher Schedler describes how Bishop Latour's Catholic church "fosters social unity while at the same time recognizing difference" (119). Cather reengages the environment's influence by choosing to have her bishop create his own piece of landscape: a rock formation in the shape of a cathedral made from local stones.

Cather's first brush strokes of Bishop Jean-Marie Latour in the desert of New Mexico show his profound response to the landscape and the way he retains his identity in the face of such influence. She illustrates how the identical, cone-shaped rock formations are "*fantastique*" to the bishop, and he has to close his eyes to the "intrusive omnipresence of the triangle" (Cather, *Death* 286). The exotic experience reinforces that he is a devout Catholic priest because when he opens his eyes, he converts the unusual juniper tree he sees into a cruciform and holds mass with "distinguished" manners, "even when he was alone in the desert" (286). The prayer seems to lead to his salvation when he discovers the homestead at Agua Secreta. Cather emphasizes Latour's relationship with the Southwest, which is opposite from his dear friend and fellow priest Joseph Valliant, who "must always have the miracle very direct and spectacular, not with Nature, but against it" (293). This characterization prepares us to read Latour seeking a relationship with and in contrast to the striking landscape around him.

Even though Latour expresses the shift in his identity required to perform his work in this region, claiming "all day I am an American in speech and thought—yes in heart too" (Cather, *Death* 297), he concedes that a properly French Christmas meal helps him maintain his original identity. This sense of himself resulting from juxtaposition with the land and community is inevitable, but for Latour, it's a less permanent influence than with Thea and Tom.

Participating in the outer regions of his social sphere, Latour understands that he must appreciate the social structure in his diocese before he can influence change. This awareness of social tolerance makes Latour an empathetic character and an obvious choice to improve the Catholic presence in New Mexico. He wrestles with the effort to bring communities together, a concept brought into focus when he travels with the Pecos Indian, Jacinto, on his way to perform mass at the pueblo on Acoma. As they discuss the multiple possibilities for the meaning in the stars, Latour realizes "there was no way in which he could transfer his own memories of European civilization into the Indian mind, and he was quite willing to believe that behind Jacinto there was a long tradition, a story of experience, which no language could translate to him" (Cather, *Death* 332). While previous Cather characters have imagined their Native American counterparts and produced those people's thoughts, such as Thea and Tom, Latour offers the nuanced realization that he cannot impose his own creative perspective on the present-day Jacinto's thoughts.

Cather turns Latour's focus away from imposing his imagination on the Indians who are present and instead sends him exploring the possibilities in the land. Her portrayal of the flat land shows her standpoint that the landscape seems unfinished and Latour has room for influence. She describes, through Latour's thoughts, how "the mesa plain has an appearance of great antiquity, and of incompleteness; as if, with all the materials for world-making assembled, the Creator had desisted, gone away and left everything on the point of being brought together" (Cather, *Death* 334). Latour's perspective creatively imagines how the landscape itself can be useful from his Catholic viewpoint. He acknowledges that the materials for "world-making" await assembly, something he brings to fruition in his crowning achievement: his cathedral. But before he can conceive of his own cathedral, he must first experience the Spaniards' previous attempt at influencing an indigenous community through construction and then a Native American example of a holy shrine.

The Spanish church on the alien rock formation of Acoma mesa seems to Latour to be "warlike" and "gaunt, grim, grey," seeming "more like a fortress than a place of worship" (Cather, *Death* 337). Relating the inappropriate architecture to the local community's response, he feels as if he were "celebrating Mass at the bottom of the sea, for antediluvian creatures…so hardened, so shut within their shells" they could hardly be saved "through any experience of their own" (337–8). He first criticizes the need for such a church, considering perhaps, his predecessors are guilty of "worldly ambition, and that they built for their own satisfaction" (338). In adding up the thousands of pounds of adobe, rocks, and massive timbers that could not have been found locally and had to be hauled to the top of the high mesa, Latour outlines the Acoma Indians' sacrifice to produce this site of worship. He realizes the Spanish priests could have fooled themselves into forgetting they were on a high desert rock inside the lush solitude of the church and their enclosed garden, but this priest learns from their misperception and chooses to sleep on a loggia that leaves him exposed to the environment around him.

This moment emphasizes the differences between his personal history and the sense of historical landscape. He experiences "homesickness for his own kind, his own epoch, for European man and his glorious history of desire and dreams" (Cather, *Death* 339). Rather than examining his personal identity by imagining the perspective of these "rock-turtles" (339), he envisions the impossibility of his task. When confronted with a world that had remained unchanged over many centuries—a time period during which so much "progress" occurred in the Western world—Latour acknowledges that his purpose in bringing the Catholic faith to these aboriginals is a struggle in the face of "something that had endured by immobility . . . crustaceans in their armour" (339). Each of Latour's realizations about the fortress-like church and the sacrifice of the Acoma Indians comes to him in the imaginative act produced by the incredible inconsistencies he finds atop the mesa. Acoma stands in stark relief as the ultimate example of the Spaniards' ambition meeting Native American untouchable resistance. Latour shapes his own ambitions accordingly. If the Spaniards had failed to realize the necessity of working with the Indians to encourage them towards a new religion, Latour would not make the same mistake. But he also does not realize just how powerful the influence of the indigenous religion is as he makes his own efforts to promote Catholicism.

When Bishop Latour spends a night at the Pecos Pueblo, Cather adds a footnote to her novel that reads, "In actual fact, the dying pueblo of Pecos was abandoned some years before the American occupation of New Mexico" (Cather, *Death* 352). The critical influence of indigenous communities in the desert Southwest requires Cather to resurrect the pueblo to allow for its impact. Cather needs this pueblo in order to give Latour his close-up experience with the Native American religion, influencing his own efforts to grow a new religion in the region. Latour launches from the resurrected pueblo to tend the seriously ill Father Valliant when a blinding snowstorm threatens his and Jacinto's lives. His guide goes against his instinct and takes Latour to a sacred Pecos site for shelter. The footholds, well-known to Jacinto, lead to a cavern the European priest can only describe in familiar terms as "a Gothic chapel" (354). Inside the "stone lips" (127) of the cave, he hears what he describes as "one of the oldest voices of the earth" when Jacinto directs him to listen to an underground river (356). While Latour keeps the secret about the Pecos cave, he remembers the shelter with "horror" noting that "no tales of wonder...would ever tempt him into a cavern hereafter" (358). The sacred site is a natural land formation that both makes the Native American religion a part of the landscape and helps Latour to understand that he should construct a religious site that is made up of the local landscape.

Accordingly, the archbishop's one "worldly ambition" is to build a cathedral in Santa Fe "worthy of a setting naturally beautiful" (Cather, *Death* 383). Latour's experience throughout the region has not only impressed upon him the effect of majestic landscape, but also the ability to influence people's sense of self through that majesty. Cather critic Joseph Urgo describes the priest's impulse to build a cathedral as "the establishment of a landscape on which history might commence" (139). With the examples of poorly wrought influence, such as the church at Acoma, juxtaposed with the gothic quality of the one native sacred site he visits, Latour has a vivid sense of his purpose in wanting to create a "Midi Romanesque" cathedral out of natural southwestern materials (423).

The priest finds the perfect indigenous rock for the church a few hours away by horseback. When he and Vaillant consider the stone, their comparisons remain European. At first the stone reminds Vaillant of St. Peter's cathedral, and with some prompting from Latour he finally recognizes its resemblance to the "Palace of the Popes at Avignon" (Cather, *Death* 423). Despite its origins in the strata of American soil, the rock will be molded and shaped by European standards to produce a "Midi Romanesque" matching the styles from Latour's and Vaillant's hometown in France (423). Latour has the opportunity to pick up the materials he noticed cast aside in the process of "world-making" (334) out on the mesa plains and form these materials into something that is both Southwestern and European in one structure.

While the work of being a priest in such an undeveloped area has required him to be an American every day (Cather, *Death* 297), Jean-Marie Latour has not lost his original sense of identity. Vaillant sees value in building any cathedral, but Latour sees the structure as more "a continuation of himself and his purpose, a physical body full of his aspirations after he had passed from the scene" (383). He joins a legacy of de la Tour priests who built similar churches in Avignon in the thirteenth century (424). Far from reforming himself into a new character based on the inspiration he feels from the desert Southwest, Latour doggedly follows the identity laid out for him centuries before. He will impose this vision on the new land, bending the participants to his will. Cather acknowledges that perhaps only the architect, Molny, and the bishop ever enjoyed the site of the building, but she insists through Molny that "'Setting...is accident. Either a building is a part of a place or it is not. Once that kinship is there, time will only make it stronger'" (441). The cathedral, as an extension of Latour, demonstrates an enduring influence as a form of a conspicuous piece of influential landscape "leap[ing] out of mountains" (441) to inspire the parishioners. And in the end, when the bishop returns to Santa Fe to die, Cather describes how "the tawny church seemed to start directly out of those rose-coloured [sic] hills—with a purpose so strong that it was like action" (441), an action that remains in people's reaction to the magnificent cathedral.

Cather's Southwest and Creative Genius

Perhaps because Cather was so forceful herself, she produces fiercely individual characters motivated by creative imaginations that stimulate them to be the best of their kind. The austere, Southwestern landscape, rich with ruins of ancient communities and expansive spaces, makes a location for these characters to gain new perspectives of themselves. Neither Thea nor Tom understood the drive towards genius until they were impelled by the influence of the Southwestern landscape as well as the remains of the people who lived there in the ancient past. While they were inspired to see themselves differently when juxtaposed with such an eternal landscape and its long-lost inhabitants, Bishop Latour recognized this effect on the people around him and used it to his advantage. As if he were actually working among the same kind of ancient people Thea and Tom only found the remnants of, Latour uses the physical materials of the landscape to inspire those people to a new religious perspective. Cather writes the inspiration of the American desert into these artists and their artistry. Thea Kronborg and Tom Outland find inspiration from the landscape to become the best among singers and engineers, while Bishop Latour builds his own portion of the landscape to inspire his parishioners in the Catholic faith. All of these characters converge on brilliance and genius, aided and influenced by the environment of the Southwestern desert.

Works Cited

Cather, Willa. *The Song of the Lark*. 1915. New York: Houghton Mifflin, 1988.

_____. *The Professor's House*. 1925. New York: Library of America, 1990.

_____. *Death Comes for the Archbishop*. 1927. New York: Library of America, 1990.

_____. "Light on Adobe Walls." 1949. *Willa Cather on Writing: Critical Studies on Writing as an Art*. Lincoln: U of Nebraska P, 1988.

_____. "The Novel Démeublé." *The Willa Cather Archive*. University of Nebraska at Lincoln, 2015. Web. 13 Nov. 2015. <http://cather.unl.edu/nf012.html>.

Moseley, Ann. "The Creative Ecology of Walnut Canyon: From the Sinagua to Thea." *Cather Studies*. Vol. 5. Lincoln: U of Nebraska P, 2003. 216–36.

Rosowski, Susan J. & Bernice Slote. "Willa Cather's 1916 Mesa Verde Essay: The Genesis of *The Professor's House*." *Prairie Schooner* 58 (Winter 1984): 81–92.

Schedler, Christopher. "Writing Culture: Willa Cather's Southwest." *Willa Cather and the American Southwest*. Ed. John N. Swift & Joseph R. Urgo. Lincoln: U of Nebraska P, 2002. 108–123.

Staples, Arthur G. "Willa Catha—Novelist." *Willa Cather in Person*. Ed. L. Brent Bohlke. Lincoln: U of Nebraska P, 1986. 158–165.

Stout, Janis. *Willa Cather: The Writer and Her World*. Charlottesville: UP of Virginia, 2000.

Trout, Steven. "Rebuilding the Outland Engine: A New Source for *The Professor's House*." *Cather Studies*. Vol. 6. Lincoln: U of Nebraska P, 2006.

Urgo, Joseph R. "Multiculturalism as Nostalgia in Cather, Faulkner, and U.S. Culture." *Willa Cather and the American Southwest*. Ed. John N. Swift & Joseph R. Urgo. Lincoln: U of Nebraska P, 2002. 136–149.

Woodress, James. *Willa Cather: A Literary Life*: Lincoln: U of Nebraska P, 1987.

Of Judges and Fairybook Beasts: The Male Mentor and Violence in Cormac McCarthy's *Blood Meridian*

Maria O'Connell

Blood Meridian is generally considered Cormac McCarthy's finest novel, although it can be quite harrowing to read. Neil Campbell asserts that it is, "an excessive, revisionist and contradictory narrative of the American West which both rewrites the myths and histories of the West inherited from Frederick Jackson Turner and maintains and utilizes many of the Western archetypes familiar in this genre of writing" (217). The novel introduces men who are paid bounties for Apache scalps, and who therefore interpret Apache rather freely and horribly. As Patricia Nelson Limerick notes, "...there was no certain way to distinguish an Apache scalp from any other dark-haired scalp; in the boom years of the bounty system, Hispanics and Indians other than Apaches were thus vulnerable to attack by scalp hunters" (n.p.). The violence and bloodiness of the novel are common subjects of criticism and interpretation, since they are sickening in the extreme, but they are also historically accurate. *Blood Meridian* cemented McCarthy's reputation as a myth-builder, since it is archetypal in its construction, so much so that the main character has no name, and, as in most of McCarthy's novels, the characters of note are men, engaged in quests and adventures to prove their manhood. The Glanton gang members are a male family or corporation who are bound by the hardships that they endure in a hellish landscape and by their respect and fear of Judge Holden. Their scalp-hunting is fueled by their own greed for more money and the judge's almost absurd sense of Manifest Destiny, which informs both their conversations with one another and Holden's monologues. Ironically, this novel, full of monologues, conversations, interpretations, and critiques, features a nearly wordless and uncommunicative main character, the kid. However, the communication that is shared within the small system of the Glanton gang shows the development of a family through the self-adaptation of gang members, particularly the kid, using the mythos of American exceptionalism. Although the Glanton gang is a corporate entity, the pedagogical and authoritative role of the judge in the gang makes him a father figure within a family structure, which shows "great ability to... determine the personal characteristics of its few members" (Luhmann 351). The family also experiences great conflict when a family member fails to perform a required adaptation. The world of the gang is "a resistance to domesticity and perhaps to heterosexuality itself... free from the demands of marriage, children, and so on" and yet establishing a certain type of order and expectation for behavior (Horrocks 64). On the borders of the southwestern United States, these men operate within frontier culture and mythos. For them, the frontier is "a vivid and memorable set of hero-tales—each a model of successful and morally justifying actions on the stage of historical conflict" (Slotkin 3). The physical boundaries of Mexico and the United States are uncertain in 1849, but the gang has clearly delineated rules about who is in it and who is not. The novel reveals an attempt to educate the kid about his role as a 'civilized' American man, and a mentor who fully justifies his 'mindless violence' and natural sense of superiority.

History Myth and Masculinity

Because the kid is a type of mythical hero, the novel begins with a conventional folk tale form; "see the child" (McCarthy 3) followed by a description of his utter abjection and want. In doing so, the novel follows a theme of descent (Frye 100), where the hero has a mysterious and oracular birth and must quest to find his true identity. His father tells his origin: "Night of your birth. Thirty-three. The Leonids, they were called. God how the stars did fall" (McCarthy 3). The image plays with both the associations with meteors and royal birth, and Native American monster-slayer tales (Peebles 241). For some Native American bands in the Southwest, the Leonids' appearance in 1833 was the signal for the arrival of a messianic figure and the end of the world. However, such mythic expectations are conditioned by the choices available to the main character. The kid has only a limited set of choices, because of his lack of education and his poverty. His biological father is a shattered, grieving, drunk, who is incapable of raising him. The kid, nameless even to his sole surviving parent, runs away at fourteen, in search of his true worth and his destiny.

As he fights his way westward, the kid is "like some fairybook beast" whose eyes are "oddly innocent behind the scars" (McCarthy 4). His physical prowess is considerable, and he wins the notice of the rough men around him and opens a space where he can interact with and find value in the violence around him. His fictional world is inextricably linked to real, historical places, and as John Sepich notes, "Cormac McCarthy's gang leader is a historical figure" (Sepich 5). Glanton is part of an embedded historical narrative in the fictive world of *Blood Meridian*, just as history often intertwines with frontier mythology. McCarthy borrowed the Glanton story from Samuel Chamberlain's memoir *My Confession*, and Chamberlain is probably also the model for the kid (Sepich 5). Nothing fictional is needed; there is abundant violence and bloodiness in the borderlands of New Mexico, Texas, and Mexico in 1849. McCarthy makes this fact clear by removing the romantic gloss of Chamberlain's memoirs. Chamberlain writes himself as Percival: a feckless boy who performs heroic deeds. He pictures himself fighting against the forces of evil and rescuing damsels in distress, but in *Blood Meridian*, all the self-justification is removed. We are left with a Chamberlain who would have laid his uncle out with an ax and felt no remorse about it (Chamberlain 24). What gets the kid to the West and enables him to survive there is a "taste for mindless violence" (McCarthy 3). His structuring myth that violence = strength is constantly reinforced by the fights that he participates in and survives. This schema is even reinforced when he is almost killed because he feels disdain both for his own vulnerability to death and for the kindness of an innkeeper while he heals. Part of tales of descent/ascent is ignorance on the part of the hero: "his origins are become remote as his destiny" (McCarthy 4), and the kid is innocent of anything but self-preservation. He must find his way by testing "whether creation may be shaped to man's will" (McCarthy 5). His reinforced schema becomes the basis of his socialization in the Glanton gang and is also the basis for a peculiar form of mentorship practiced by the judge, aimed at preparing the kid as a possible successor.

Mentoring and Communication

In a mentoring situation, the results are contingent upon communication, which could be seen as utterance (what is said), information (what is heard), and understanding (interpretation). All social systems use these selections to establish who is inside and who is outside the system. Every element of the system and "every communication in a social system... contributes to determining or changing the system's boundaries" (Luhmann 195). When the kid joins the Glanton gang, he becomes one element from which it is composed, and the relation of his communication to other elements is a challenge to the boundaries of the system. His communications reveal "which ... communications can be risked" (Luhmann 195). What communication can be risked in a system and how systems function are what bring this otherwise traditional western narrative into the real world of contingency and uncertainty. The gang's values depend on interpretation and understanding and can be seen differently, just as the Mexican border is more or less "real" depending upon who is describing it. Captain White, a recalcitrant US soldier, refuses to recognize the government in Mexico or the border, even denying the end of the war. When he first comes to the desert, the kid signs up with Captain White to "whip up on the Mexicans" (McCarthy 29), even though the war is over because "Hell, there is no God in Mexico. Never will be. We are dealing with a people manifestly incapable of governing themselves" (McCarthy 34). Men like Captain White applied to the Mexico "reasoning that resembled the persistent way of thinking about the Indians—that they were not using the land productively and properly and that, therefore dispossession would not only be easy but also right" (Limerick n.p.). Like the border with Mexico, the boundaries that form the Glanton gang are always contingent on the story being told and how each man hears and interprets the story. There are limits to the communication and reproduction of myth. In *Blood Meridian,* Judge Holden's one weakness is that he seems to believe in the pedagogical methods applicable to boys during this time. For American culture, men's virility and capability went hand in hand with the virility and strength of the nation. The pedagogy of what would come to be known as 'boyology' reinforced the national myth. Young men, like their young nation, needed a redemption of the spirit. The process included a "separation [from civilization, including the influence of women] temporary regression to a more primitive or 'natural' state and *regeneration through violence*" (Slotkin 12, italics original). Judge Holden, under this scenario, is the embodiment of the American myth.

The judge is a mythological figure, either hero or monster, depending upon the interpretation of his character. He is archetypally dominant, and he acts as a father figure for the men in the Glanton gang, and even in their violent manner of life, they are a family, "[which] acts as an executive organ of society, and a conduit for the channeling of ideological messages" (Horrocks 16). Holden represents and communicates the ideals of the Euro-American social system, and the desire of that system to reproduce itself wherever it may. Some critics, such as John Cant and Sara Spurgeon, find that *Blood Meridian* undermines the myth in exposing its violence and its destruction of the Native Americans and environment, providing "an indictment, bloody and accusatory, of an American national(ist) identity based on the violent conquest of both racialized Others and feminized nature" (Spurgeon 19). However, while today's reader might judge this story that way, men of the time would not have done so. Judge Holden would certainly consider himself an exceptional man, using violence against those who are less "fit" to rule or even to exist. In addition, like a Teddy Roosevelt, Robert Baden Powell, or Buffalo Bill, he considers it his duty to indoctrinate the right type of boy (white, intelligent, charismatic, and violent) into his values.

Socializing Through Myth

Hearkening back to the warrior Spartans (and to Joseph Campbell's rites of manhood), he says that the "way of raising a child" is that "they should be put in a pit with wild dogs. They should be set to puzzle out from their proper clues the one of the three doors that does not harbor wild lions. They should be made to run naked in the desert...." (McCarthy 146). Holden does not denigrate culture and education for a man. He himself values those qualities in himself and others. In Chihuahua to discuss business and turn in some of their scalps, the men are treated to a state dinner. While the Glanton boys wreak havoc and destroy the hotel, Holden comports himself differently. As the ex-priest Tobin notes, "Him and the governor they sat up till breakfast and it was Paris this and London that in five languages...." (McCarthy 123). However, for Holden, as for any proponent of savage war, a man is also a feral predator against those whom he considers inferiors or who are in his way. The judge sees a Darwinian world and teaches that dominant males should be both cultured and, when necessary, violent. As Horrocks writes, the Euro-American social system 'requires' masculinity and needs to ensure masculine outputs (Horrocks 15). Kenneth Kidd notes that purveyors of 'boyology' have, especially since the nineteenth century, been attempting to mold boys in the 'right' masculine direction for a modern, imperial, society, including the proper use of violence. Wildness in boy-tales and in the mock feral movements of organizations like Boy Scouts is "no longer a liability but an asset" and "boy-rearing handbooks draw directly from the mythopoetic movement [and] take issue with feminism" (Kidd 6). Masculinity has been discussed and debated since the nineteenth century and informs current anxieties about children's literature and boys. Anxiety about masculine roles and behaviors persists because disdain or esteem of other men is one way that the system perpetuates itself. One quality esteemed by the judge and that he encourages in the kid is control of emotion, particularly control of fear. Horrocks' description of this control as "male autism" (68) resonates with the kid and his stunted ability to feel or communicate. His 'autism' is not a disability in the Glanton gang, but a requirement. When the kid is warned about punishment from the guards in a border jail, his response is spitting and saying that "[t]hey aint about to come in here and eat no whips" (McCarthy 71). The kid is the very model of iconic Western masculinity. His ability to control his own fear and to inspire fear in others makes the gang value him. It signals his exceptional nature. The idea of regeneration through violence in the American mythos is that once the feral stage is over, then the violence should no longer be necessary. However, in the novel, as in history, the use of violence to control others becomes habitual. The judge's essential violence and need for domination is illuminated through his treatment of children and animals. He kills puppies for sport and habitually rapes and murders children. When he finds an orphan Apache child, he keeps him in his tent, and "in the morning he was dandling it on one knee while the men saddled their horses…but when [Toadvine] came back ten minutes later leading his horse the child was dead and the judge had scalped it" (McCarthy 164). Because the Indians and Mexicans were 'savages' in Judge Holden's view, he had the right to what Slotkin, in *Gunfighter Nation* calls "savage war," including the 'right' to kill children.

One of the justifications for savage war is the idea that white, European males are responding to Indian savagery in order to civilize them. In one critical early passage of *Blood Meridian*, the Comanche appear almost as a costumed tableau of the history of the West, playing traditional flutes, riding ponies painted with fish and bones, and dressed in everything from buffalo skins to traditionally European wedding dresses and veils to the armor of Spanish conquistadors (McCarthy 52). In these oddly assorted historical costumes, with the traditional feather headdresses, as well as curiously Viking-like horns of bison, the Comanche constitute "death hilarious" (52). Their costumes represent centuries of exchange, commerce, and warfare with the Europeans who attempted to enter their territories (Hämäläinen). Considering that they were not conquered by other Native Americans, the Spanish, nor anyone else until the systematic destruction of the buffalo and the collapse of their environment weakened them in the 1870s, the tableau is a good reminder of a successful native culture that not only resisted invasion, but also expanded their own imperial boundaries. As early converts to horse culture, "the Comanche ascent turned interior North America into a nomad's realm and yanked it beyond Spain's imperial grip" (Hämäläinen 183), and incidentally, for quite a while, that of the United States as well. By the mid-nineteenth century, the Comanche had still managed to avoid much European contact and had only had a few outbreaks of illness so that "the Comanche population hovered between twenty and thirty thousand... making them by far the most populous indigenous society in the Colonial southwest" (Hämäläinen 188). The Comanche wipe out Captain White and his soldiers because they are protecting their boundaries from military invaders. Their garb and their ease in dealing with an American military contingent are reminders that the myth of American exceptionalism and Manifest Destiny depends upon erasing history. The Comanche were not only as strong and imperial as Europeans in the past, but they also have not disappeared.

The judge actively engages in removing history by removing a petroglyph on the rock walls they pass, "leaving no trace of it only a raw place on the stone where it had been" (McCarthy 173). Juliana Barr writes that the Comanche carvings of "images of warfare, mounted horsemen, Franciscan missionaries, Anglo wagon trains, and what is believed to be a Comanche reading of the 1758 San Sabá massacre make for an arresting historical narrative" (34). Even now, myths of American dominance overlook the fact that native peoples and buffalo still survive, and even the eventual defeat of many tribes depended on things beyond military might and "fitness" for rule. The petroglyphs are a challenge to the nationalist myth, which wants to consign the Comanche to a distant, romantic past as primitive horsemen and hunters. The petroglyphs illustrate the history of the Comanche as a sophisticated political entity that controlled the land Americans wanted to possess. The encounters with people like Captain White show them as a still-present and living people. Indians were easier to deal with as objects of nostalgia; "the image— the noble, happy, pristine, uncontaminated Indian—had always been a great deal easier to live with than the diverse and complicated human beings who had come to be known as Indians" (Limerick n.p.). Spurgeon writes that "myths are what we wish history had been—a compressed, simplified, sometimes outright false vision of the past but a vision intended to serve a specific purpose in the present, and, just as importantly, to bequeath a specific shape to the future" (3), even if it has to erase parts of the past to do so.

Judge Holden's attempted education of the kid into the violent masculine family depends upon his belief in the power and attraction of myth and its ability to organize the world. However, his ultimate failure to transform the kid into a "fairybook beast" like himself illustrates the way that the outcome of pedagogy and mentorship depends upon a receiver and how the receiver understands and interprets the myth. The social system has many ways to bring the individual into line with its expectations. They can include expressions of esteem or of disdain, legal values, and inclusion or exclusion from a group. The Chihuahuan government's fear of the Comanche raids at the border allows the Glanton gang to justify a regime of terror because they are "defending" the Mexicans. The citizenry beg for rescue from their rescuers and "[c]harcoal scrawls appeared on the limewashed walls. Mejor los indios" (McCarthy 171). The judge communicates a particularly Western and Euro-American set of values, which relishes "that man who sets himself the task of singling out the thread of order from the tapestry [who] will by the decision alone have taken charge of the world" (199) rather than the Indians and Mexicans that he believes are weak and worthless. In articulating his beliefs, he attempts to educate the kid. However, the kid's emotional reaction to others, a feckless (and often useless) kindness, is an immunization against the complete coldness of the judge. The judge believes him to be weak:

> I know too that you've not the heart of a common assassin. . . No assassin, called the judge. And no partisan either. There's a flawed place in the fabric of your heart. Do you think I could not know? You alone were mutinous. You alone reserved in your soul some corner of clemency for the heathen. (McCarthy 299)

The kid paradoxically communicates his mutiny by refusing to shoot the judge, even as he is being urged on by Tobin (McCarthy 285). The kid, in a traditional western fashion should kill the judge or be killed by him to establish who is right. Instead, the novel ends ambiguously. The ending is usually read as a rape/murder by the judge, who then returns to the bar. However, it could also be a triumph for the kid, who as the fully grown man warns people away from the jakes and then turns and walks toward the light. The triumphant reading makes perfect sense when connected to the prophecy at the kid's birth. In the Yuman legend, the Hero Twins return to the human world after their sojourn against the monsters. However, this kid is no storybook hero, any more than he is a fairybook beast. Instead, his own development and resistance are contingent upon the choices available to him and what stories he finds acceptable.

Clemency and Social Health

Before the final confrontation, the kid has to escape from the judge and his verdict, so that he can travel freely on his quest. He must become "a coldforger who worked with hammer and die, perhaps under indictment and an exile from men's fires, hammering out like his own conjectural destiny all through the night of his becoming for a dawn that would not be" (McCarthy 310). He has to forge his own way. In San Diego, the kid finds his way out of jail with a story about treasure, finally using his voice when he has no other choice and showing his latent charisma. The fact that he can weave such a convincing story shows how similar he is to the judge and how powerful his words can be. Violence surrounds him and does not simply disappear from life because he wishes it would, nor do the social systems' expectations disappear just because the judge is not with him. The epilogue is read by some critics as a clear triumph of American exceptionalism (Josyph 107). However, the kid's experience and the ends of his companions do not seem like triumph or manifest destiny. Only the judge and the kid are alive at the end of the gang's reign of terror.

Luhmann notes that the inability to fit into a system is often seen as sickness (Luhmann 271). However, the kid decides that system, not he, is sick. In the romance world, as explicated by Northrop Frye—and which corresponds to traditional westerns— the kid, who has been traveling through a hellish underworld since his childhood, eventually will return to his real world. In order to recognize himself and regain that world, he acquires objects that remind him of his true self. One is the bible that he finds at a mining camp and "he carried this book with him no word of which he could

---

read" (McCarthy 305). The other is Toadvine's necklace of ears. Although, as the necklace shows, Toadvine nourished no clemency towards heathens, he did care, in a rudimentary way, for the kid. He even calls the kid, in the southern way, "honey," acknowledging childhood and innocence where few others would have. These talismans reinforce what the judge has taught him, which is that he indeed has a corner of clemency in his heart that sets him apart from others in his dark world. In order to claim that corner, he must confront the judge, for better or worse. Although many critics see the meeting in the jakes as the end of the kid's life and any hope for change, its ambiguity suggests a different reading. The man on the path, who warns others not to go into the jakes, is the kid as a fully adult male, who is ready to leave the darkness behind and turned "and went up the walk towards the lights" (McCarthy 334). This reading is not only supported by the Yuman mythology, but also by the memoirs that McCarthy followed. Samuel Chamberlain, the model for the kid, also turned away from his life in the West. After the Civil War, he left the violence behind to become a painter of some note, a family man, and warden of prisons in Massachusetts.

The kid, a fairybook beast at the beginning, must find his true identity at the end, but because this is a fairytale based in reality, that identity is not simple. The judge's teaching is that men are beasts and that the world is inherently evil. The Gnostic worldview that appears so often in McCarthy's earlier novels, however, also teaches that there is something beyond the bestial in man and that the only way to see God is to see those glimpses of spirit. For the kid, those glimpses include the rough kindness of Toadvine and the faith of the *penitentes* that he finds in the cave, who died praying. His bible is as much a memory of their faith as a representation of his own rough and rudimentary kindness. When he kills Elrod on the bonefield, it hearkens back to the killing of the idiot child in *Child of God.* It is an act of mercy, rather than mindless violence. For the kid, Elrod is the world of darkness and the dark side of himself, and he knows that such a violent youngster "wouldnt of lived anyway" (McCarthy 314). The kid himself has died to his past. When the kid and the judge meet, the kid (now grown) knows that the world is bestial and carnal, and he can accept that because he hopes that it is also something more.

His joining with the judge in the jakes is necessary because he can now face the ultimate truth: although he is bestial, he is also capable of goodness. He emerges unharmed and turns toward the distant light because, although he knows that he has all the darkness of the judge, he also has that "flawed place in the fabric of [his] heart" (McCarthy 299). It is enough to save him and to make him look for the light. The judge, empty of spirit, reappears naked (a sign of bestiality) and takes the place of the dancing bear in a bar that Stacey Peebles has persuasively argued is a dance hall of the dead. He can never die because he is already dead. His mentorship is rejected because the kid interprets his own clement heart not as weakness, but as hope. Their horrific joining in the end signals that the kid and the judge, both of them violent, resourceful, charismatic, and intelligent, have the same possibilities, but they made different choices. Despite the judge's mentoring and the kid's own belief in the Western masculine myth, the kid made his own path, based upon how he understood the idea of a good man.

Conclusion

Joseph Campbell writes that "the totality—the fullness of man—is not in the separate member, but in the body of the society as a whole" (383). Such an individual cannot exist outside of society, and he cannot break the connection. The striving of man, in such a mythological view, is to "embrace the form of the super-individual" (383) and so be supported in the appropriateness of his role in his world. Glanton and his band seek the judge's esteem and are surprised when the kid disobeys the judge. The ex-priest Tobin tells the kid "Fool...God will not love ye forever" (McCarthy 162), equating the judge's verdicts with the judgment of God. Acceptable or unacceptable behaviors depend on who one accepts as his judge, and the kid decides that his masculinity and/or his heroism do not depend on the judge's esteem, thus charting his own path in life.

Works Cited

Barr, Juliana. "Geographies of Power: Mapping Indian Borders in the 'Borderlands' of the Early Southwest." *The William and Mary Quarterly* 68.1 (Jan. 2011). 5–46.

Campbell, Joseph. *The Hero with a Thousand Faces.* 2nd ed. Princeton: Princeton UP, 1971. Bollingen Ser., 17.

Campbell, Neil. "Liberty Beyond Its Proper Bounds: Cormac McCarthy's History of the West in *Blood Meridian*." *Myth, Legend, Dust: Critical Responses to Cormac McCarthy.* Ed. Rich Wallach. Manchester, UK: Manchester UP, 2000. 217–226.

Cant, John. *Cormac McCarthy and the Myth of American Exceptionalism.* Ed. William E. Cain. New York: Routledge, 2008. Studies in Major Literary Authors Ser.

Chamberlain, Samuel. *My Confession: Recollections of a Rogue.* New York: Harper & Bros., 1956.

Frye, Northrop. *The Secular Scripture: A Study of the Structure of Romance.* Cambridge, MA: Harvard UP, 1976.

Hämäläinen, Pekka. "The Politics of Grass: European Expansion, Ecological Change, and Indigenous Power in the Southwest Borderlands." *The William and Mary Quarterly* 67.2 (Apr. 2010): 173–208.

Horrocks, Roger. *Male Myths and Icons: Masculinity in Popular Culture.* London: Macmillan Press, 1995.

Josyph, Peter. *Adventures in Reading Cormac McCarthy.* Lanham, MD: Scarecrow Press, 2010.

Kidd, Kenneth B. *Making American Boys: Boyology and the Feral Tale.* Minneapolis: U of Minnesota P, 2004.

Limerick, Patricia Nelson. *The Legacy of Conquest: The Unbroken Past of the American West.* New York: W.W. Norton & Company, 1987. Kindle Edition.

Luhmann, Niklas. *Social Systems.* Rev. ed. Trans. John Bednarz, Jr. & Dirk Baeker. Stanford, CA: Stanford UP, 2005.

McCarthy, Cormac. *Blood Meridian: Or the Evening Redness in the West.* First Vintage International Ed. New York: Vintage Books, 1992.

Slotkin, Richard. *Gunfighter Nation: The Myth of the Frontier in Twentieth-Century America.* Norman: U of Oklahoma P, 1998.

Spurgeon, Sara L. *Exploding the Western: Myths of Empire on the Postmodern Frontier.* College Station, TX: A&M UP, 2005. Tarleton State University Southwestern Studies in the Humanities Ser., 19.

Wallach, Rick. *Myth, Legend, Dust: Critical Responses to Cormac McCarthy.* Manchester, UK: Manchester UP, 2000.

The Haunted Frontier: Cormac McCarthy's Border Trilogy_____

Cordelia E. Barrera

Cormac McCarthy's Border Trilogy is a unified body of work comprised of *All the Pretty Horses* (1992), *The Crossing* (1994), and *Cities of the Plain* (1998). The novels, along with *Blood Meridian* (1985), mark a shift from McCarthy's earlier works set in the American South and his later 'western' novels. The trilogy epitomizes the hallmarks of McCarthy's oeuvre: a poetic and highly lyrical narrative style; unpunctuated dialogue and minimalist realism; and an expansive, almost cinematic attention to details of landscape. The bookend novels are devoted to the protagonist John Grady Cole, and the hinge novel is devoted to the story of Billy Parham. The novels do not require that they be read as a whole, as a distinct plot sustains each. However, reading the works as a trilogy broadens the tone, scope, and narrative complexity of McCarthy's extended treatment of frontier mythologies and border spaces in the American Southwest.

In the trilogy, John Grady Cole and Billy Parham assume mythic roles common to historical western narratives situated between two key frontier paradigms: the myth of progress, and the primitive-pastoral myth. At the heart of *All the Pretty Horses* is the myth of American progress and individual promise, a "rose-colored and stereotyped cliché of the national symbolic," in which the "sacred cowboy" image is revered and romanticized (Spurgeon 89, 86). This mask is all but destroyed in *The Cities of the Plain*. In the hinge novel, *The Crossing,* Billy Parham is tempted by the heroic possibilities of a primitive-pastoral dream that begins with returning a she-wolf to her home in Mexico and ends in desolation and loss while hinting at the promise of regeneration—a theme picked up once again in the final pages of *Cities of the Plain.* The boys' adventurous quests, typical of the *Bildungsroman*, enable their move from innocence to experience as they push forth into unknown territories. The novels combined present a Euro-American point of view associated with the driving forces of a frontier mythology of self-reliance, promise, and renewal. However, all three works are situated along the US-Mexico borderlands. Thus, when both Billy Parham and John Grady Cole seek adventure and the fulfillment of personal dreams and goals by moving south into Mexico, readers are urged to conceptualize stories and histories from both sides of the border.

Inherent in the American Southwest is an east/west paradigm of early settler movement as well as a north/south paradigm of US-Mexico race relations and racial politics. José David Saldívar calls this region a "*transfrontera* contact zone" (13). Similarly, Patricia Nelson Limerick concedes that the term "borderland" or the Spanish *frontera,* is the more "frank and direct version" of the frontier because it suggests a "continuous running story," where two or more groups meet, contest with each other, and try to settle relationships of power and influence (8–9). Because the Border Trilogy is held together by the power of stories and the way stories both organize and impose order on our worlds, a fruitful way to imagine the region is in terms of what I call the "bordered frontier." In this way, we can account for ideologies, mythologies, and histories inherent in both the frontier and the border. This course allows us to engage the American Southwest in terms of ideas that embody space, place, and time in the historical as well as modern imagination, ideas that coalesce in the influential ideas of the geographer Yi-Fu Tuan. Tuan writes, "from the security and stability of place we are aware of the openness, freedom, and threat of space, and vice versa." Space encompasses movement, and place represents a "pause" in movement. Each pause in movement, argues Tuan, "makes it possible for location to be transformed into place" (6). Place, then, signifies security and attachment, and space corresponds to movement and freedom. Space and place are co-dependent, and as humans, we require both. They are poles by which we organize behaviors, thoughts, and experiences.

Studies that discuss the Border Trilogy in terms of the border and the frontier as distinct, possibly incompatible ways to experience and know the world are wanting. However, both John Grady and

Billy are continually confronted with scenarios that culminate in lessons indicating how frontier myths associated with freedom and vast spaces lose their currency in Mexico—a place rife with a history and cultural legacy of its own. Mexico is more than the place where much of the action of the trilogy takes place, and the extensive use of Spanish throughout the novels is a cultural reminder that the boys are in a foreign country. When we engage a dialogue that highlights ideas central to both border and frontier studies, we can better understand how the boys' identities are continually haunted by "impossible memories and unwritten histories" that demand attention, seek justice, and challenge the way they encounter their world (Ferreday & Kuntsman 1).

All the Pretty Horses and Cities of the Plain

Space in the Southwest was often mis-taken from those—Mexicans, Chicana/os, and American Indians—who revered the land as a distinct place: their cultural and ancestral home. When we look to border places as part of a system "caught up in [a] swirl of histories, temporalities, and narratives" (Brady 52), we better understand the bordered frontier as a site where the production of place often supersedes the imperatives of space wherein American Adam-like heroes played out, or performed, frontier stories. With this in mind, John Grady Cole's and Billy Parham's stories are rooted in a southwestern geography and in the ideologies that have shaped the landscape. "The American Adam," as R. W. B. Lewis calls him, is self-reliant and confident, the "inventor of his own character" (Owens 111). In the first chapter of All the Pretty Horses, John Grady Cole leaves the ranch he grew up on in San Angelo, Texas, after the death of his grandfather in 1949. In so doing, he enacts the myth of American progress when he sets out on horseback to make a life for himself as a hired cowboy. He does not consider, however, that when he travels south to Mexico he will encounter codes, histories, and truths of a culture beyond the scope of American laws, values, and ideals. As part of his reading of Mexico as a mythologized space in the novel, Cooper-Alarcón suggests that the "Manichean Mexican landscape that John Grady moves through [is] a projection of the tension between his steadfast romantic ideals, and the cruel, capricious world around him" (144).

John Grady travels southward in an attempt to move backwards in time to a place where the codes of the Old West still hold some value. With his grandfather's death comes the dissolution of the San Angelo ranch he grew up on. Because the cowboy myth can no longer be had in Texas, he and his friend Lacey Rawlins venture south to seek "paradise," a promised land filled with ranches, horses, and opportunity. While still in the US, they meet Jimmy Blevins, a young "gunsel." Once they cross the physical border of Mexico, stripping naked to suggest what Harold Bloom calls a "baptismal scene" (24) that symbolizes rebirth, a broader theme of metaphoric borders—such as those between the US/Mexico, civilization/wilderness, present/past, and myth/truth—takes shape.

The reoccurring theme of metaphoric borders in the novel is significant, as character and setting are deeply tied in all of the novels. For example, when the boys reach the *Hacienda de Nuestra Señora de la Purísima Concepción* in Coahuila, they believe they will be free to live out their fantasy of cattle ranching in an Old West paradise. Moreover, John Grady immediately has eyes for more than the ranch; he falls in love with the beautiful Alejandra, the *hacendado's* daughter. Although John Grady proves his worth as a skilled horseman with the *hacendado,* Don Héctor, earning a private room and the boss's good favor, he will soon learn that Mexico is not paradise, and he is not Adam. The crossing into Mexico represents the movement from myth to truth in the novel: John Grady will not "own" horses, land, or Alejandra because, as a *norteamericano,* he has no right to them. There are other borders, too. The borders of race and class are made evident in the eventual failed relationship between John Grady and Alejandra. John Grady oversteps his ground when he partakes too boldly of the fruits of paradise, signified by his love affair with the aristocratic Alejandra.

Mexico is a region of memory, and these memories continually haunt John Grady's maturation. Mark Busby writes about Mexico as a land of history and the Southwest as one that deemphasizes history. He writes, "If the American frontier hero pushes west into a historyless land, then when that figure turns south and crosses the border, he encounters a land with a strong and troubling past, for Mexico represents a country with a lengthy and distressing history (144–145). Throughout the trilogy, the Southwest is described as a historyless space where John Grady and Billy withdraw from familial memories in search of American ideals; the border and Mexico, conversely, are signified as places with long histories. This underscores the idea that although the frontier vision is one of promise, it is nonetheless a static vision because it subsumes historical and familial memories in favor of national ideals.

National fantasies drive John Grady Cole's border crossings, but the absence of familial histories and memories to situate his identity-in-the-making leave him, as Gail Moore Morrison has argued, "adrift in time and space" (179). Although John Grady's lineage is entrenched in the Texas landscape, a longer history that echoes of displaced nations and buried places will haunt him throughout both *All the Pretty Horses* and *Cities of the Plain*. His grandfather's death announces the end of the Grady name: "the boy's mother was born and that was all the borning that there was" (McCarthy, *Pretty Horses* 7). After the funeral, John Grady rides out west, where he encounters a "dream of the past" that speaks of an earlier time. In the passage, McCarthy's lyrical prose conjure riders of "lost nations" who have come down out of the north,

> all of them pledged in blood and redeemable in blood only. When the wind was in the north you could hear them…nation and ghost of nation passing in a soft chorale across that mineral waste to darkness bearing lost to all history and all remembrance like a grail the sum of their secular and transitory and violent lives. (*Pretty Horses* 5)

Later, when John Grady stops to survey the landscape, he remains haunted, "like a man come to the end of something" (McCarthy, *Pretty Horses* 5). As readers, we, too, feel the weight of the lingering spirits of ancient Indian nations. In mythologizing these nations, specifically, Indian warriors, McCarthy suggests that violent, colonizing histories do not simply remain as memories, but as constants that suffuse a powerful sense of place and history onto the landscape: "but the warriors would ride on in that darkness they'd become, rattling past with their stone-age tools of war in default of all substance and singing softly in blood and longing south across the plains to Mexico" (6).

The crossings John Grady and Lacey Rawlins undergo in *All the Pretty Horses* are rife with neither history nor memory. In fact, the frontier visions that spur them onward are continually subsumed by memories of other peoples and other nations. John Grady's "code" is like so much clothing when he crosses the border. He is stripped of the false promises pledged in the cowboy code of endless space and romantic dreams when he crosses the border; his code means nothing in Mexico. While in Mexico, the boys are not bound by the time period in which the novel's action takes place, 1949–51; instead, they cross into the past. Cooper-Alarcón writes, the "farther into Mexico the Americans ride, the farther back in time they ride as well, culminating with their arrival at the hacienda" (148). When John Grady begins his doomed affair with Alejandra, he attracts the attention of the Dueña Alfonsa, Alejandra's great-aunt, who speaks at length with John Grady about her early idealism, the martyred Francisco Madero, and the Mexican Revolution. Her complex stories foreground a history of loss in Mexico as well as instill in John Grady a lesson about differentiating between dreams and realities. Her story underscores a main conflict in the trilogy: the tension between our idealized visions and the not-so-ideal realities they often engender. The Dueña tells him: "In the end we all come to be cured of our sentiments…The world is quite ruthless in selecting between the dream and the reality, even where we will not. Between the wish and thing the world lies waiting" (McCarthy, *Pretty Horses* 238). This foreshadows another painful history lesson—the one provided by Eduardo the pimp in the trilogy's final installment, *Cities of the Plain*.

Soon after John Grady begins his affair with Alejandra, he and Rawlins are arrested and taken to a Saltillo prison, where the outlaw Blevins is also being held. Blevins is killed and both John Grady and Rawlins manage to escape. We later learn that the Dueña Alfonsa has been instrumental in their release; she buys John Grady out of prison in return for Alejandra's promise that she will not see him again. Tom Pilkington reminds us that Alejandra ends the affair because she acknowledges "the obduracy of centuries-old conventions and customs" (320). What Alejandra seems to understand and John Grady does not is that there are limitations to their affair, and these are based in family, class, and nationality. In the trilogy, love alone is insufficient when crossing such borders.

Upon his return to the US, in the final pages of the novel, John Grady is confronted with a vision similar to the one he encounters after his grandfather's death. This time, the indigenous people he sees are Indians camped just outside of Iraan, Texas, "a scattered group of their wickiups propped upon that scoured and trembling waste" (McCarthy, *Pretty Horses* 301). These Indians have "no curiosity about him at all. As if they knew all that they needed to know. They stood and watched him pass and watched him vanish upon that landscape solely because he was passing. Solely because he would vanish" (301). Unlike McCarthy's earlier description of warriors who "would ride on in that darkness they'd become," John Grady, at the novel's end, is described as only one man, not a "nation" or "ghost of nation," but one man, one shadow—albeit one shadow composed of horse and rider. This final image of John Grady who rides and passes "like the shadow of a single being. Passed and paled into the darkening land, the world to come" (302) provides a thematic close to the novel. John Grady's vision is peopled not by *his* ancestors, but by Indians who once roamed the land freely, nations whose domestic ties are directly linked to the ground under their feet, and, as such, remain.

In *All the Pretty Horses* and *Cities of the Plain* John Grady makes remarkably unreasonable choices in the two romantic quests that structure each novel; both Alejandra and Magdalena, the prostitute in *Cities of the Plain*, are well out of his reach. As the *hacendado* notes in *All the Pretty Horses*, John Grady's living out the "idea of Quixote" is at odds with the "monster" that is "reason" (146). Moreover, the *hacendado* also notes, "one country is not another country" (145). These remarks speak to the "odd durability for something not quite real," that John Grady is cautioned about by the Dueña Alfonsa. By the time we encounter John Grady in *Cities of the Plain,* which opens in 1952, his plans for reclaiming his grandfather's lost ranch that first set him in Alejandra's direction have all but vanished; his plans now are to fix up an old domestic space on the New Mexico ranch he works with Billy Parham. Although John Grady's longings are quite reasonable: a home of his own with a woman he loves, he remains haunted by the constraining space of a frontier mythology that cannot contain his imaginings. Eduardo the pimp, who "owns" John Grady's love interest, the doomed Mexican prostitute, Magdalena, imparts this lesson, but it comes too late.

John Grady's guiding principles in *All the Pretty Horses* and *Cities of the Plain* are grounded in the ideals of a frontier mythology predicated on a future vision; they do not easily accommodate familial memories or alternative historical narratives. In fact, the road metaphor in these novels stifles or even negates individual histories. This is one message among many that the old traveler imparts to Billy in the final pages of *The Crossing.* "Our waking life's desire to shape the world to our convenience," says the old man, "invites all manner of paradox and difficulty" (McCarthy, *Cities of the Plain* 283). The past in *All the Pretty Horses* and *Cities of the Plain* is circumscribed and gives way only to the dream. This is important when we consider Jay Ellis's observation that "[d]reams in McCarthy point more to delusions, beliefs, and provisional truths, more than to larger truths" (5).

The central action of *Cities of the Plain* surrounds a team of cowboys who face an uncertain future in a dying industry. In the novel, Billy Parham, whom we meet as a young boy in *The Crossing,* is a world-weary twenty-eight-year-old, and John Grady Cole is nineteen. The men make regular forays into Ciudad Juárez, and it is here where John Grady meets and falls in love with Magdalena. Once again, however, his romanticized expectations and lack of knowledge of Mexican history and culture force the conclusion that the "the chivalric roles promised by cowboy mythology are ultimately impossible to fill" (Ellis 221).

In the novel, Billy Parham visits Juaréz to ask Eduardo the pimp if he can "buy" Magdalena so that she and John Grady may marry in the US. Eduardo tells Billy that John Grady "has in his head a certain story. Of how things will be." (McCarthy, *Cities of the Plain* 134). But Eduardo also cautions Billy that the thing that "is wrong with this story is that it is not a true story. Men have in their minds a picture of how the world will be. How they will be in that world. The world may be many different ways for them, but there is one world that will never be and that is the world they dream of" (134). These lines hark back to one of the Dueña's harsh lessons is *All the Pretty Horses*: Mexico is "another country" (136). The frontier is the bedrock of John Grady's identity, but the tension between his desires and Mexico as a place with a geography, culture, and heritage of its own is more powerful, and ultimately deterministic than lofty ideals. In *Cities of the Plain,* John Grady must suffer the unintended consequences bound by this truth.

At the end of the novel, during his fight to the death with Eduardo, Eduardo reproves John Grady once again for underestimating the reality of the Mexico in favor of imagined dreams rooted in a frontier ideology of limitless pursuit and increase. Eduardo says: "Your kind cannot bear that the world be ordinary. That it contain nothing save what stands before one" (McCarthy, *Cities of the Plain* 253). He continues, juxtaposing the vast spaces of the frontier with Mexico as a place with a solid make-up: "But the Mexican world is a world of adornment only and underneath it is very plain indeed. While your world—your world totters upon an unspoken labyrinth of questions. And we will devour you, my friend. You and all your pale empire" (253). Indeed, Eduardo "sees" what John Grady and Magdalena cannot, or will not see—that their love is based on false promises that cannot be reconciled given the violent subjugation of space that has become constrained by the imperatives of a historically contained Mexican place.

The border and the frontier are alternate ways to experience and know the world. Memories are like scars, reminders of a past that will always remain, however changed. The Mexican police officer, the captain whom Billy visits after he identifies the body of

Magdalena, reminds us that the past must bleed into the present in order that events in the past are given their true weight. The captain tells Billy, "Every male in my family for three generations has been killed in defense of this republic. Grandfather, father, uncles, brothers. Eleven men in all. Any beliefs they may have had now reside in me. Any Hopes …They are my Mexico and I pray to them and I answer to them and to them alone" (McCarthy, *Cities of the Plain* 243).

The Crossing

In *All the Pretty Horses* and *Cities of the Plain*, John Grady leaves his homeland and encounters a cultural and ethnic Other. In *The Crossing*, which takes place before and during World War II, Billy encounters the Other in nature, a she-wolf that he traps and intends to deliver to her Mexican homeland. The novel is composed of four sections, each consisting of an instance of crossing the border from the central character's home in New Mexico into northern Mexico, around the state of Chihuahua. The main protagonist, Billy Parham, first travels into Mexico to return a she-wolf he has trapped; the second time, Billy enters Mexico with his brother Boyd to search for his family's stolen horses after his parents have been murdered; the third and fourth crossings revolve around the search for Boyd and Billy's subsequent return to the US to bury his brother's bones. Entwined in these sections are various stories told by different travelers. Time and again, in the form of stories from so many people, it seems that we are heading toward some inescapable conclusion of McCarthy's. "Bits of wreckage. Some bones. The words of the dead. How make a world of this? How live in that world once made?" says the *gitano* to Billy (McCarthy, *Crossing* 411). *The Crossing* is perhaps the most haunted, and haunting, novel of the trilogy.

As we have seen, the bookend novels of McCarthy's Border Trilogy reveal what John Cant has called a "self-consciously mythic manner" (206). In these works, Cant writes, McCarthy "depicts the American side of the border as an arid wasteland, a sterile limbo, home to a myth that has lost its power. His Mexico is a mythic and exotic other that is increasingly shown to be as much a product of American fantasies as of indigenous reality" (206). Additionally, by recasting, indeed subverting, the codes inherent in frontier imaginings, Susan Kollin argues that in *The Crossing*, "Mexico becomes a region where the hero from the north of the border loses his bearings and his sense of identity." (580). Mexico, and the various Mexican and Indian characters, as well as the she-wolf Billy attempts to return to the place he imagines is her rightful home, represent "the wild, the inscrutable, the unknown" (Kollin 580). As Barcley Owens so effectively describes, Billy represents the primitive-pastoral hero who discovers paradise in an inscrutable wilderness setting that becomes a "purgatory of loneliness" where "he must purge his soul" and make ready for mythic battle (67). At the novel's end, however, Billy remains haunted by the pastoral vision represented by the she-wolf, as he cannot save that which has already been lost. The she-wolf symbolizes what Owens calls the "sins of mankind" (79). Wolves in the novel, and the she-wolf with a belly full of pups that Billy tries so desperately to save, signify the obliteration of wildlife and wild spaces ushered by the unfettered encroachment of the cattle and ranching industry in the southwest.

In the novel, Billy hears tales and stories in many guises and from diverse travelers, but he heeds little of the narrative messages he "witnesses." As such, Cant surmises that he remains outside of the "cultural matrix" that both he and Dianne C. Luce explore in McCarthy's oeuvre. The capability for narrative, says Luce of *The Crossing*, is the means by which human beings formulate the stories that contain our past and give meaning to our present (208). In this regard, the final book of the trilogy "is the story of a boy who discovers too early and too crushingly what cannot be held and whose spirit suffers a grievous wound" (Luce 211). Billy's capacity for taking part in his own narrative or the world's "matrix" is not restored in either this novel or *Cities of the Plain*, where, as an old man of seventy-eight, he is still homeless—a *huerfano*. In both novels, "Billy picks up the road metaphor with its connotations of wandering, avoidance and entrapment within the illusion of linear time-boundness" (Luce 212). This being said, it is Billy's desolation at the end of *The Crossing* that empties the Southwest

---

most poignantly of any sacred qualities it once held—whether real or in dreams. It is the final image of Billy holding his face in his hands and weeping for an old dog—"[r]epository of ten thousand indignities and the harbinger of God knew what" (McCarthy, *Crossing* 424)—that illuminates the vast frontier space before him as one fully defiled and profaned. The irony that the "false" dawn—ostensibly the nuclear explosion at the Trinity site that occurred on July 16, 1945—is what prompts Billy to call the dog back from the growing darkness is not lost on readers. The atomic detonation in the final pages of *The Crossing* further sets in stone that which can never be right again. Billy recognizes that his fate is tied to that of the old dog's—both are part and parcel of the world's matrix, regardless of Billy's desolation at the novel's end.

Time and again, the travelers Billy meets on the road in Mexico allude to a space between, a thing he cannot know. Sometime before Boyd's death, a Mexican *ganadero* "hold[s] his hands forward one above the other, a space between. As if he held something unseen shut within an unseen box." With this gesture, he tells Billy: "You do not know what things you set in motion. No man can know. No prophet foresee" (McCarthy, *Crossing* 202). In the novel, Billy tries "to see the world the wolf saw" (51). His attempts to restore order to the wolf's world by seeking to deposit her safely home in Mexico mirror his own attempts to find a place in the world, a home of his own. In seeking to connect with this wolf-Other, he seeks to connect with a mythic narrative in which he might secure direct knowledge of the world. But this need will cost him the wolf, his family, and his home. His alignment with the wolf is one of responsibility, and he knows he is "a man entrusted with the keeping of something which he hardly knew the use of" (McCarthy, *Crossing* 79). As such, just as "the wolf knew nothing of boundaries" (119) neither does Billy. But he will learn, and this lesson will cost him any sense of place he once embodied. The consequences of Billy's quest to restore the wolf to her place in the world cost him any sense of home, of security and attachment, he once had—however tenuous.

As readers, we must acknowledge that, with the wolf's death, Billy comes to know "what cannot be held," and perhaps it is for this reason that he continues to pursue a nomadic existence. As Billy's dreams increasingly become nightmares, and as he loses everything he once had, we are forced to reckon with the limits of our human power over the wild. By the novel's end, we realize that Billy has paid an insurmountable cost for the price of his primitive-pastoral dream. Just as the crippled old dog he sees at the end of the novel has written across its body, "ten thousand indignities" (McCarthy, Crossing 424), so too is Billy's body thus writ in the language of travel and the road. Toward the end of *Cities of the Plain*, we are privy to Billy's hands as an old man, full with "ropy veins that bound them to his heart. There was map enough for men to read. There God's plenty of signs and wonders to make a landscape. To make a world" (McCarthy, *Cities of the Plain* 291). Perhaps the homeless dog, like the she-wolf, is more attuned to the heart of things, and Billy's driving away the dog remains, as Luce points out "a cowardly disavowal of his connectedness to the matrix of the world that includes horror and loss and grief" (212). This appears to be evidence of McCarthy's own ambivalence regarding the fatal nature of the southwestern mythology that informs the actions of old cowboys like Billy. Even so, Billy's ultimate failure rests in the "doomed enterprise" that is his initial quest, and it is this which gives power and resonance to the final image of Billy as he weeps, alone, on a road that will, once again, take him to no place, but, rather, more empty spaces.

The Border Trilogy is replete with universal meanings about human nature and significant lessons of western and national history. The West is full of stories grounded in a pastoral-primitive nostalgia where the hero's idyllic dreams come to fruition in a wilderness setting. But Billy's quest, like John Grady's, is a doomed enterprise. Billy represents the primitive-pastoral hero who, tested and almost spiritually broken by the wilderness experience, remains a wanderer, *un huerfano* at the conclusion of *Cities of the Plain*. Like John Grady, Billy must learn that there exists an essential continuity between our present concerns and the concerns of history. The boys' dreams, which encompass so much of the spatial imagery of the southwest, and the figurative imagery of borders and frontiers—*la frontera*—are singular, and, as such, little match against the social and cultural backdrop of a Mexican landscape steeped in history and memory. In the trilogy, the boys' willful dreams are continually overshadowed by powerful Mexican and indigenous realities told to them in the form of stories or embedded in a landscape that disrupts their idyllic pursuits. In this sense, the boys remain haunted by unsettled, unresolved histories of collective violence and cultural and social issues signified by their crossings into Mexico.

Works Cited

Bloom, Harold, ed. *Bloom's Guides: Cormac McCarthy's "All the Pretty Horses."* Philadelphia: Chelsea House Publishers, 2004.

Brady, Mary Pat. *Extinct Lands, Temporal Geographies: Chicana Literature and the Urgency of Space.* Durham, NC: Duke UP, 2002.

Busby, Mark. "Into the Darkening Land: the World to Come." *Modern Critical Views: Cormac McCarthy.* Ed. Harold Bloom. Philadelphia: Chelsea House, 2002. 141–167.

Cant, John. *Cormac McCarthy and the Myth of American Exceptionalism.* New York: Routledge, 2008.

Cooper-Alarcón, Daniel. "All the Pretty Mexicos: Cormac McCarthy's Mexican Representations." *Cormac McCarthy: New Directions.* Ed. James D. Lilley. Albuquerque: U of New Mexico P. 2014. 141–152.

Ellis, Jay. *No Place for Home: Spatial Constraint and Character Flight in the Novels of Cormac McCarthy.* New York: Routledge, 2006.

Ferreday, Debra & Adi Kuntsman. "Haunted Futurities." *borderlands e-journal* 10.2 (2011): 1–14.

Kollin, Susan. "Genre and the Geographies of Violence: Cormac McCarthy and the Contemporary Western." *Contemporary Literature* 42.3 (2001): 557–88.

Lilley, James D. "There Was Map Enough for Men to Read: Storytelling, the Border Trilogy, and *New Directions.*" *Cormac McCarthy: New Directions.* Ed. James D. Lilley. Albuquerque: U of New Mexico P. 2014. 1–15.

Limerick, Patricia Nelson. "Borderland vs. Frontier: Redefining the West." *Humanities.* 17.7 (Oct. 1996): 4–9.

Luce, Dianne C. "The Road and the Matrix: The World as Tale in *The Crossing.*" *Perspectives on "The Crossing."* Eds. Edwin T. Arnold & Dianne C. Luce. Jackson: UP of Mississippi, 1999. 195–219.

McCarthy, Cormac. *All the Pretty Horses.* New York: Vintage International, 1992.

_____. *The Crossing.* New York: Knopf, 1994.

_____. *Cities of the Plain.* New York: Knopf, 1998.

Morrison, Gail Moore. "*All the Pretty Horses:* John Grady Cole's Expulsion from Paradise." *Perspectives on Cormac McCarthy.* Eds. Edwin T. Arnold & Dianne C. Luce. Jackson: UP of Mississippi, 1999. 175–94.

Owens, Barcley. *Cormac McCarthy's Western Novels.* Tucson: U of Arizona P, 2000.

Pilkington, Tom. "Fate and Free Will on the American Frontier: Cormac McCarthy's Western Fiction." *Western American Literature.* 27.4 (Winter 1993): 311–322.

Pilkington, William T. *My Blood's Country: Studies in Southwestern Literature.* Fort Worth: Texas Christian UP, 1973.

Saldívar, José David. *Border Matters: Remapping American Cultural Studies.* Berkeley: U of California P, 1997.

Spurgeon, Sara. "On Truth and Redemption." *Bloom's Guides: Cormac McCarthy's "All the Pretty Horses."* Philadelphia: Chelsea House Publishers, 2004. 86–92.

Tuan, Yi-Fu. *Space and Place: The Perspective of Experience.* Minneapolis: U of Minnesota P, 1977.

Coming to Terms with Death in the West: Anticipation of Death and the Effects of Loss in the Novels of Larry McMurtry

Roger Walton Jones

Death be not proud, though some have called thee
Mighty and dreadful, for thou art not so;
For those whom thou think'st thou dost overthrow
Die not, poor Death, nor yet canst thou kill me.

(John Donne)

To go west, as far west as you can go, west of everything, is to die.

(Jane Tompkins)

Texas may be the country's best state in which to be lonesome.

(Fred Setterberg)

Texas author Larry McMurtry, like Mark Twain or William Faulkner, is very much identified with the particular region of the country where he grew up, even as he transcends it. His existential concern with death and its consequences is only heightened by his childhood on what was once the barren southwestern frontier bereft of churches and the restrictive comforts civilization may provide. In its place was a world where, as critic Jane Tompkins pithily puts it in *West of Everything*, "strength counts more than prayer" (34). McMurtry's early ambivalence to such a male-dominated world[1] does not negate his sense of emotional loss associated with it from a young age. As McMurtry wrote, "the place where all my stories start is the heart faced with the loss of 'its country, its customary and legendary range'" (*Film Flam* 148). While McMurtry may be said to transcend his environment and the simplistic macho stereotypes often associated with it via western pulp fiction and film, he nevertheless finds ample means to exploit his rich western heritage and his intimate familiarity with its desolate landscape. He does this in part by examining in fiction the enduring strength of southwestern men and women as they face the undeniable reality of death in their lives. In *Streets of Laredo*, McMurtry has Charles Goodnight tell a younger cowboy, "Life's but a knife edge.... Sooner or later people slip and get cut" (585). As the quote suggests, a factor that distinguishes McMurtry from other writers dealing with the same material is the nuanced sensitivity to human fragility he brings to such portrayals. Additionally, McMurtry takes a particular interest in how women may triumph over loss while living in the Southwest, not only in the past but in the present.

In his review of Larry McMurtry's *Terms of Endearment*, O. B. Hardison stresses how the modern Houston mother and daughter who form the novel's main focus find enormous strength to cope with life's inevitable losses. According to Hardison: "They have the strength to accept repeated loss, a powerful will to create order even when the effort seems futile, and the instinctive urge... to give love wherever it is accepted (38). Hardison further notes how the small Renoir that the mother Aurora ends up hanging in her dying daughter's hospital room serves both women at different times in their lives as a spiritual touchstone upon which they can project their dreams and desires. For example, at a culminating moment in the novel, Aurora finds herself gazing at the painting she inherited from her mother as she attempts to come to terms with her inescapable awareness of the inevitable losses associated with middle-age:

> ...she took her hairbrush and stood for a while in front of her Renoir, brushing and looking at the two gay young women in their yellow hats.... Then the young women blurred and the painting became like an open window, the window of memory, and Aurora looked through it and saw her own happiness—with her mother in Paris, with Trevor on his boat, with Rudyard beneath the mosses of Charleston. It seemed to her that it had mostly been all happiness then, before quite so much had been said and done. (McMurtry, *Terms of Endearment* 323)

Similarly, in a more extreme context, shortly before her death, her daughter Emma discovers temporary imaginative escape from the disorienting ravages of cancer as she gazes at the same Renoir in her hospital room:

In time, as Emma faded, her mother became lost in the Renoir. Often Emma couldn't tell whether there were two shimmering women in the room or three.... Sometimes she dreamed she was living in the picture, walking in Paris in a pretty hat. At times she felt herself awakening in it instead of a bed covered with hair that had fallen out during the night. (McMurtry, *Terms of Endearment* 368–369)

What attracts both Emma and her affluent mother Aurora, a transplanted northeasterner, to the Renoir is the attractive possibility it seems to hold out in their mutual hours of need of a meaningful spiritual realm inspired by beauty that will transcend time and death. Just as some might achieve a similar transcendent sense of the sublime while contemplating the grandeur of the southwestern landscape, so Aurora, reflecting her effete New Haven heritage, turns to art. In this respect, it is appropriate that McMurtry chose as his epigraph for *Terms of Endearment* an excerpt from a sonnet by Shakespeare, for Shakespeare's sonnets are famous for wrestling with the painful question of the relationship between love and human mortality and the role art may play in ensuring a kind of worldly immortality. Yet in this context, the except from the sonnet that McMurtry chose from Shakespeare is also ironic, for it deals not with the promise of immortality associated with art, but with the more pragmatic possibility of immortality achieved by having children. The epigraph reads: "Thou art thy mother's glass, and she in thee/Calls back the lovely Aprill of her prime;/So thou through windowes of thine age shalt see,/Dispight of wrinkles, this thy goulden time....—Shakespeare, Sonnet III" (McMurtry, *Terms of Endearment* n.p.). Of course, in contrast to the above sonnet's fictional daughter, who embodies her mother's youthful beauty and "golden time," McMurtry's neglected Emma lacks not only her narcissistic mother's outward beauty, but bears the added burden of dying of cancer before her mother.

Following her daughter's death, Aurora tries more urgently to explore her hope that art may hold a key to transcending time and death. In *Terms of Endearment*'s sequel, *The Evening Star*, she approaches the end of her long life wishing that she could emulate a great author like Marcel Proust, who seemingly conquered time itself via his vividly detailed narratives. Aurora does her best to record her life for posterity, yet she lacks ultimately the unique ability of a great artist to take past incongruities and transform them into some kind of meaningful, immortal whole:

> Despite the playbills and the concert programs, despite the diaries and the scrapbooks, she had to admit that she could remember practically nothing of her long experience of life. The analysis of high moments, whether ecstatic or terrible, that Monsieur Proust was so good at was far beyond her. She could not get back in her memory the life of her emotions, or of her senses, or even her society, to any important degree. (McMurtry, *The Evening Star* 593)

Ironically, the worldly immortality Aurora craves will come not through her literary experiments to record her past, but through a special artistic connection with her baby great-grandson Henry. With him, she shares repeatedly Johannes Brahms's *Requiem* (a work appropriately inspired by the death of the composer's mother). As Aurora holds the baby in her arms listening to the music, she and he discover together a beautiful all-encompassing spiritual realm:

> The sounds became the world, became his life, for the course of the special time, and he and the old woman were in them together. The old woman offered him a finger, and Henry took it and held it very tight. He wanted to stay with the old woman, and to have her stay with him. He did not want to be lost. (McMurtry, *The Evening Star* 609)

Many years later, as a young man on a concert date, the mature Henry will suddenly become overwhelmed with an inexplicable sense of emotional loss when Brahms's *Requiem* is played, even as he remains unable to access the unconscious memory of his special spiritual connection to his great-grandmother enabled by art:

> Before he knew it, the music had taken him to another place—to an old place in his memory, to a place so old that he could not really even find the memory, or put a picture to it, or a face. He just had the emptying sense that he had once had something or someone very

important: someone or something that he could not even remember, except as a loss—something or someone that he would never have again. (McMurtry, *The Evening Star* 612–13)

Larry McMurtry's thematic concern with innocence and loss combined with anticipating the ultimate loss death entails and its ego-shattering effects on the people left behind had early origins. In his 1984 memoir, *Walter Benjamin at the Dairy Queen*, he admits to the traumatic effect a neighboring farmer's suicide had upon him when he was only five:

I remember the shock of that event because, up to then, it had never occurred to me that it was permissible, or even possible, to kill oneself. Up to that point... I assumed that, once alive, you were required to stay alive until a horse fell on you or lightning struck you or something. (McMurtry, *Walter Benjamin* 27)

Rather than finding his elders a source of wisdom or comfort in his hour of need, what only added to young McMurtry's horror and confusion were the hardened responses of the cowboys surrounding him. What interested them primarily was not the issue of suicide itself (which, in their eyes, was an understandable way out considering the farmer's hard, lonely life on the prairie), much less the fate of the poor abandoned farmer's wife, but, instead, the surprisingly ironic, if trivial, circumstances that surrounded both: namely, why did the young dairy farmer bother to go through the trouble of completing his milking chores before killing himself? McMurtry states:

... I never forgot the suicide of the nice Dutchman up the road. What was his despair, and why did it culminate just after milking on that particular morning? And his wife, about whom I know nothing? The cowboys never talked about her. To them the milk cows, not the wife, were the interesting part of the story. (McMurtry, *Walter Benjamin* 28)

McMurtry's unrelieved early existential anxiety evoked by his neighbor's suicide, combined with his protective interest in the woman left behind, would lead to the lifelong creation of fiction set in the Southwest and involving, as a major concern, the anticipation of death and its chilling after-effects. For references to death in all its forms, including suicide, occur over and over in McMurtry's more than thirty novels, whether set in the past or in the present. [2] That this fixation and its spiritual implications remained with him into the new millennium is reinforced by McMurtry's suggestion in his 2001 memoir, *Paradise*, that something called "ego-chill" has always been a part of his emotional make-up. In *Young Man Luther*, psychologist Erik Erikson defines that condition as "the chill that occurs when one is suddenly faced with the possibility of one's non-existence" (147).

One of McMurtry's insights in relation to this chill is how it challenges the ego's habitual desire to feel powerful and in control. Growing up in the Southwest, with its harsh environment and weather extremes, could only have contributed to McMurtry's constant awareness of how little control over destiny the individual actually has. This idea is wittily underscored at one point in his Hollywood novel *Somebody's Darling*. When Hollywood insider Jilly Legendre explains why the solipsistic movie star Sherry Solare could not cope with the accidental killing of her son and therefore commits suicide, he tersely points out, "Death is not a camera" (McMurtry, *Somebody's Darling* 288). Death disorients, for it refuses to accommodate the bloated demands of one's ego for a reassuring sense of order, forcing one to constantly renegotiate one's identity and its often highly tenuous relationship to the ever-shifting, unrelenting demands of the external world. An example of this challenge to always accommodate reality, no matter what occurs, appears at the end of *Terms of Endearment*, when Emma is on her deathbed and wisely warns her feckless husband regarding the future welfare of their children: "We're thinking of them....We're not thinking of how we'd like to think of ourselves" (361). This idea of the need for humility in the face of death is further illustrated by her devastated mother, Aurora, who achieves a rare moment of humble self-insight standing above her daughter's grave.

McMurtry's interest in the damage to the ego that death can cause—forcing one to discover a fresh connection to the world—is likewise dramatized through his sensitive depiction of Jacy Farrow in *The Last Picture Show*'s sequel *Texasville*. At the death-haunted core of the novel are delicate hints of Jacy's spiritual journey to reconnect with her rural southwestern roots following her years of tumultuous self-absorption as a minor celebrity—a period culminating in the accidental electrocution of her son on a European movie set. Jacy's journey away from the devastating effects of her son's death towards a newly grounded life is ironically framed by the heady materialism that has overtaken her tiny hometown of Thalia (based on McMurtry's hometown of Archer City). For, in the years since she left, the Texas oil boom of the 1980's that swept the Southwest has financially invigorated the desolate town of her youth with disorienting results. For example, it has left her formally poor boyfriend Duane not knowing how to cope with either his newfound wealth or encroaching debt, much less his suddenly inflated status as the famous town multimillionaire whose spiritual emptiness mirrors Jacy's own.

Everywhere Jacy looks, however, the same brutal, unforgiving West Texas landscape she once fled seems intent on teaching her humility. When Duane takes her with him on a business trip to Odessa to meet a fellow oilman, she gets no further than Big Springs before being overcome by the overwhelming bleakness of the land:

> Jacy slumped against the door....she seemed without energy. The countryside was dotted with oil pumps. In places the thin grass itself looked as if it had been smeared with oil.
> "You're right, it's getting uglier," Jacy said. (McMurtry, *Texasville* 210)

Checking into a cheap hotel in an effort to escape her forlorn environment, Jacy soon fixates on a television game show that only further seems to confirm the meaningless, arbitrary nature of her existence. As she explains to Duane, in contrast to escapist soap operas based on cleverly manufactured illusions: "Game shows are what's really like life. You win things that look great at the time but turn out to be junk, and you lose things you might want to keep forever, just because you're unlucky" (McMurtry, *Texasville* 220).

At another, equally dark point in *Texasville*, McMurtry specifically echoes the early trauma he once experienced as the result of his neighboring farmer's suicide. This is when Duane realizes how incalculable the ever-expanding effects of taking one's life are. Listening to his economically beleaguered old friend Lester, the town banker, casually contemplating suicide, Duane suddenly realizes how Lester could inadvertently:

> ... ruin his two nice daughters' lives. It might drive Jenny over the edge she seemed to live on. It might even have a ripple effect in Thalia itself. People who had never particularly liked Lester might blame themselves for his death. The whole town might slip into an emotional decline matching its economic decline. (McMurtry, *Texasville* 388)

The unnerving chill Duane experiences as a result of his idle speculation is likewise felt by his own children later in the novel as they innocently bring up the subject of Jacy's son's accidental death:

> "Her little boy was younger than me and he got killed," Jack said, once Jacy was gone.
> No one had anything to say to that.
> "I'd never get killed," Jack said, kicking the table leg nervously.
> "Hush, it's bad luck to talk about it," Karla said. (McMurtry, *Texasville* 496)

Yet in the midst of all the darkness, there are signs of Jacy's personal growth from the shallow girl she once was. Standing on a parade float with Duane, she realizes as never before their importance as meaningful role models for the rural community. And at her high school reunion, she quotes from Keats' famous poem "Ode on a Grecian Urn," suggesting that, like Aurora, she, too, is at least open to exploring the possibility of an immortal spiritual realm hinted at by art.

The ultimately bittersweet conclusion of *Texasville* suggests that—despite the sobering lesson that death can happen to anyone at any time—Jacy's painfully slow journey towards a new, healthier sense of being integrated and engaged with real life has been granted renewed impetus.

In contrast to the cautiously deliberate soul-searching that informs Jacy's grieving process against a backdrop of modern existential ennui in *Texasville* are the abruptly uncharacteristic actions Captain Call reflexively adopts as part of his unacknowledged grieving process in response to his long-time friend's sudden death in *Lonesome Dove*. Call's emphasis on instinctive action reflects the fact that Larry McMurtry's novel is set in the Old West, a world where death is prevalent and, therefore, survival is paramount. Jane Tompkins describes it as "without God, without ideas, without institutions, without what is commonly recognized as culture" (37). This dangerously barren world of McMurtry's ancestors, unmediated by civilization, is not particularly conducive to inner self-reflection. Yet McMurtry's fiction reveals how the ever-present reality of death on the frontier only highlights the most basic human need to find an outlet for grief while constantly rediscovering a crucial inner balance between hope and despair.

Early in *Lonesome Dove*, McMurtry introduces this idea through the black cowboy Deets' misgivings regarding Call's reckless dream to go on one final cattle drive: a drive that will take the Hatcreek outfit far from the relative safety of their home in the town of Lonesome Dove:

> Deets felt a foreboding, a sense that they were starting on a hard journey to a far place. And now here was the boy, too excited to keep his mind on the work.... The boy was young and had his hopes, while Deets was older and had fewer. Newt sometimes had so many questions that Deets had to laugh.... Some Deets answered and some he didn't.... He didn't tell him that when life seemed easy, it kept on getting harder.... He had known several men who blew their heads off, and he had pondered it much. It seemed to him it was probably because they could not take enough happiness just from the sky and the moon to carry them over the low feelings that came to all men. (203–204)

Deets' paternal interest in preserving Newt's innocence as long as possible—particularly with regard to death—recalls the innocence McMurtry lost at an early age as a result of his neighbor's suicide. McMurtry's special empathy for Newt's character is furthermore suggested by the author's statement in his 2010 preface to *Lonesome Dove* that "the lonesome dove is Newt, a lonely teenager who is the unacknowledged son of Captain Call."[3] Of course, Deets' protective impulse proves prophetic, considering the tragic deaths that take place during the cattle drive, including Deets' own. Not surprisingly, the naïve, homesick Irish boy, Sean O'Brien, dies first, followed later by the older and more experienced cowboy. Upon Deets' death, McMurtry shows how thoughts of self-extinction can be a legitimate response to the shock of recognizing someone close is gone. Newt, slowly waking up from sleep, spies Deet's remains and "wished they would all die, if that was the best they could do" (McMurtry, *Lonesome Dove* 804). Then, as reality breaks through his efforts at denial, none of the preoccupied adults surrounding the boy attempt to relieve his growing despair:

> Newt sat on his blankets, feeling alone. No one noticed him or spoke to him. No one explained Deet's death. Newt began to cry, but no one noticed that either.... He didn't look at the corpse again, but he wondered if Deets had kept on knowing, somehow.... He felt if anyone was taking any notice of him, it was probably Deets, who had always been his friend. It was only the thought that Deets was still knowing him, somehow, that kept him from feeling totally alone. (McMurtry, *Lonesome Dove* 805)

Newt's youthful disillusionment serves as an ironic counterpoint to his father Call's later despair upon his close friend Gus' death. Call, despite his differences from Jacy in *Texasville*, must, nonetheless, similarly cope with the highly disorienting suggestion that his life has no meaning:

> He felt so alone that he didn't really want to go back to the outfit.... For his part he would just as soon have ridden around Montana alone until the Indians jumped him, too.... Gus had died and left the world

without taking him with him, so that once again he was left to do the work. He had always done the work.... All his work, and it hadn't saved anyone, or slowed the moment of their going by a minute. (McMurtry, *Lonesome Dove* 885)

As if embodying the traditional western hero, Call maintains the taciturn silence of one who distrusts language, preferring action over words. Yet when Deets' dies, Call finds himself spending hours carving words in tribute to him. Then when Gus dies, Call defies all expectations by verbally agreeing to actions on his friend's behalf, which violate his practical nature. The depth of Call's feelings for his friend, which have no formal outlet on the frontier, are illustrated by his heart-felt promise to transport his friend's body all the way back to Texas from Montana. Don Graham observes that the sequence turns into "the most moving...in the novel" (316). Even more surprising, for a man who had so little use for language that he refused to acknowledge his illegitimate only son Newt with the gift of his name, Call agrees not only to deliver Gus' final two hand-written letters to the ladies in his life, but to bring back to Texas his friend's enigmatic, Latin-inscribed wooden sign to serve as his gravestone. Even though it turns out that the erudite language Gus intended to impress strangers with (even though he himself did not know what the words meant) is worn away by nature over the course of the long trip, Call's willingness to faithfully include on his journey what his friend claimed was his greatest achievement suggests the need for greater cultural outlets in the face of death on the frontier.[4]

The ending of *Lonesome Dove* further underscores Call's devastating loss as well the need for a renewed sense of balance and reconciliation as a prerequisite for healing. Having carried out his promise to bury Gus in the Texas orchard where he first courted Clara Allen, Call returns to the abandoned town of Lonesome Dove, where he immediately encounters Bol, his outfit's former cook. The chance encounter resonates in a number of important ways. Like Jacy at the beginning of *Texasville*, Call feels both disoriented and ambivalent about being around people. Also like Jacy, Call instinctively returns to his roots: the closest thing to a home he has ever known. But in Bol, Call discovers a man even more in need of human contact than himself. The pathetic nature of Bol's situation is underscored by the fact that when Call encounters him, he is in the process ringing the dinner bell, as he once did every evening, even though no one is around to hear it:

> When Call dismounted and dropped his reins old Bolivar walked over, trembling, a look of disbelief on his face. "Oh, Capitan, Capitan," he said, and began to blubber. Tears of relief rolled down his rough cheeks. He clutched at Call's arms, as if he were worn out and might fall.
> "That's all right, Bol," Call said. He led the shaking man to the house.... (McMurtry, *Lonesome Dove* 943)

It is both moving and ironic that the formally stoic and independent Call is able to offer words of comfort to Bol, himself highly independent, enabling hints of Call's own potential for spiritual healing in the process. The danger of unchecked social isolation is further emphasized in the novel's closing lines, which serve as a reminder of McMurtry's vicarious childhood brush with suicide. Standing before the ruins of the town saloon, Call learns that its owner committed suicide by burning it down around him when the beautiful prostitute he worshipped abandoned him. Just as the young McMurtry was horrified by the coolly indifferent responses of the adult cowboys to his neighbor's suicide, so the hypocritical church folks in the town of Lonesome Dove are equally blind to the high degree of inner pain leading to the saloon owner's death: "'The pi-aner burnt up with him,' Dillard said. 'Made the church folks mad. They thought if he was gonna roast himself he ought to have at least rolled the pi-aner out the door. They've had to sing hymns to a fiddle ever since'" (McMurtry, *Lonesome Dove* 944).

As these excerpts from McMurtry's fiction suggest, a special quality exists in the manner in which McMurtry portrays the anticipation of death and its aftermath on the frontier in both the present and the past. In depicting modern Texas, McMurtry reveals his conviction in the important role art may play when focusing on female privileged characters, such as Aurora and Jacy, who possess the time and luxury to reflect on the possible relationship between art and their own mortality. When he goes to the other extreme and returns to the Southwest's primitive past, he does so in a way that subtly highlights human beings' unmet emotional and spiritual needs. This despite the fact that, as Jane Tompkins explains, traditional westerns believe that "reality is material, not spiritual" and "celebrate the suppression of feeling" (6). Nonetheless, McMurtry unabashedly shows, via characters like Woodrow Call and his unrecognized son Newt, the painfully high price that denial of reality can cause by encouraging the repression of very real, if unacknowledged, needs. In the process, McMurtry convincingly links America's human past to its human present in an authentic way that transcends common stereotypes.

Larry McMurtry's ever-present interest in how death in the West may force one to reconsider one's relationship to the world in a spiritual and aesthetic context was fully evident his first published novel, *Horseman, Pass By*. Appropriately, it culminates with a scene set in a church where the only spiritual consolation comes, ironically, from the artistry of the church soloist, as McMurtry sensitively portrays the devastated reaction of young Lonnie Bannon to the loss of his beloved grandfather. Upon taking in the news of his grandfather Homer's death, Lonnie must combat the initial shock characterized by a deadening of all feeling: "I dried up then. I felt like I didn't have anything else to say, to Hud or anybody, ever... I was just pushed back in myself like a two-bit variety-store telescope" (McMurtry, *Horseman* 160). The danger for Lonnie as it is for Jacy in *Texasville* or Call in *Lonesome Dove* is that he will disconnect from those around him and lose the best part of what makes him human as a result: the heartfelt ability to reach out to others.

But Lonnie's healthy desire to metaphorically embrace all the people who make up his life and form his sense of identity in his hour of profound loss ultimately wins out in the novel's final pages when he discovers that he "had them all, those faces who made my days" (McMurtry, *Horseman* 179). Lonnie's impulse to reach out to others significantly parallels the behavior of Larry McMurtry's arguably most autobiographical character: the fiction writer Danny Deck in *All My Friends are Going to Be Strangers* in his own hour of extreme spiritual confusion. At the end of that novel, even as McMurtry's artistic alter-ego contemplates drowning himself in the Rio Grande, Danny's healthy side cannot help but be illuminated, perhaps for the last time, by all the faces in his life he is effectively abandoning. Their treasured faces form a moving panoply in stark contrast to the impersonal words that have overtaken his life as an artist. Through the process of visualizing his friends, Danny can picture their shared inability after the fact to understand why he drowned himself. The only lingering exception Danny can picture is that singular face of the special lady who succeeded in breaking his heart:

> All sorts of.... faces troubled me. Emma, Jenny, Wu—also Jill. I turned south.... if they came, my friends, if Wu came, for some reason, or Godwin, or Jenny, they wouldn't get it from him, he wouldn't know... why I loved any of the people I loved, they wouldn't get it from him and none of them could guess, only maybe Jill could,... if I had stayed..... if she had stayed, I could tell her, she might guess, she had the clearest eyes, the straightest look, the most honest face, I missed it so—but ah no, no chance, better just to want rivers—Jill was gone. (McMurtry, *All My Friends* 285–6)

In his book *Shakespeare and the Nature of Time*, Frederick Turner concludes that, in Shakespeare's sonnets, the great author "eventually accepts the terrible temporal forces that are pitted against what he holds dear. But at the end he realizes that they are irrelevant to love" (26). Similarly, over and over in Larry McMurtry's death-filled novels, whether set in the past or the present, while he may show initially self-centered characters like Aurora Greenway in anticipation of death toy with the tempting promise of art to arrest time's inevitable advances and insure a kind of worldly immortality, he also shows how art may more immediately serve as a welcome catalyst for bringing people together through their common desire to believe in a spiritual, artistic realm transcending time and space. But what McMurtry perhaps stresses most through his memorable characters is the fundamental power of the human heart to transcend loss through its affirmation of a powerful connection with others, which enables it to overcome despair and the lure of self-destruction. For repeatedly, McMurtry emotionally invests his readers in characters whose tenuous, often lonely lives are suddenly shattered by the loss of someone whose very presence formed their sense—and, vicariously, the reader's sense—of the world around them. More often than not, McMurtry shows how each character, in his or her own way, eventually finds the inner strength to avoid self-destruction by using his or her pain and disorientation as an impetus for spiritual renewal. For whether it's Aurora in *Terms of Endearment* coping with the death of her daughter; or Jacy in *Texasville* coping with the death of her son; or Newt in *Lonesome Dove* coping with the death of his friend Deets; or his father Call coping with the death of his friend Gus; or Lonnie in *Horseman, Pass By* coping with the death of his grandfather; or—perhaps most revealing of all—Danny in *All My Friends Are Going to Be Strangers* coping with the temptation to escape through suicide versus his inescapable recognition that all the people he loved would never fully understand; Larry McMurtry's perpetually death-haunted southwestern fiction serves as an important reminder to everyone of how loss may, in the final analysis, ultimately lead to redemption.

Notes

1. In McMurtry's first memoir, entitled *In a Narrow Grave*, he stresses the early sense of alienation he experienced within his own family due to his sensitive nature (158–9).

2. While my essay, for reasons of space, dwells on only a few pertinent examples, anticipation of death in one form or another, directly or indirectly, and its devastating after effects infuses virtually all of McMurtry's fiction. To mention just two additional examples, McMurtry's second novel, *Leaving Cheyenne*, set in the modern era, ends with the three gravestones of its major protagonists. Furthermore, McMurtry's multi-novel opus, entitled *The Berrybender Narratives*, set in the nineteenth century, contains multiple deaths, including the tragic death of Pomp Charbonneau, a man in contrast to James Fenimore Cooper's Hawkeye, who is too gentle and kind-hearted to survive life on the frontier.

3. See McMurtry's new preface to the twenty-fifth anniversary edition of *Lonesome Dove*, published by Simon & Schuster, 2010.

4. This need for greater cultural outlets for death on the frontier is further underscored early on in the novel when the Irish boy, Sean O'Brien, dies and the men lament the fact they cannot provide a proper funeral (*Lonesome Dove* 306–307).

Works Cited

Graham, Don. "*Lonesome Dove*: Butch and Sundance Go on a Cattle Drive." *Taking Stock: A Larry McMurtry Casebook*. Ed. Clay Reynolds. Dallas: Southern Methodist UP, 1989.

Hardison, O. B., Jr. "Terms of Endearment." *New Republic* 173.22 (29 Nov. 1975): 37.

McMurtry, Larry. *All My Friends Are Going To Be Strangers*. Albuquerque: U of New Mexico P, 1971.

_____. *The Evening Star*. New York: Pocket Books/Simon & Schuster, 1992.

_____. *Film Flam*. New York: Simon & Schuster, 1987.

_____. *Horseman, Pass By*. College Station: Texas A&M UP, 1985.

_____. *In a Narrow Grave*. Austin, TX: Encino Press, 1968.

_____. *Lonesome Dove*. New York: Signet/Simon & Schuster, 1985.

_____. *Paradise*. New York: Simon & Schuster, 2001.

_____. *Somebody's Darling*. New York: Touchstone/Simon & Schuster, 1987.

_____. *Streets of Laredo*. New York: Simon & Schuster, 1983.

_____. *Terms of Endearment*. New York: Signet/Simon & Schuster, 1975.

_____. *Texasville*. New York: Simon & Schuster, 1987.

_____. *Walter Benjamin at the Dairy Queen*. New York: Simon & Schuster, 1999.

Setterberg, Fred. *The Roads Taken: Travels Through America's Literary Landscapes*. Athens, Georgia: U of Georgia P, 1993.

Tompkins, Jane. *West of Everything: The Inner Life of Westerns*. Oxford, UK: Oxford UP, 1992.

Turner, Frederick. *Shakespeare and the Nature of Time*. Oxford, UK: Oxford UP, 1971.

RESOURCES

Additional Works of Southwestern Literature___

Long Fiction

Grey, Zane. *Riders of the Purple Sage*. 1912.

Waters, Frank. *The Man Who Killed the Deer*. 1942.

Niggli, Josefina. *Mexican Village*. 1945.

Abbey, Edward. *Fire on the Mountain*. 1962.

Momaday, N. Scott. *The Way to Rainy Mountain*. 1969.

Rivera, Tomás. *...y no se lo tragó la tierra/And the Earth Did Not Part*. 1971.

Kelton, Elmer. *The Time It Never Rained*. 1973.

Nichols, John. *The Milagro Beanfield War*. 1974.

Candelaria, Nash. *Not By the Sword*. 1982.

Allen, Paula Gunn. *The Woman Who Owned the Shadows*. 1983.

Islas, Arturo. *Rain God*. 1984.

Hillerman, Tony. *A Thief of Time*. 1988.

Kingsolver, Barbara. *The Bean Trees*. 1988.

Hogan, Linda. *Mean Spirit: A Novel*. 1990.

Silko, Leslie Marmon. *Almanac of the Dead*. 1991.

McMillan, Terry. *Waiting To Exhale*. 1992.

Véa, Alfredo, Jr. *Gods Go Begging*. 1999.

McCarthy, Cormac. *No Country for Old Men*. 2005.

Castillo, Ana. *The Guardians*. 2007.

Short Fiction

Porter, Katherine Anne. *The Collected Stories of Katherine Anne Porter*. 1965.

Silko, Leslie Marmon. *Storyteller*. 1981.

Ríos, Albert. *The Iguana Killer: Twelve Stories of the Heart*. 1984.

Viramontes, Helen María. *The Moths and Other Stories*. 1985.

Chávez, Denise. *Last of the Menu Girls*. 1986.

Gilb, Dagoberto. *The Magic of Blood*. 1993.

Cantú, Norma Elia. *Canícula: Snapshots of a Girlhood en la Frontera.* 1995.

Tapahonso, Luci. *Blue Horses Rush In.* 1997.

Hinojosa, Rolando. *The Valley/Estampas del Valle.* 2014.

Poetry

Nye, Naomi Shihab. *Different Ways to Pray: Poems.* 1980.

Ortiz, Simon J. *From Sand Creek: Rising In This Heart Which Is Our America.* 1981.

Mora, Pat. *Borders.* 1986.

Baca, Jimmy Santiago. *Martín & Meditations on the South Valley.* 1987.

Cisneros, Sandra. *My Wicked, Wicked Ways.* 1987.

Villanueva, Tino. *Scene from the Movie* GIANT. 1993.

Herrera, Juan Felipe. *Border-Crosser with a Lamborghini Dream.* 1999.

Cortez, Sarah. *How to Undress a Cop.* 2000.

Tafolla, Carmen. *Sonnets and Salsa.* 2001.

Harjo, Joy. *How We Became Human: New and Selected Poems: 1975– 2001.* 2004.

Drama

Medoff, Mark. *When You Comin' Back, Red Ryder?* 1973.
Jones, Preston. *A Texas Trilogy.* 1976.

Geiogamah, Hanay. *New Native American Drama: Three Plays.* 1980.

Morton, Carlos. *Johnny Tenorio and Other* Plays. 1992.

Valdez, Luis. *Zoot Suit and Other Plays.* 1992.

Nonfiction

Van Dyke, John C. *Nature for Its Own Sake.* 1898.

Austin, Mary Hunter. *The Land of Journeys' Ending.* 1924.

Krutch, Joseph Wood. *The Desert Year.* 1952.

Bowden, Charles. *Blue Desert.* 1986.

Harrigan, Stephen. *Comanche Midnight.* 1995.

Williams, Terry Tempest. *Red: Passion and Patience in the Desert.* 2002.

Urrea, Luis Alberto. *The Devil's Highway: A True Story.* 2004.

Bibliography

Allen, Paula Gunn. *The Sacred Hoop: Recovering the Feminine in Native American Traditions.* Boston: Beacon Press, 1986.

_____, ed. *Spider Woman's Granddaughters.* New York: Fawcett Columbine, 1989.

Anaya, Rudolfo. *Aztlán: Essays on the Chicano Homeland.* Albuquerque: El Norte P, 1989.

Anzaldúa, Gloria. *Borderlands/La Frontera: The New Mestiza.* San Francisco: Aunt Lute, 1987.

Anzaldúa, Gloria E. & AnaLouise Keating, eds. *This Bridge We Call Home: Radical Visions For Transformation.* New York: Routledge, 2002.

Anzaldúa, Gloria & Cherrie Moraga, eds. *This Bridge Called My Back: Writings by Radical Women of Color.* 4th ed. Albany: State U of New York P, 2015.

Arnold, Edwin T. & Dianne C. Luce, eds. *A Cormac McCarthy Companion: The Border Trilogy.* Jackson: U of Mississippi P, 2001.

Busby, Mark, ed. *The Greenwood Encyclopedia of American Regional Cultures: The Southwest.* Westport, CT: Greenwood, 2004.

_____. "'I Don't Know, But I Ain't Lost:' Defining the Southwest." *Regionalism and the Humanities.* Ed. Timothy R. Mahoney & Wendy J. Katz. Lincoln: U of Nebraska P, 2009: 44–55.

_____. "Texas and the Great Southwest." *A Companion to the Regional Literatures of the United States.* Ed. Charles Crow. New York: Blackwell, 2003. 432–457.

Calderón, Héctor & José David Saldívar eds. *Criticism in the Borderlands: Studies in Chicano Literature, Culture, and Ideology.* Durham & London: Duke UP, 1991.

Campbell, Neil. *The Cultures of the American New West.* Edinburgh, UK: Edinburgh UP, 2000.

Castillo, Ana. *Massacre of the Dreamers: Essays on Xicanisma.* New York: Plume/Penguin, 1995.

Dasenbrock, Reed Way. "Southwest of What?: Southwestern Literature as a form of Frontier Literature." *Desert, Garden, Margin, Range:*

Literature on the American Frontier. Ed. Eric Heyne. New York: Twayne, 1992.

Dobie, J. Frank. *Guide to Life and Literature of the Southwest*. Dallas: Southern Methodist UP, 1952.

Dunaway, David King & Sara Spurgeon, eds. *Writing the Southwest*. Rev. ed. Albuquerque: U of New Mexico P, 2003.

Ferguson, Erna. *Our Southwest*. New York & London: A. A. Knopf, 1940.

Gaston, Edwin. *The Early Novel of the Southwest*. Albuquerque: U of New Mexico P, 1991.

Gilb, Dagoberto, ed. *Hecho in Tejas: An Anthology of Texas Mexican Literature*. Albuquerque: U of New Mexico P, 2008. Southwestern Writers Collection Ser.

Goodwyn, Larry. "The Frontier Myth and Southwestern Literature." *American Libraries* (Feb. 1971): 161–7; (Apr. 1971): 359–66. Rpt. in John Gordon Burke, ed. *Regional Perspectives: An Examination of America's Literary Heritage*. Chicago: ALA, 1973. 175–206.

Hollon, W. Eugene. *The Southwest: Old and New*. New York: Knopf, 1961.

Kolodny, A. *The Land Before Her: Fantasy and Experience of the American Frontiers, 1630–1860*. Chapel Hill & London: U of North Carolina P, 1984.

Lensink, Judy Nolte, ed. *Old Southwest/New Southwest: Essays on a Region and Its Literature*. Tuscon: Tuscon Public Library, 1987.

Lynch, Tom. *Xerophilia: Ecocritical Explorations in Southwestern Literature*. Lubbock: Texas Tech UP, 2008.

McCracken, Ellen. *New Latina Narrative: The Feminine Space of Postmodern Ethnicity*. Tucson: U of Arizona P, 1999.

Major, Mabel & T. M. Pearce. *Southwest Heritage: A Literary History with Bibliographies*. 3rd Rev. ed. Albuquerque: U of New Mexico P, 1972.

Norwood, Vera & Janice Monk, eds. *The Desert Is No Lady: Southwestern Landscapes in Women's Writing and Art*. New Haven: Yale UP, 1987.

Pilkington, William T. *My Blood's Country: Studies in Southwestern Literature*. Fort Worth: Texas Christian UP, 1973.

Powell, Lawrence Clark. *Southwest Classics: The Creative Literature of the Arid Lands: Essays on the Books and Their Writers*. Los Angeles: W. Ritchie Press, 1974.

Reisner, Marc. *Cadillac Desert: The American West and Its Disappearing Water*. New York: Viking Penguin, 1986.

Siringo, Charlie. *A Texas Cowboy: Or, Fifteen Years On The Hurricane Deck of A Spanish Pony*. 1885. New York: Penguin, 2000.

Slotkin, Richard. *The Fatal Environment: The Myth of the Frontier in the Age of Industrialization, 1800–1890*. Middleton, CT: Wesleyan UP, 1985.

_____. *Gunfighter Nation: The Myth of the Frontier in Twentieth-Century America*. New York: Atheneum, 1992.

_____. *Regeneration Through Violence: The Mythology of the American Frontier, 1600–1860*. Norman: U of Oklahoma P, 2000.

Smith, Henry Nash. *Virgin Land: The American West as Symbol and Myth*. Cambridge, MA: Harvard UP, 1950.

Sonnichson, C. L. *The Southwest in Life and Literature*. New York: Devin-Adair, 1962.

Swift, John N. & Joseph R. Urgo. *Willa Cather and the American Southwest*. Lincoln & London: U of Nebraska P, 2002.

Turner, Frederick Jackson. "The Significance of the Frontier in American History." 1947. *The Frontier in American History*. Tucson: U of Arizona P, 1997. 1–38.

Vizenor, Gerald. *Fugitive Poses: Native American Indian Scenes of Absence and Presence*. Lincoln: U of Nebraska P, 1998. Abraham Lincoln Lecture Ser.

Wallach, Rick. Ed. *Myth, Legend, Dust: Critical Responses to Cormac McCarthy*. New York: Manchester UP, 2000.

About the Editor

William Brannon is a professor of English at Collin College in Texas. He received his PhD from Texas Tech University in 2003, where his dissertation examined genre, myth, and ideology in Cormac McCarthy's western novels. He completed his MA in English from Texas A&M University–Commerce, where his thesis considered the depiction of family relationships in McCarthy's *Suttree* (1979) and *Blood Meridian* (1985). While completing his MA, Brannon taught high school English and Spanish. In addition to his research interests in Cormac McCarthy studies, Brannon's scholarly work focuses on other Southwestern authors, including Leslie Marmon Silko and Sandra Cisneros. He is a member of the Western Literature Association.

Contributors

Cordelia E. Barrera earned her PhD from The University of Texas San Antonio in 2009. An assistant professor of Latina/o literature at Texas Tech University, Barrera specializes in literature of the American Southwest as well as US border theory, third-space feminist theory, popular culture, and film. Her work has appeared in *The Quarterly Review of Film and Video*, *Western American Literature,* and *Chicana/Latina Studies.* Her latest project explores cyber technologies, social justice, and forms of oppositional consciousness in borderlands science fiction. Her first scholarly encounter with Cormac McCarthy's *Border Trilogy* was in her dissertation, in which she discussed the trilogy from the perspective of border theory.

Mark Busby is professor of English at Texas State University–San Marcos and previously was director of the Center for the Study of the Southwest and the Jerome H. and Catherine E. Supple Professor of Southwestern Studies. He received his PhD from the University of Colorado, Boulder, and his BA and MA from Texas A&M University–Commerce. He is author of *Larry McMurtry and the West: An Ambivalent Relationship* and *Ralph Ellison* and *Preston Jones* and *Lanford Wilson* in the Western Writers Series. He edited *The Greenwood Encyclopedia of Regional American Culture: The Southwest* and coedited *From Texas to the World and Back: Essays on the Journeys of Katherine Anne Porter*; *John Graves, Writer*; *The Frontier Experience and the American Dream*; and the journals *Southwestern American Literature* and *Texas Books in Review*. He is the author of two novels, *Fort Benning Blues* and *Cedar Crossing*.

T. Jackie Cuevas is an assistant professor of Latina/o literary and cultural studies in the Department of English at the University of Texas at San Antonio (UTSA). Prior to joining UTSA in 2013, Cuevas taught in the Department of Women's and Gender Studies at Syracuse University. Cuevas coedited *El Mundo Zurdo 4: Selected Works from the 2013 Meeting of The Society for the Study of Gloria Anzaldúa,* published in 2015 by Aunt Lute Press. Cuevas is also a cofounder of Evelyn Street Press and a member of Macondo, the creative writing collective founded by author Sandra Cisneros.

Max Despain is an associate professor of English at the US Air Force Academy. She studies questions about the role of memory in identity formation, especially how different forms of memory expose fears and limitations about characters' present-day moments. She specializes in autobiography and women's writing from the turn of the nineteenth to the twentieth century. She teaches English-major seminars on topics such as American literature, American modernism, novels, food in literature, and minority literature, as well as the core senior capstone course on war literature and speech.

Paul Guajardo teaches literature at the University of Houston. He has published more than eighty articles, essays, and reviews. He is the author of *Chicano Controversy: Oscar Acosta and Richard Rodriguez* (2002) and is currently at work on *The Myth of Memoir: Mexican-American Masks*. His teaching interests include minority literature, immigrant narratives, memoir, literature of the sea, travel literature, and the British novel.

Roger Walton Jones is professor of English at Ranger College. He earned a BA in English from Kenyon College, an MA in English from Southern Illinois University, and a PhD in English from Texas A&M University, where his dissertation was on Larry McMurtry. His revised dissertation was published as *Larry McMurtry and the Victorian Novel* (1994). In recent years, in addition to publishing scholarly articles and book reviews, he regularly presents papers at the PCA/ACA annual convention.

Mike Lemon is a doctoral student at Texas Tech University. He studies literature, social justice, and the environment and investigates moments in which social movements intersect with environmental concerns. His dissertation focuses on turn-of-the-twentieth-century regional American literature and looks for convergence points between local issues and national interests.

Maria O'Connell is an assistant professor of English in the School of Languages and Literature at Wayland Baptist University, and she has taught American and world literature on various levels, from undergraduate to graduate. She has also taught beginning Spanish. Her research interests are interdisciplinary, including systems theory, gender, translation, and social constructions of persons in Western/Southwestern literature. Her dissertation explored the role of story and myth in Cormac McCarthy's novels and how they are used to teach young men their roles.

Annette Portillo, assistant professor of English and Native American studies at the University of Texas, San Antonio (UTSA) received her MA and PhD from Cornell University. Her interdisciplinary research focuses on life stories, *testimonios*, memoirs, and autobiographies by women of color. Her current book project is tentatively titled *Sovereign Stories: (Un) mapping, Unearthing and (Re)righting Native American Women's Blood Memories.* She has taught Chican@, Native American and Ethnic Studies courses at Cornell, Mount Holyoke, Oberlin, Nevada State, and UTSA. She is especially dedicated to student-centered learning and integrates *testimonio* into her classes, where she values and validates everyone's lived experiences.

John Samson (PhD, Cornell, 1980) is concerned with historical and theoretical approaches to American novels and nonfictional prose narratives. He is the author of *White Lies: Melville's Narratives of Facts* (Cornell University Press) and of many articles and book chapters on eighteenth-, nineteenth-, and twentieth-century American literature. From 1995 to 2003, he contributed the "Melville" chapter to *American Literary Scholarship.* He is currently engaged in a project tracing the cultural roots of the movement from realism to modernism in the American novel from 1870 to 1920 in relation to their political and philosophical contexts.

Wilma Shires is an assistant professor of English at Southeastern Oklahoma State University in Durant, Oklahoma, where she teaches Native American literatures, introduction to literature, creative writing, and freshman composition. Her specific interests include contemporary American, Native American, medieval, and Eastern European literatures. She has published articles in each of these areas as well as original poetry. She also enjoys science fiction and fantasy. She has presented papers at regional and international conferences on topics ranging from Louise Erdrich's novels to humor in *Le Morte D'Arthur*. Shires earned her BA at Southeastern Oklahoma State University and her MA and PhD at Texas A&M University–Commerce.

Laura Smith is lecturer in human geography at the University of Exeter. Her present research focuses on how literature (especially nature and natural history writing) can contribute to ecological restoration debates, examining the link between literature and ecological and political reform. Her articles have appeared in *Ethics, Policy & Environment, Ecological Restoration*, and *Transactions of the Institute of British Geographers*. She received her PhD, MSc, and BSc from Cardiff University.

Randi Lynn Tanglen is associate professor of English at Austin College in Sherman, Texas. She teaches pre-1900 American literature, including classes on women writers, frontier literature, and captivity narratives. Her articles have appeared in *Western American Literature* and *Tulsa Studies in Women's Literature*.

Index

Miller, Vassar 14
Milner, Clyde, Jr. 123
Mitchell, Carol 78
modernism x, xiv, xxv, 144, 155,
    156, 228, 229
Mojica, José 41
Momaday, N. Scott xv, xx, 12, 14,
    17, 27, 28
M.O.M.A.S. 139, 140, 141
Mondale, Clarence xiii, xxvi
monopolies 113, 114, 120
Montejano, David 36
Moraga, Cherríe 97
Mora, Pat 14, 97
Morrison, Gail Moore 190
Moyers, Bill 14
Munguia, Flavio 30
myth ix, xi, 5, 6, 15, 17, 18, 22,
    23, 35, 36, 47, 49, 73, 77,
    81, 108, 110, 133, 172, 174,
    175, 176, 179, 180, 183,
    186, 188, 189, 195, 225, 229

nature xxi, xxv, 4, 9, 16, 25, 26,
    27, 31, 43, 53, 55, 56, 63,
    83, 84, 85, 88, 102, 127,
    130, 135, 136, 143, 149,
    177, 195, 198, 207, 211,
    212, 215, 230
Nestor, Sarah 148, 157
N., José Ángel 94
Nocona, Peta 66
Nusbaum, Jesse 154
Nye, Naomi Shihab 14, 17

Oatman, Olive 67, 68, 69, 74
O'Brien, Sean 210, 216
O'Brien, Sharon 143
O. Henry 6

O'Keeffe, Georgia 144, 155
Oliphant, Dave 14
Olmstead, Frederick Law vii
Osborn, Carolyn 17
O'Shea, Elena Zamora 91
Ossana, Diana 8
Otero, Miguel 91
Outland, Tom 147, 152, 158, 161,
    162, 164, 170
Owens, Barcley 196
Owens, William xxii

Padilla, Genaro 102, 122
Paredes, Américo xx, 10
Parham, Billy xi, 186, 187, 188,
    193, 194, 195
Parker, Cynthia Ann 65, 66, 67
Parker, James W. 65, 67
Parker, Quanah 66
pastoralism 16, 17
Pearce, T. M. 21, 31, 222
Peebles, Stacey 183
Pérez, Emma 109
Pérez, Gail 130
Perez, Luis 91
Pérez, Ramón "Tianguis" 94
Pérez, Rolando 37
Pérez, Severo 10
perspective 26, 28, 63, 94, 109,
    113, 115, 117, 146, 159,
    161, 165, 166, 167, 170, 227
Peter, Godfrey St. 162
Peterson, Carla 118
Philippon, Daniel J. 53
Pilkington, Tom 192
Pilkington, William T. xxiv, 4
Platt, Kamala 127
Plummer, Rachel 65, 67, 75

Critical Insights